DESIGNERS

Marie Wallin • Kaffe Fassett • Martin Storey
Erika Knight • Sarah Dallas • Lisa Richardson
Grace Melville • Jennie Atkinson • Brandon Mably
Sarah Hatton • Amanda Crawford

INCLUDES 39 DESIGNS

ROWAN

EDITOR'S LETTER

Dear Rowan Knitters

I am proud to welcome you to the 50th issue of the Rowan Magazine.

I wonder how many of you have Magazines 1 to 50 and now have a full book case!

What a journey we have been on from the beaches of Brighton in the first issue ...to South Africa and Sicily, there are now few places left where the Rowan team have not explored to find the magical backdrop for the Rowan designs. I would hope you would agree that throughout the years Rowan has kept true to its ethos by offering a magazine that is not just a knitting magazine but a creative escape from the every day ups and downs that life throws our way. We have also kept an evolutionary yet consistent team of designers who continue to invent new and exciting fabrics and shapes for us to explore.

For the first time to mark the 50th edition of the Rowan Magazine, we have produced an interactive online version for our website. You will be able to browse the stories, editoral content and regular features. As an added bonus, wherever you see the @, click on the logo to view video footage of the behind the scenes from the photography shoots, interviews with the designers, some of the shetland knitters and myself. We are really excited to bring you this new feature and hope to make it a regular part of the magazine. We are also re- launching our Rowan International club. It will be divided to make a Rowan Subscription and on-line club Row@n with lots of added benefits that will be absolutely free.

In Magazine 50 we talk to your favourite designers about what Rowan means to them and as always we have the three main stories which are all completely different and I love each of them for different reasons.

Wildwood for the colour, pattern and fantastic backdrop of the perfect autumn day with incandescent sunshine streaming through the trees. Finesse for its elegance, grace and playfulness. And lastly Winter Essentials for its timeless simplicity.

As always I hope you find something that you enjoy knitting and wearing and here's to another 50 issues of the Rowan Magazine.

Kate Buller
Kate Buller
Rowan Brand Manager

ON THE COVER
Hawthorn Cape by Marie Wallin
Beech Mittens by Erika Knight
Photographer Sheila Rock
Art Direction & Styling Marie Wallin
Hair & Make-up Frances Prescott (One Make Up)
Model Anna Tatton (Bookings)

Rowan Brand Manager Kate Buller
Rowan Head Designer Marie Wallin
Design Room Manager David MacLeod
Publications Co-ordinator Paul Calvert
Graphic Designer James Knapton
Rowan Designer & Pattern Editor Lisa Richardson
Yarn & Photoshoot Co-ordinator Ann Hinchliffe
Garment Co-ordinator Vicky Sedgwick
Knitting Co-ordinator Andrea McHugh
Garment finishing Lisa Parnaby & Pauline Ellis

Rowan Magazine Design Layout Simon Wagstaff

Sales Manager Emma Mychajlowskyj
Consumer Manager Emma Irving

With special thanks to the following handknitters:
Andrea McHugh, Ann Banks, Elizabeth Jones, Margaret Morris,
Janet Oakey, Ella Taylor, Audrey Kidd, Val Deeks,
Marjorie Pickering, Mary Wilmot, Jyoti More, Violet Ellis,
Julie Ferguson, Marjorie Pickering, Wendy Shipman,
Glenis Garnett, Ann Newton, Honey Ingram, Sandra Richardson,
Wendy Shipman, Elsie Eland, Helen Betts, Ros Miller,
Sandra Taylor, Cynthia Noble, Clare Landi, Joan Broadbent,
Margaret Goddard, Pat Cooper, Jacqueline Silvester, Margaret
Oswald, Joyce Limon

First published in Great Britain in 2011 by Rowan Yarns Ltd.
Green Lane Mill,
Holmfirth,
West Yorkshire,
England,
HD9 2DX
E-mail: mag50@knitrowan.com

British Library Cataloguing in Publication Data
Rowan Yarns.
Rowan Knitting & Crochet Magazine Number 50
ISSN 2045-340X

Copyright Rowan 2011
Printed in the UK
Reprographics by Gloss Solutions

CONTENTS

Visit our website – www.knitrowan.com for further information on the new clubs: Row@n, Rowan Subscription and the new interactive on-line Magazine 50.

ROWAN

wildwood

Inspired by an ornate tapestry of
time worn florals and heritage
countrywear, WILDWOOD is a
beautiful collection of heirloom arans,
exquisite florals and handcrafted crochet
using the rich autumnal colours of the
British rural countryside.

HOLLY
Felted Tweed
Kaffe Fassett
🧶159

HAWTHORN CAPE
Felted Tweed Aran
Marie Wallin
126

BEECH MITTENS
Felted Tweed Chunky
Erika Knight
126

HORNBEAM
Felted Tweed Aran
Martin Storey
178

BIRCH
Felted Tweed Aran
Martin Storey
🧶 176

LAUREL
Kid Classic
Marie Wallin
🧶165

23

YEW SCARF
Felted Tweed &
Cashsoft 4 ply
Martin Storey
🧶 125

ELM
Felted Tweed & Cashsoft 4 ply
Martin Storey
183

29

LARCH
Felted Tweed Aran
Marie Wallin
⟳ 187

Photographer: Sheila Rock. **Styling:** Marie Wallin. **Hair & Make Up:** Frances Prescott (One Photographic). **Art Direction:** Marie Wallin.
Model: Anna Tartoni (Booking). **Location:** Westonbirt - The National Arboretum, Gloucestershire.

Shetland Lace in a new light

Words by
Dr Kate Davies

THE GREAT INDUSTRIAL EXHIBITION OF 1851.
Plate 3. The British Nave.

What could be more traditional than Shetland Lace? On hearing those two words, the first image that probably springs to a knitter's mind is a fine, white, openwork shawl, which, in construction, style, motifs, and commemorative function, might seem the very essence of 'tradition'.

Over the past half-century or so, a host of books and articles have compounded our 'traditional' view of openwork knitting, celebrating the incredible beauty and complexity of the fine shawls that were produced on the Shetland Islands during the Victorian era. These accounts have improved the contemporary understanding of knitted lace immeasurably, but sometimes, in their championing of set methods, and their emphasis on tradition, their approach can rather tend toward the Victorian as well. Indeed, at their worst, such accounts may convey a sense of Shetland as an isolated, inward-looking culture where particular styles of knitting have been practised, unchanged, since time immemorial. This is, of course, far from being the case. In truth, Shetland lace knitting—like many other 'traditional' textiles— has always been extremely fluid and adaptable. The fine openwork Shetland shawls and stoles that adorned the shoulders of wealthy Victorian ladies were profoundly

innovatory accessories, developed in response to the demands of a rapidly changing market, and prey, like any other nineteenth-century garment, to the fickle fortunes of fashion. Perhaps it is time to see *Shetland lace in a new light*.

Though one may think of Shetland as geographically remote, in the Seventeenth Century it was actually far better connected than most English provincial towns. The sea brought the outside world to Shetland, and took Shetland to the world. The islands maintained strong links with Northern Europe via the Hanseatic trade, and, through seaborne commerce, Shetlanders encountered many different kinds of people and commodities. It was the thriving trade routes of the North and Baltic seas, rather than domestic British influences, which first enlivened the distinctive skills and styles of Shetland's hand knitters. In the absence of their seafaring men folk, the women

of Shetland had to be extremely resourceful. As well as working their crofts and managing their families, they rooed the soft fleece of the islands' hardy native sheep, and knitted their hand-spun yarn into small articles for sale. Several seventeenth-century accounts mention women knitting caps, gloves, mittens and, most frequently, stockings, to exchange with Dutch merchants. According to one early eighteenth-century Shetland landowner, these merchants frequently bought "a considerable quantity of coarse stockings, for ready money at a tolerable price." The sale of their hand-knitting meant that Shetland crofters might have a small stock of foreign currency with which to pay rent or buy provisions. However this important source of income was not to last. At the turn of the Eighteenth Century, trade restrictions were enforced by the British Government, Shetland saw far fewer Dutch and Scandinavian merchants, and the hand-knitters lost their small but lucrative export market. Several thousand pairs of Shetland socks were still sent annually to Leith, but, under competition from knitters on the British mainland, the price Shetlanders received for their hosiery was increasingly poor.

Shetland's hand knitters found that they had to change and innovate in order to continue to profit from their craft, and, by the middle of the Eighteenth Century, there are several brief but tantalising references, which suggest that the industry had begun to divide and specialise. On the one hand, sources make frequent mention of Shetland's "coarse woollen hose" a pair of which would gain the knitter a few pence, or which more frequently, she might barter in Lerwick for tea or tobacco. On the other, there are several references to "fine worked" stockings, which seem to have been produced on special commission for wealthy customers, and whose appearance marks the inception of Shetland hand-knit goods as luxury commodities. In *The Wealth of Nations* (1776), Adam Smith mentions such stockings being priced at "a guinea and upward"; while the writer of *A True and Exact Description of the Islands of Shetland* (1753) suggests that a Shetland knitter producing extremely "fine" hose might expect to be paid "four guineas a pair." For stockings to fetch the maker four guineas in the 1750s, the work must have been extremely "fine" (in the mid-eighteenth century sense of "fine" as "delicately wrought") and it seems likely that Shetland's distinctive openwork designs were beginning to be developed and incorporated into the islands' hand-knitting at around this time. Openwork motifs had already begun to feature in the folk knitting of Scandinavia and the Baltic—the Northern world to which Shetland remained importantly connected. Further references to the "extremely fine" hand-knitting of Unst at the close of the eighteenth century reveal that, while the market for coarse hose had seriously declined, Shetland openwork was beginning to find its feet in a niche luxury market.

Sharon Miller (a renowned lace authority) has persuasively argued that, by the end of the Eighteenth Century, Shetland knitters were incorporating now-familiar openwork motifs into their own hap shawls and kerchiefs. But while the working women of Shetland were proud to wear the practical and attractive hap, this was not the case with the fashionable women of Regency Britain. In costume history, the thirty-year period from the 1790s through the 1820s is notable for its singular lack of lace. For the fashionable woman, the emphasis was on simple, neo-classical lines; fabrics tended toward the plain and sheer, and the decorative excesses of the latter half of the Eighteenth Century were seen as terribly outmoded. Not until the reign of Queen Victoria did lace really begin to make a

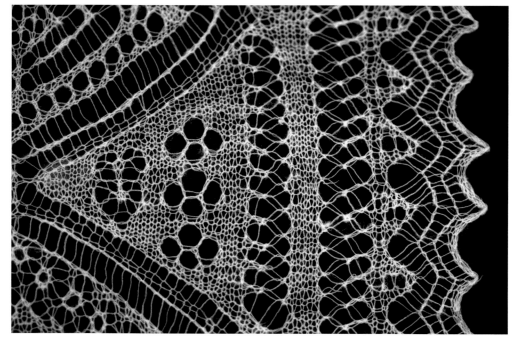

Above
An example of a black 'crepe' mourning lace from the early 20th century.

Left and Top Right
A fine lace stole from the mid 19th century.

Middle Right
A Shetland lace shawl from the 1880's.

All the images shown here are reproduced with the courtesy of the Shetland Museum and Archives.

comeback, and Shetland's innovative hand-knitters were more than ready for this shift in trend.

By the middle of the 1830s, technical advancements, such as Samuel Fergusson's adaptation of the jacquard loom, meant that crude, but striking-looking openwork could now be produced relatively cheaply, and in quantity. Lace suddenly became incredibly fashionable and, rather than the expensive preserve of the court and aristocracy it had been a century earlier, it trickled down the social ranks to adorn the dress of Britain's middle classes. While traditional bobbin-lace makers suffered from the introduction of the new machines, other forms of fine handmade openwork came to be regarded as exclusive, luxury products, and were hence increasingly sought-after. These craft laces—usually made in small, and often impoverished, regional communities—began to carry their own distinctive cachet. For, in true Victorian style, a woman who wore the craft lace of Madeira, of Malta, or of Limerick, not only displayed her status as a wealthy individual, capable of affording such singular hand-crafted luxuries, but might also advertise her status as a figure of charity or of sentiment, assisting the Empire's poor.

In the collections of the Shetland Museum and Archives, the earliest example of what we would now recognise as Shetland "fine" lace is a Christening shawl dated 1837. In the method of its construction, the arrangement of its patterns, and the complexity of its motifs, it suggests a refinement of skills that had been in development for several generations. Shetland fine lace did not suddenly appear in the Victorian era, fully formed like Athena from the head of Zeus, but rather drew on well-established local practice—the techniques and patterns that the islands' talented craftswomen had been devising and honing for a century or more. In the 1830s, fine shawls were already being produced as luxury heirlooms for babies, and it was merely a shift in direction for Shetland's innovative hand-knitters to capitalise on fashionable demand, and create beautiful shawls in which to wrap the women of metropolitan Britain.

By the 1840s, Shetland found itself connected to the mainland by a steamer and postal service that made communication and commerce much more efficient. Prompted by the new trend for lace, Shetland's fine openwork knitting became a thing of curiosity, and British merchants visiting the islands discovered beautiful examples of a niche product they knew they could sell to wealthy customers. Competing stories began to circulate, (and are still repeated today) claiming

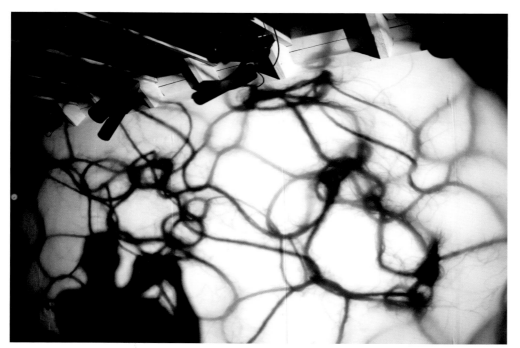

Above Left
A projection of a lace swatch knitted by Joan Manson. Photograph by Mark Sinclair. Mirrie Dancers Project.

Above Right
Lace Hat, design by Angela Irvine.

Right
A projection of a lace swatch by Christine Smith. Photograph by Mark Sinclair. Mirrie Dancers Project.

Far Right - Top to Bottom
Dress with lace bodice, design by Angela Irvine.
Hazel Laurenson. Photograph by Billy Fox.
Mary Kay. Photograph by Billy Fox.

this or that 1840s merchant or patron as the 'originator' of Shetland fine lace. If not prompted entirely by commercial self-interest, these narratives certainly suggest a degree of partiality. In truth, there is only one source of the innovative artistry of Shetland lace, and that is the women of Shetland. As Eliza Edmonston put it in 1856:

"The open work knitting now so attractive to the public is an invention for which the Shetland females themselves deserve all the credit. From the simplest beginnings, led on and encouraged by some ladies as a pastime, it has progressed from one thing to another till it has attained its present celebrity, without the aid either of pattern-book or of other instruction than the diligence and taste of the natives themselves."

Several examples of Shetland fine lace were showcased and celebrated at the Great

Exhibition of 1851, and there was a sudden boom in their fashionable appeal. Shops describing themselves as "Shetland warehouses" began to appear on London's Mayfair and Edinburgh's Frederick Street, and famous figures, like author and critic Elizabeth Rigby, were photographed wearing their fine Shetland shawls displayed prominently for the camera. The censuses for Unst (where the finest knitted lace was—and perhaps still is—produced) reveal a remarkable degree of specialisation among the knitting community, as women adapted their skills to fashion's changing demands. Early in the Nineteenth Century, Unst was home to just a handful of stocking knitters, but by the 1861 census, the stocking knitters had been overtaken by more than a hundred women who described 'shawl knitting' as their principal occupation. And, in 1881, at the height of the trend for knitted lace, Unst's fine shawl knitters outnumbered those producing plain stockings by two to one.

Any expert knitter is, by necessity, an innovator: working with pattern means that one constantly encounters problems with construction and shaping, and is always having to devise new design solutions. With their tremendous technical ability and aesthetic sense, the lace knitters of nineteenth-century Shetland were innovators *par excellence*; continually refining and developing their craft with a distinctive, and very shrewd, artistry. Such characteristics not only made these women superlative designers, but also meant that they were capable of responding and adapting to whatever the market threw at them. Though Shetland may have seemed far removed from the culture of mainland Britain, there was nothing remote about Shetland lace knitters' sense of the contemporary.

While the 'traditional' view of Shetland lace is generally of fine, white openwork shawls, the collections of the Shetland Museum and Archives reveal just how varied and wide-ranging the

output of the islands' nineteenth-century knitters really was. As well as many 'traditional' examples of gossamer-fine lace stoles and shawls, there are also tray cloths and underclothes, spencers and bonnets, jumpers and booties, often featuring intriguing and novel methods of construction. Shetland lace was not, despite popular conception, limited to being knitted in natural white yarn, but was frequently produced in the lurid hues much favoured by the Victorians. Toward the end of the Nineteenth Century, as lace shawls began to fall out of favour among the fashionable, Shetland's knitters changed tack again, and began to produce the black stoles, veils and tippets that were still worn by the elderly or those in mourning. The Shetland Museum's collections reveal that, far from being a static tradition, lace knitting was actually a craft very much bound up with fashion's shifting trends. In fact, the only thing that was outmoded about Shetland's hand-knitting industry was the archaic and exploitative Truck system by which women were paid for their work in commodities rather than cash.

The 1920s and 30s saw the fashionable rise of Fairisle knitting, but Shetland lace never really went away. Innovative local knitter/designers, such as Lerwick hairdresser, Ethel Henry, clearly loved the challenge of enlivening traditional lace with new techniques. She incorporated many familiar Shetland motifs into her neat, well-constructed jerseys, even combining complicated openwork with zips. Today, many Shetland women follow in the innovative footsteps of their forebears, and, as highly skilled knitters, continue to transform the traditions of Shetland lace. On Unst, Hazel Laurenson and Minne Mouatt are spearheading a local project to recreate the patterns of some breathtakingly beautiful Victorian garments that had lain untouched since the 1880s. Meanwhile, in Lerwick, lace knitters such as Mary Kay (former teacher, and designer of patterns for *Woman's Weekly*) have lent their hands and talents to the Shetland Amenity Trust's *Fine Lace Project*, in which the contribution of knitters to the islands' heritage is promoted and celebrated. Hazel, Minnie and Mary are all incredible knitters with several decades of experience behind them, but they are also forward-looking women with a careful eye on the future of their craft. Perhaps the most inspiring thing about Shetland lace today is the way that these women are sharing their considerable expertise with lace knitters of a new generation, encouraging and supporting dynamic new ideas.

One source of such ideas is designer, Angela Irvine, whose work typifies Shetland's combination of traditional practice with contemporary innovation. Like most Shetland girls, Angela grew up in a family of knitters, but her interest in fine lace was sparked when she began designing garments during her degree in Textiles. Her beautiful dresses mix digitally printed silk with fine hand-knitting—a striking mingling of old methods with new technology. Angela thrives on a technical challenge, and says that getting to grips with complicated lace patterns and digital processes involves much the same thing. "I had no idea that it was so tricky to transform

Shetland back-and-forth lace for working in the round," she says, "the older lace knitters were very impressed when I showed them what I'd done with my purl rows." Much of the visual energy of Angela's work seems to spring from her mastery and transformation of traditional patterns; incorporating in-the-round shaping into a print o' the wave bodice; showcasing birds-eye lace with a ballooning sleeve; enlivening fine openwork with beaded embellishment. Angela's designs have already won several awards, and, from her studio on the small easterly island of Whalsay, her work continues to speak both to local traditions and contemporary trends.

Angela is one of twenty-two women involved in an original endeavour which illustrates how collaborative and forward-looking Shetland lace knitting is today. The "Mirrie Dancers" Project (named for the dialect term for the Northern Lights) celebrates the innovatory culture of Shetland lace on an impressively large scale. Artists Nayan Kulkarni and Roxane Permar began by organising lively cross-generational "lace labs", in which knitters were challenged to think about their craft as a vehicle for the diffusion of light and shade. Experimenting with pattern, and using twine and microfilament as well as traditional laceweight yarns, the knitters designed swatches, which were then projected to create a beautiful and dramatic lacy lightshow. With its complex patterning and elaborate detail, Shetland fine lace seems perhaps a definitively private medium. But here, through the use of projected light, lace is opened up in an immersive and intriguing way, enabling public eyes to look at it anew. Four years in the making, the project will culminate this year with a permanent installation in Lerwick's new music and cinema venue, Mareel. "The building will be completely lit up with lace," says Roxane, explaining how visitors will find themselves wrapped up in illuminated knitted stitches. The talented knitters and artists involved in this exciting project will truly enable us to see Shetland lace in a new light.

Go to **www.knitrowan.com** to visit our new interactive on-line Rowan Magazine and to see video interviews with some of the Shetland knitters.

Links and Further Reading
Eliza Edmonston,
Sketches and Tales of the Shetland Isles (1856)

Linda G Fryer,
Knitting by the Fireside and on the Hillside (1995)

Sharon Miller,
Heirloom Knitting (2002) and *Shetland's Hap Shawl then and Now* (2006)

Shetland Museum and Archives
http://www.shetland-museum.org.uk

Mirrie Dancers
http://www.mirriedancers.com

finesse

Inspired by the retro influences of the
late 1950's and early 1960's, FINESSE is
a collection that heralds a return to
feminine curves. Classically understated,
the knits in FINESSE are sleek and lean
hugging the body, creating a beautiful
collection of designs which are flattering
and a joy to wear.

LORETTA
Pure Wool DK
Marie Wallin
🧶 147

CARRIE
Wool Cotton
Marie Wallin
🧶151

BONNIE
Cashsoft DK
Martin Storey
🧶182

JOYCE
Cashsoft DK
Lisa Richardson
166

PEGGY
Cashsoft 4 ply
Marie Wallin
✿ 136

66

NANCY
Cashsoft 4 ply
Erika Knight
🧶157

Photographer: Peter Christian Christensen. **Styling:** Marie Wallin. **Hair & Make Up:** Frances Prescott (One Photographic).
Art Direction: Marie Wallin. **Model:** Catherine Hudson (Tess Model Management).
Location: Calke Abbey, Derbyshire. Many thanks to the National Trust, Nigel and John for all their help.

in 1986.....

Pope John Paul II made history by entering a synagogue and Margaret Thatcher and Francois Mitterand did the same by entering into an agreement to link England with France via the Channel Tunnel. Picasso's 'Weeping Woman' was lost then found, in an Australian railway station and, 72 seconds after take-off, American space shuttle 'Challenger' was lost period. The first computer virus, 'The Brain', started to spread and Prince Andrew married Sarah Fergusson, Carrie Grant and Simone de Beauvoir died. Lady Gaga and The Rowan Magazine were born.

It cost £3.45, featured on the front cover a boxy, short-sleeved, jumper and a list of contributing designers including 'Kaffe Fassett and others'. Cut to The Rowan Knitting and Crochet Magazine 50, and it features on the front cover a lovely chunky cabled cape and, inside, contributions from a selection of designers including 'Kaffe Fassett and others'. Some marriages are plainly made in heaven and this Golden Anniversary issue celebrates Rowan's long-running relationship with many of its favourite designers.

Kaffe Fassett

First design - *Ikon* - Magazine 1.

Favourite design - *Kilim* - modelled by Kate Moss in Magazine 10.

Amazing how far you can travel in 10 steps. Kilburn pavement - grey slabs, grey sky, drizzling rain. Through Kaffe's front door- the cobalt blues of a mosaic table, the bright mix of an Indian wall hanging, the rich tones of

traditional Turkish carpets; and that's just the hallway! Another world!

Kaffe, the living antonym to monochrome, is rather more than one of Rowan's favourite designers - his input helped make the company what it is today. In the late '70s, Stephen Sheard and Simon Cockin started a Yorkshire company selling rug making kits. Distinctly superior kits, it has to be said, with a stunning yarn collection of 96 colours. Kaffe was becoming increasingly well known for his own wizardry with colour and, when the trio met at a showcasing event, the outcome was a request for Kaffe to colour some hand knitting yarns. He was particularly delighted to accept; driven by his artist's need for an ever-expanding palette, he'd been working with anything he could get his hands on and that included rug yarns so rough they were stripping the skin off his hands!

In 1983, the cover of 'Woman and Home' magazine featured Kaffe's 'Super Triangles' jacket. Sales massively exceeded expectations and Rowan Weavers was reborn as Rowan Yarns. Things then happened fast; Rowan started producing patterns by other designers, it moved eventually from kits to open-stock yarn and, finally, established a world-wide distribution and consultancy network. Kaffe's early abrasive experiments were over, leaving him with a preference for working in fine, 4-ply, natural

yarns and an abiding respect for what Rowan has achieved!

"Knitters around the world really responded to the products coming out of Rowan. You knew there was something extraordinary going on in the middle of this small, creative community in the middle of Yorkshire."

The invention has never stopped. Kaffe was recently commissioned to produce a new range of 100% lambs wool yarn - 'Colourscape Chunky' - and found himself back in the Yorkshire landscape:

"There I was, surrounded by old Victorian machinery, and I was just tying together bits of all my favourite colours and the guy was figuring out how to segue them together and concentrating so hard he couldn't speak." Each hank (and the production process means no two are exactly the same) produces a' repeat rainbow-like effect'. Relax! It's a rainbow blended by Kaffe; you're guaranteed success.

"When I started with Rowan there were no shareholders, we didn't have much to lose so we were prepared to try things, but nothing in this life stays the same!"

"Now I tend to work with Rowan doing special collections and that lets me really express myself and produce what I love. I have tremendous respect for that very interesting group of people in that wild landscape full of great hills, stones and wonderful mosses, and I'm glad that Rowan, after a few years of looking outward, is now turning back to really celebrate that landscape, its heritage and intense Englishness. I am loving the palettes it's bringing out now. My hope is there will always be room for someone as outrageous and theatrical as myself and I look forward to going on and on and on."

Marie Wallin

First design - *Regency* dress - Magazine 39

Favourite design - *Inga* - Magazine 48

An ad in 'Draper's Record', a week-long interview that involved producing a collection using some 'horrendous yarns' and, in 2005, Marie Wallin took over from Kim Hargreaves as Rowan's head designer. She was looking for a challenge. She wasn't disappointed.

"I was thrown in the deep end and it was a really steep learning curve. Not so much on the design side but dealing with the magazine. And I had some real disasters. On the 'Kidsilk Dream' shoot, for example, I hadn't cast the model and, honestly, the only time she looked good was when she was lying down! I had a lot to learn.

"I'd always been a fan of Rowan, and admired what Kim Hargreaves did with the brand. Actually I was completely in awe and terrified when I first got to meet Kaffe and the other designers. Now they're just good friends."

This petite lady, with a ready smile and a constant twinkle in her eye, has a real knack for making friends and, as a modus operandi, declares she 'only works with people she likes'.

You get what that means if you watch the ease with which she now runs a photo-shoot and gets the stunning results she is famed for. She chats quietly to the impossibly tall model about her university interviews; congratulates the photographer on his latest shot, reassures a colleague planning an afternoon shoot and still manages to check what people want for lunch. Calm, cheerful, relaxed, encouraging. Marie brings out the best in people so excellent work

gets done, and she manages to look as if she's just dropped in for tea!

But don't be fooled, she's acquired her own brand of assertiveness and knows exactly what she wants - making sure Rowan maintains its position as an iconic British brand and grounds that iconography in developing real British skills.

"It's important we maintain the quality and integrity of the yarns we buy. My passion has been the Purelife yarns and we're planning to extend this range in the coming seasons. The British Sheep Breeds yarns are dear to my heart. My aim would be to have more of our yarn range British, but it's a challenge as there is currently limited UK production."

"Rowan is not just about getting people knitting but about presenting knitting in a different, aspirational way. We're at the forefront of knitting design – we do classics, mainstream and catwalk, and maintaining that diversity, the way we do the photography and styling, is an edge we have to keep. In my opinion, if we lose that, we lose Rowan."

A good year before they're seen by consumers, Marie works with Kate Buller, Rowan's brand manager, on putting together the yarns and designs for the new season.

"I do trend research and decide on possible stories. Even at this stage I have a vision of the whole look and exactly how I want to shoot it. Then I give it a name and start to put together a story board and a pretty comprehensive design brief for the freelancers and the in house team. They submit designs and the design committee make the choice."

"There's a revival of interest in knitting across all ages and we need to embrace different ways of reaching people to keep the brand up there. It's really important that we keep ahead of what is happening on the internet, so it's great that we are launching our new website and that we carry on promoting new designers."

She's smiling. But she's determined!

patterns you're working on. They want to download patterns and buy yarns, and they want to do it now! They might still go into a wool shop to feel the wools but craft is becoming more of a communal thing and the way people shop is changing. Every town now has a 'Knit and Natter' or a 'Stitch and Bitch' group, where you can buy yarns and have a coffee, and then people get together online as well, to get advice and share what they're doing. All that networking is creating a new demand."

"I use technology quite a bit. It's great! I can work for Rowan but live in the West Country. You need to be out there to keep up your profile and I do use Facebook and Twitter but I'm quite careful what I put up there. I also use a software package, a really ancient one I've had for years, to help with the technical side of things."

"I'm researching all the time looking at trends. I look at shape and pattern, picking out things I think are nice, then the yarn, colour and texture come together after that. I think I do things the opposite way round to most people. And I think I am quite concerned with what people are wearing on the street. It's a really fine balance between getting the fashion element yet maintaining the classic Rowan approach that people love. It's a sort of symbiosis. You need to be right up there with the High Street but people also want to keep what they've made in their wardrobe for many years."

"It's important to think of the novice knitter and include entry level patterns in the mix; you just have to make them so beautiful even the experienced knitters want to make them!"

"I love the fact that you can get a completely different look from the same garment depending on how you style them. Someone might wear a jumper with a long skirt and someone else wear it with micro-shorts and it works perfectly for both."

Martin Storey

First design – *Dales Aran* **– Magazine 6**
Favourite design – *Valentina* **– Magazine 48**

Stephen Sheard was developing a denim yarn. Martin Storey was working for design house, Artwork, which was keen to develop a range of denim knitwear. A collaboration ensued. Stephen clocked Martin's potential and, when he went freelance in the early 90's, asked him to do some designs for the magazine. Ten year's later he was taken on as a full-time in-house designer and, many Classic brochures, books, magazine designs and website offerings later, he's still at it.

"We've never been able to perfect a profile of the 'typical' Rowan knitter – but we do know that instead of asking 'Where can I get a brochure?' now they're asking 'Have you got a website?' The Internet is changing things and it's all happening so fast. It has really brought people into the knitting community and, even for the traditional knitter, it's fast becoming their first port of call."

"The social networking sites, like 'Ravelry', have brought a whole new dimension to things. People are getting positively voyeuristic. They want to get involved with every detail of what you're doing, what colours you're using, what

"We need to keep revisiting our roots all the time – the heart of Yorkshire and the heritage of Rowan, that very British thing that international markets appreciate. We have to keep refreshing it but, if you move too far away from your roots, you risk losing everything."

Erika Knight

First design – *New England* **– Magazine 4**
Favourite design – *New England* **– Magazine 4**

Another designer who's been there right from the start. When she started her own company, 'Molto', in the '80s, it was Rowan yarns she used. "It was the only yarn company to recognise the needs of the small designer. And it's still there after 30 years because of its choice of yarns, the selection and diversity of designs, the patterns, which are well conceived and engineered to accommodate the breadth of knowledge of the knitter, and the fact they are all graded for ten or twelve sizes and thoroughly pattern checked.

Bit of a lateral jump here as Erika thinks about a place you can go to get patterns that don't have quite that stamp of quality.

"The internet is fantastic. Having loads of free patterns available is all good and it's great that you can go to a homely instruction site and learn how to knit or crochet. Bit disconcerting to be talking crochet and then suddenly switch topic to someone's cat, and you have to be careful what you select, but it's stimulating an amazing culture of craft, that's going to grow as we try and balance all the technology in our lives."

At this point Erika admits to being a bit of a 'tweeter': "Not just about knitting, but anything. Since kindergarten we've all enjoyed doing 'show and tell', looking for our peers' approval, and we naturally seek to exchange ideas. People want instant access to something that engages them – whether that's a recipe for tonight or a new knitting project. There's a global reach now with fascinating patterns coming from Israel, Japan, Scandinavia, the Baltic States. Everything is out there, you just have to choose what suits you."

"The next big thing is Backing Britain, and Rowan has always been a beacon for supporting British industry. That beacon needs to be shining bright and it must never forget its heritage and that it has a story to tell. Rowan has always been about promoting awareness of natural fibres. It stands for expertise, experience and innovation. Long may that last."

Sarah Dallas

First design – *Oak Leaves* – Magazine 4
Favourite design – *Ioannina* – Magazine 7

I've never seen Sarah Dallas in anything other than shades of black; extremely elegant and beautifully put together, as befits the founder and senior tutor of the Fashion Knitwear course at the Royal College of Art, but always, well, dark.

"I think that started with ease of packing for trade fairs and it just stuck!" Slight pause; "Actually I do wear fuschia pink when the sun's out!"

And it's definitely colour that gets her creative juices flowing. Just as well or her first brief from Rowan, 'using no less than eight colours', which resulted in a Fair Isle sweater inspired by Greek embroidery, may well have been her last!

"Now I get three trends from Rowan, with suggestions of yarns and palettes, and then I just sit down and start doing lots of rough sketches. I start with colour, think of the yarn, then approach the garment. I work on one, start on another and, in the end, have lots of things on the go at once."

"I don't use technology at all in the design process – I go to books, galleries and museums for inspiration. I like to take all that back to the students."

Talking of museums, Sarah donated her entire archive, not just garments but fashion sketches, designs, technical drawings and correspondence, to the Bath Fashion Museum where they form part of the permanent exhibition; proof of just how far knitwear has come.

"The best bit of knit is that you are in control of the whole process, you decide on the shape, the colour, everything; there are no parameters."

"Rowan's projects with the RCA have been really important for the industry. The competitions introduce students to hand knitting, they discover the possibilities and then incorporate it into their final collections. Companies see the talent and take on knitwear designers for their fashion collections. Things have changed and there's an awareness that knitwear isn't just something anyone can do. It's now very firmly part of fashion and I hope we've all helped to put it there."

Lisa Richardson

First design – *Dream* – Magazine 34
Favourite design – *O'Malley* – Magazine 38

Lisa was experiencing a distinct sense of déjà vue. A photoshoot – check. A gathering of designers – check. An interview – check. Magazine 34, which featured her first design, (not knitwear at all but a quilted, embroidered bag), involved all of these and Lisa was sitting in the London studio, surrounded by Rowan colleagues, feeling as if she had come full circle.

Always a hobby knitter and crocheter (thank you Grandma!), she first used her design skills doing knitted art pieces for ' A' levels. College added some tailoring knowledge and she then worked as a freelancer in homeware design. Her first job with Rowan was on the admin side in the design room and, since then, there's not many jobs - from pattern writing and grading to original designs - that she couldn't turn her hand to. It's actually Lisa who is overall pattern editor for anything that goes out under the Rowan name.

"I suppose designing has finally brought my tailoring and knitting skills together. When I get a brief I think of the shape and the texture first and work from there."

Suggest that yarn and colour come later and Lisa laughs as she realises she hasn't mentioned them because they are such an intrinsic part of her life that she doesn't even consider them as separate from the process.

"At the office party I was nominated for the 'Messiest Desk' prize. I have shade cards, half-knitted swatches and needles all over the place. I work completely surrounded by yarns so I don't exactly start with them, they are always there."

"The internet does draw in people who want to share but I think knitters will always like the sort of sensory experience you get from the Rowan books. They are so beautiful you can flick through them and

you're guaranteed to find inspiration. They offer timeless pieces and your part as a designer is to help people create something they'll have for years and years. That's what I love about working with Rowan."

Brandon Mably

First design - *Rice Paper* - **Magazine 23**
Favourite design - *Ease* - **Magazine 49**

History just doesn't seem to be the right place to start with Brandon; he is quintessentially a man of the moment. His favourite pattern – the one he's working on now. His favourite yarn - the one he's using to complete the one he's working on now... His favourite colours - the ones he's using... You get the picture? And 'picture' really is the key word. It wouldn't make sense to remove the plural in the 'favourite colours' question. When Brandon works with textiles he may be knitting, working with needlepoint, or designing a new fabric, but what he is actually doing is 'painting with yarns'.

"If I was asked to knit a beige sweater it would be the equivalent of asking me to knit up a bowl of cold porridge." 'Nuff said!

His disgust at working in monotone demonstrates a clear path to his mentor and inspiration, Kaffe. It was a chance meeting with Kaffe that seduced Brandon away from his erstwhile career as a chef (and I'll wager he didn't spend too long on porridge in that incarnation either!) and opened his eyes to Art.

"I walked into Kaffe's studio and it was like entering a nursery school that hadn't been tidied up." He manages to convey the eye-popping excitement of such a visual feast and, at the same time, hints at another side of his character. He'd be inspired by the chaos but there's a little bit of Brandon that, having absorbed the pattern the colours made, would really like to get stuck in and clear up the mess.

It's those organisational skills that turned him, as he puts it, 'into the 'O' in the Kaffe Fassett Studio in London'. Kaffe gave him a job, taught him to do simple stocking stitch and, together with Rowan's Stephen Sheard, encouraged

Brandon to 'have a go' at developing what proved to be an innate talent for design. He's never looked back. On the knitting technique side he will say he hasn't developed much either. His designs get their impact from the palette he uses but still rely on a basic stitch. He's not keen on 'bunches of grapes'!

"I can show anyone how to add colour in five seconds. You only knit using manageable lengths of yarn. I don't want to see anyone with balls or I'll cut them off!"

Basic language. Undeniably inspirational effect!

Amanda Crawford

First design - *Betty, Daisy and Plaid* – **Magazine 38**
Favourite design - *Minnie* - **Magazine 39**

Amanda's life as a knitwear designer was nearly thwarted by a owl. A Brown Owl, to be precise, in the guise of her Mum, who forced her to knit

endless squares for charity blankets. She got her Brownie Badge and a strong aversion to needles.

But hormones do strange things and, aged 12, her Mother's stash suddenly looked irresistible and one 'Frankenstein jumper' later (no shape, lots of stitching together – the latter an abiding pleasure) she was off and hasn't stopped since. She worked her way through Wendy, Sirdar and Patons' designs for pocket money, designed for M&S, then something happened: "I opened a Rowan Magazine and I knew that's where I wanted to be."

Where there's a will there's a way. Slightly circuitous in this case, via a job in the haberdashery department at John Lewis, Nottingham, impressing the Rowan consultant there and finally being given four balls of 'Cork' (now defunct) and asked to come up with a design for a 'free gift with every subscription' promotion. A cabled, mini-poncho, 'Freda', obviously hit the right buttons. Eight years on, light years from the original 'Frankenstein', and much beading and lace work later, Amanda's very firmly where she wanted to be.

"When I receive a design brief from Marie I get my yarns together in a big pile in front of me and group them all into the stories; I pull pictures from magazines that influence the stories - shapes, patterns and textures. Then I go through all my books listing all the stitches I want and I'm away - knitting like a woman possessed!"

"Today's knitters are quite fearless, they'll take on a massive project. They see something they like on the internet and that's it. And they use blogs to get help so, instead of leaving something to die in a corner, they actually finish it."

"One piece garments with no seams are already around but I think circular and 4-needle knitting will become more popular."

"The Rowan look is quite purist in a way, it's like a little piece of the Yorkshire countryside."

"It needs to stay true to itself and keep its core values – beautiful, natural fibres and as much as possible British."

Jennie Atkinson

First design - *Butterfly* dress - **Magazine 37**
Favourite design - *Stanwyck* - **Magazine 44**

Get yourself down to the famous London Vintage Fashion Fair (Hammersmith Town Hall, once every five weeks) and while wandering through the rails of beaded gowns, lace work trimmings, gloves, and textiles from the 1800s to the 1980s, you are quite likely to bump into Jennie Atkinson, prowling the displays in search of inspiration.

"You walk into this room and are surrounded by all these things that have had so much love and work put into them. It's fantastic."

It's been eight years since Jennie, who already had her own shop in Islington offering hand and machine knits, joined the Rowan band and has been pouring love and work into her own creations.

"I was first asked to contribute to a feature on

freelance, but all her energies are still focussed on knitwear. And technology!

"I think it has taken people by surprise, because knitting is a craft, but knitters are very tech savvy; they're a clever bunch and that's the way ahead."

"I've just launched an App that's like a knitting book - it starts with a scarf and ends with a simple sweater and has videos of all the techniques you need. I'm trying to encourage people along so they'll start with a scarf but then carry on."

edgings and braids and then my next design, The Butterfly Dress, a lacy dress in Kidsilk Haze with beading worked in, ended up on the front cover."

"Knitting can either be a way of making your own garments quickly or it can be about making something really beautiful. I did a dissertation on the history of the knitting pattern and loved the way the Victorians knitted such intricate things. I prefer the challenge of using fine needles and fine yarns and including lots of detail."

"You don't often find knitted things at the vintage fairs, though, because knits didn't really become part of fashion until women's role in society started to change and their dress code became a bit more relaxed."

Jennie may look backwards for inspiration but she's enthusiastic about the positive changes the latest technologies are having on the future of knitting.

"The internet has been really important to the current comeback. It was bought home to me when I went to work on my annual project with the RCA students. Usually, I start by teaching skills but last year I found they'd all been online and everyone already knew how to knit. That's a great change. And a good one."

Sarah Hatton

First design - *Charley* - Magazine 37
Favourite design - *Martha* - Studio 2

"I'm a knitting slave!" Sarah announces, but with a peal of laughter that makes bondage sound fun. After eight years of in-house designing and pattern writing, she's gone

"People used to think you knitted a front, a back, two sleeves then sewed them together but now the younger crowd want to knit top down or use magic loops; it's crazy and really exciting."

"The industry is getting flooded at the moment with everyone thinking they can be a designer, but I think things will calm down and there will be a realisation there's a skill and a talent in being a designer and only the good ones will come through."

"A few years ago, at the fashion shows, there were celebrities on the front row, now there are 13-year old bloggers with a huge amount of power. Suddenly you have people like Ysolde Teague and Jared Flood who have just created themselves. But bring them all on and let's see what happens."

"Blogging's great but it can also get quite personal. People have had a bad day at work and vent on the pattern they are trying to do. They can't scream at their boss so they have a go at a designer on line. They forget we're real people and it can be a bit hurtful."

"The defining thing about a Rowan customer is that she's an individual who's quite happy with

herself and doesn't want to follow the crowd. Rowan is the pinnacle of the knitting world and it's just great to continue to be involved with what they are doing."

Kim Hargreaves

First design was in the 'Cotton Collection' published in 1987.
Favourite design - *Kiri* - Magazine 28

Garter stitch tea cosy at eight; Rowan designer in the eighties – Kim did a week of 'work experience' at the Holmfirth Mill at the tender age of 17 and was thoroughly hooked. Back in the day, part of the mill was rented out to a furniture maker and Kim's Mum, Kathleen, (engaged at the time in sewing leather upholstery for yachts), got to know Stephen, swapped jobs, ended up as design room manager for Rowan and organised the week for Kim. The week turned into a holiday job helping to put together the printed canvas needlepoint kits. Her enthusiasm was spotted, she was offered a full-time job and left school with her "A" level in Art (" I was rubbish at drawing anyway.") to start what turned into a twenty-year association with Rowan .

"Kaffe happened, Rowan moved into knitwear and I showed some designs I'd done to Stephen. He muttered something polite but he must have remembered them because the next thing I knew I was asked to do some for the magazine. It was amazing!

"It was called 'The Cotton Collection' and involved lots of stripes, bold colours and unstructured shapes. In fact, they were the only

shapes I could do to start with; it took years of practice before I could do anything more body conscious."

Practice clearly makes perfect and Kim ended up as Rowan's in-house designer and brand co-ordinator.

"I don't see that Rowan has changed hugely. Fashions obviously move with the times but there is always that undercurrent of where the company came from. The quality and colours of the yarns, and the magazines, are still absolutely wonderful."

In 2005 Kim branched out and, with her mother, started her own internet design company that now publishes four books each year so loyal followers can still get their Hargreaves hit. And she certainly has followers – one lady regularly 'frogs' less favoured knits to convert them into Hargreaves garments (think the term 'frogging' comes from upper class English frogs who go 'rip it, rip it' – well, they're hardly going to croak 'unravel' are they?) Kim is also a firm favourite of The Sexy Knitter's Club – her shaping skills are much admired, and the yarns she insists on using for all her patterns? Nothing but Rowan!

young talent available, and as the retail landscape changes, methods of communication and self promotion become ever more rapid and globally accessible through the internet, Rowan will make ever greater efforts to source emerging trends and talents through the popular social networking sites such as Ravelry and Facebook.

The times that we now live in are forever changing and at an ever increasing pace, but Rowan has always believed change to be a good thing and evolution of the brand is essential to securing our long term position in the hand knitting market. We will always embrace change and new ideas, but the one thing that will remain the same is that we will always endeavour to communicate with you first and foremost as passionate knitters who will always remain just like all our designers, part of Rowan's extended family.

CONCLUSION
Kate Buller

The Rowan brand has built its name through the unique talents of a fantastic stable of designers. As Rowan's brand manager it has been my privilege to have the support and ongoing creative enthusiasm of the best designers in hand knitting. We have also been thrilled to be able to spot new talent and through our editorials and workshop programme been able to promote these new designers.

From Magazine 1 onwards designers have always been a huge part of Rowan's success. Names have changed throughout the 33 years but the core designers have remained the same, Kaffe Fassett, Martin Storey and Erika Knight to name a few. Some designers have moved onto become best selling authors, whilst others have launched their own yarn ranges and some have set themselves up independently but still sponsored by Rowan, such as Kim Hargreaves. However we have always firmly believed that even these independent designers remain part of the Rowan extended family.

As Rowan's journey continues through the next 50 issues of the Rowan magazine, we will continue to search out and nurture the best

Go to **www.knitrowan.com** to visit our new interactive on-line Rowan Magazine and to see video interviews with the designers.

the british are turning soft!

Words by Dr Margy Cockburn. Photography by Peter Christian Christensen

The Wool Cycle – from mud to tactile magnificence – is nothing short of miraculous and, frankly, deserves more attention. I'm not talking 'low temperatures and a short spin' here, but the conversion of sunshine, air, rain and grass, into fleece that's shorn to provide wool, that can be spun into yarn, and finally morphed into cloth, clothes, insulation, carpets, bedding, furniture – the possibilities are endless.

Sheep manage this marvellous conversion – in fact about 2.2 kilos - every year. That makes wool not just one of the most effective natural forms of all-weather protection known to man but also a totally renewable source of fibre. So that part of the conversion works just perfectly and ticks every box for the ultimate modern material. The bit that urgently needs to be tackled is the retail end and the conversion of consumers to appreciate the qualities of wool and so restore worldwide demand for this fantastically versatile material. The appalling truth is that it can currently cost a UK farmer more to sheer a sheep than he will make from selling its wool. Not a prospect that offers much appeal to prospective shepherds.

And if sheep farmers were to disappear because their life style becomes unsustainable – (no vague, pseudo-ecological, marketing use of the term here, but sustain as in 'afford to put food on the table!') - the impact would extend way beyond the world of textiles. One casualty would be the classic UK landscape. Imagine the transformation in your garden if it was left to its own devices for a decade. That gives an inkling of just how dependent our rolling countryside is on Nature's natural and constant ruminant lawnmowers! No shepherds equals no sheep and no wool but an awful lot of brambles!
'Sustainable, biodegradable, and inextricably linked to the heart of the rural British countryside' - no surprise, then, that the Prince of Wales got involved and, last year, convened the "Campaign for Wool"- a five-year, cross-industry initiative that is pulling together wool organisations from around the world – growers, manufacturers, designers and retailers - to try and turn around its declining popularity.

'Natural, traditional, eco-aware, designer, and luxurious ' and there's another British institution that it's no surprise to find wholeheartedly behind the Campaign – Rowan Yarns, which kicked off its involvement by running a design competition for students at the Royal College of Art and linking with Liberty of London to showcase the results. The students were tasked with 'challenging the perception of hand knitting by exploring new uses for knitting, in designs for garments, accessories for the person or the home, or textile art.' The key word was 'Freedom' and the pieces had to link to the 50th anniversary of London's icon of the Swinging Sixties, Carnaby Street – an area still setting the trends and celebrating individualism and independence – from reworking vintage fashion at 'FCNK' (Fur Coat No Knickers!) to Liam Gallagher's 'Pretty Green'.

Freedom and students is obviously a felicitous mix. Bridgette Kelly from the British Wool Marketing board, one of the prize donors to the competition, took one look at the in-store display of the six finalists' pieces and instantly doubled the prize money! She explains why:

"The standard of work and creativity from the students was just excellent and really showcased the natural colours and potential of wool from Rowan's British Sheep Breeds range of yarns. The British Wool Marketing Board believes that students have a key position in taking wool forward in both fashion and interiors and it's their fresh ideas and innovative approach that will give wool a new lease of life,"

Not a lot of people know that wool...

- offers naturally high UV protection,
- is flame retardant, due to its high water and nitrogen content, has a higher ignition threshold than many other fibres and gives off fewer toxic and noxious fumes when burnt
- is biodegradable so won't contribute to the landfill problem
- can absorb up to 30% of its own weight in moisture without feeling damp to the touch
- fibre can be bent 20,000 times without breaking and still have the power to recover
- is naturally elastic, able to stretch one third of its length so cloth returns to its original shape after wear
- 29 million kilos of British Wool was sold last year

Joint- winner, **Claire Anne O'Brien**, *(Royal College of Art - MA Textiles graduate)* is currently busy setting up a design studio in Bethnal Green, and had taken Rowan's Purelife British Sheep Breeds Chunky, and an old chair and... and... had some fun. She explains:

"The piece is a humorous play on scale and the chair celebrates the very structure of the knitted stitch and combines attention to detail with an exaggerated scale. At the fabric level, it is knitted in rib to give very precise stitch definition, and then this is manipulated into a repeat pattern to give the illusion of a giant knitted chair. I loved the opportunity to work with the chunky wools. They're a really versatile yarn for interiors."

Helen Turner, *(Royal College of Art - MA Fashion Knitwear - Womenswear)* the second joint winner, went one better than this year's craze for 'coatigans' and, in a piece that reflected the hippy fringing of the 60's and offered at least a nod in the direction of the one-time ubiquitous Afghan coat, practically knitted up a whole sheep.

"I started with the intarsia base of the coat and the fringing was worked in on top. It took rather a long time to build up to the thickness I wanted – to be honest I lost count of the hours it took and I must have used about 60 balls of wool - but it was amazing working with the British Sheep Breed yarns (Helen used 5 varieties of Chunky and DK yarns, all undyed, including Steel Grey Suffolk, Mid Brown Jacob and Bluefaced Leicester). You'd think British wool would produce something hard but it's amazing how soft the yarn is and how many different textures you can exploit."

Second prize went to **Ruth Green** (Royal College of Art - MA Fashion Knitwear - Womenswear) who took inspiration from the checked weaves of Pierre Cardin, using hand knit to recreate the weavers' patterns, and Flower Power style queen, Mary Quant. She created a unique dress using a mix of British Sheep Breeds yarn - Mid Brown Jacob, Bluefaced Leicester, Black Welsh, Shetland Moorit and Steel Grey Suffolk Chunky - that combined intarsia and interweaving stitch and juxtaposed 60's 3-D felted flowers (the result of commandeering the oven and a little outré cooking!) and geometric patterns.

"I've always loved the freedom of hand knitting," explained runner-up **Catherine Tremellen** *(Royal College of Art - MA Textiles)* "there are no limits and you can do absolutely anything with it." So she did, and the result was a stunning dress echoing the fluidity of Art Nouveau curves, full of movement and tactile 3-D forms, and perfect for exploiting the structural qualities and softness of the British Sheep Breed yarns. She used the natural colour palette of Bluefaced Leicester and Mid Brown Bluefaced Leicester DK and a variety of needle sizes.

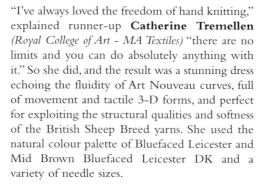

Emma Bradbury *(Royal College of Art - MA Textiles graduate)*, also a runner-up, started with a retro tea cosy pattern, Bluefaced Leicester and Black Welsh Chunky yarn and, inspired by 60's optical patterns and psychedelic colours, started knitting and went on and on and on.... The end result was a fully reversible continuous loop scarf, long enough to twist round the head or contort round the body to offer maximum wear opportunities. "I love natural wool – the handle of it, even the way it smells, and the environmental benefits far outweigh those of man-made materials."

Emma's next project is a visit to Shetland College, in the north of Scotland, where she will be working with students to explore combining Shetland and Scandinavian patterns to produce a new take on some old traditions.

Lucy Falke *(Royal College of Art - MA Textiles)*, final runner-up, presented a shift dress made from hair-pin lace and crochet and, though still rigorously 60's-based, she looked a little further afield than Carnaby Street for her ideas. The Japanese Metabolist movement in architecture (lots of modular, flexible and adaptable megastructures) was one inspiration and the other was Paco Rabanne (lots of experimenting with unconventional materials and famous for his 'Unwearables' collection which featured those quintessentially 60's, hi-tech, dresses with discs of metal, vinyl and plastic linked together by chains). Nothing unwearable about Lucy's design, though. While the literal structure for the dress was provided by split metal rings these were used to link together sections of knitting done with softest Purelife yarn to produce an eminently wearable end result.

Perhaps it's time, in an entirely upbeat way, to declare that 'Britain is going soft!' We have long been famed for the hard-wearing wool of British hill breeds and top quality carpets. There are now an increasing number of farmers proving they can successfully raise a variety of breeds to offer a much more extensive range of yarns and they are aiming to raise UK wool production to altogether more elevated positions. Wool underfoot is good but add wool to walk around in, wool to insulate our buildings and wool to sit on, 40,000 feet above sea level on a transatlantic flight, and that's got to be even better.

Early last year, yarn specialists Laxtons, another supporter of the Rowan competition, flew in the face of the majority of manufacturers who have been turning East for their supplies and production, and invested in a new yarn manufacturing facility in Yorkshire. James Laxton, great grandson of the company's founder, is definitely on a mission to restore England's place in the world of wool.

"Some people said it was a bold move, some people said it was crazy, but we knew it was now or never so we took the decision to bring back our raw material purchasing and production to the UK to support what is left of the textile infrastructure and we are going to build on that."

Initial reactions have been good. Wool spun by Laxtons from British sheep breeds has been sold into Savile Row and has already hit the shops in a range of top quality women's jackets from Jigsaw. James is allowing himself to feel "really excited about the future. The UK can provide everything the consumer demands, we just have to get them to buy it!"

So Rowan continues its commitment to support young designers to push the boundaries of an age-old artisan craft to offer a whole new look at what, and where, wool can feature in our lives. Farmers are experimenting with breeding programmes to extend the range of wools offered by UK producers so they will be ready to service new demand, whatever that is, and to command a price that will make sheep farming a viable proposition. Yorkshire has a champion putting his energies into a stimulating a renaissance of the UK textile industry. The Campaign for Wool has Royal patronage to help raise awareness of wool's natural properties – it's warm, durable, naturally thermo-regulating, wicks away moisture, and makes environmental sense on a number of levels. And the wool producers and sellers round the world are joining together to shout the message far and wide and make sure a fibre with a history reaching back thousands of years is also very much a fibre with a future.

Go to **www.knitrowan.com** to visit our new interactive on-line Rowan Magazine and to see more information on Wool Week including the Savile Row Field Day in October 2010.

winter
essentials

is a collection of the key shapes and textures on trend, designed into more simple, easy to wear styles that will compliment the season's ESSENTIAL looks. Using a warm neutral colour palette, ranging from ochre and terracotta to dark earthy browns this is the 'must have' collection of the season.

THE
TIE FRONT
TUNIC

COMPASSION
Cocoon
Martin Storey
128

SINCERE
Kid Classic
Marie Wallin
🧶163

THE
HERITAGE
CABLE

LOVE
Kidsilk Haze & Baby Alpaca DK
Marie Wallin
175

THE
DRAPE
TOP

THE
CROPPED
SWEATER

AFFECTION
Lima
Sarah Hatton
🧶 142

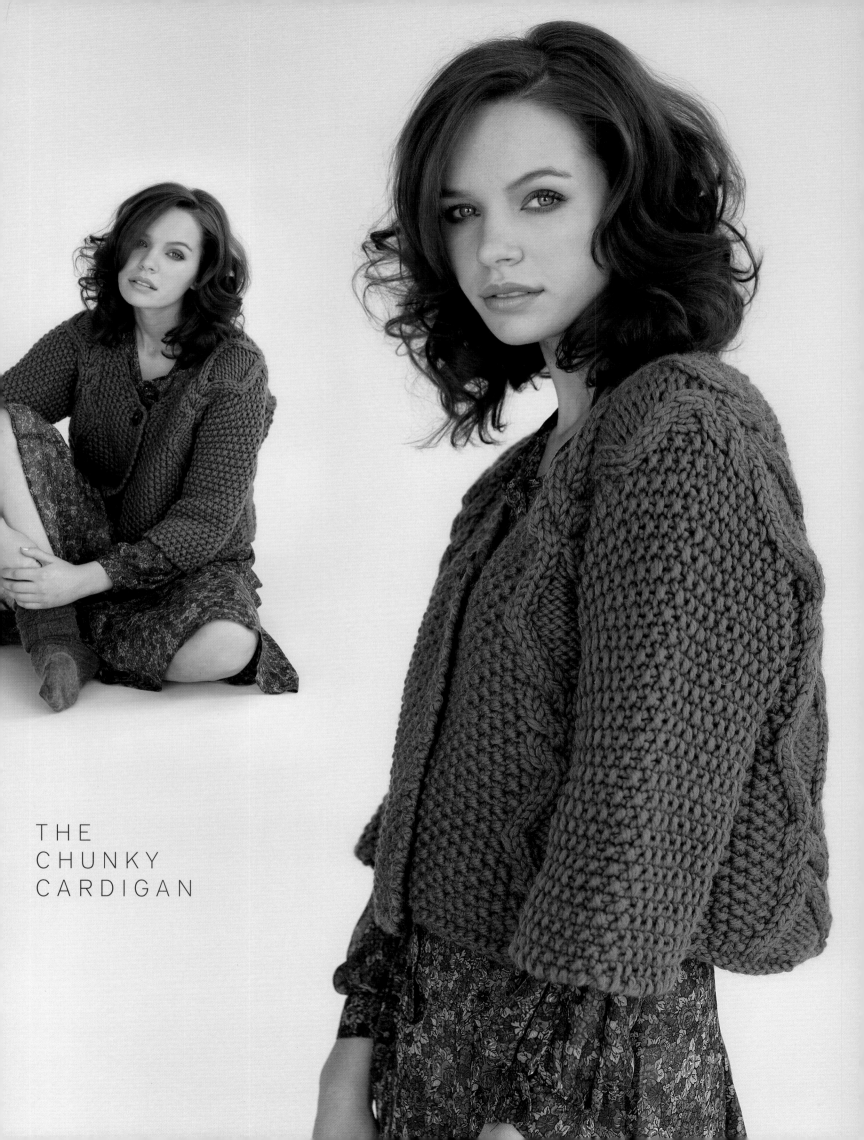

THE
CHUNKY
CARDIGAN

THE
LACE
TUNIC

THE
BELTED
CARDIGAN

THE
TEXTURED
CARDIGAN

KIND
Lima
Marie Wallin
🧶170

THE
CAPE
SWEATER

TENDER
Kid Classic
Grace Melville
173

Photographer: Peter Christian Christensen.
Styling: Marie Wallin.
Hair & Make Up: Carol Morley (One Photographic).
Art Direction: Marie Wallin.
Model: Abigail Gotts (First Model Management).

THE
CAPE
JACKET

Quilts in Sweden

Words and Photography by Debbie Patterson

Skansen is one man's vision. Artur Hazelius, a Swedish academic, founded Skansen in 1891, "the world's first open air museum" of a bygone way of life. Artur wanted to show traditional folk-life in living brushstrokes (so Kaffe, I think!) and so this very restrained Swedish-style "theme park" was born. A sense of loss about the old Swedish ways had compelled Artur to start collecting all things domestic and agricultural (hey, I love the guy he's a fellow hoarder!) until he eventually collected entire buildings representing all periods and ways of Swedish life, rebuilding them and furnishing them on the island of Djurgarden, overlooking Stockholm. Skansen Museum was born.

Below top, left to right
The Alvros farmstead 17th century loft.
A view of Stockholm.
Romantic Shawl Quilt by Mary Mashuta.

Below bottom, left to right
Sunlight In The Forest Quilt by Kaffe Fassett.
Painted cupboards in the Delsbo farmhouse.
The traditional shuttered windows of the Petissan Cafe.

In Stockholm, September 2010, enter Kaffe and team in the lobby of a nearby hotel, armed with a new and glorious collection of quilts. Kaffe and Brandon are responsible for manhandling two huge suitcases crammed with these treasures; I am armed with camera and tripod, while Pauline brings the most important thing.....the shoot list, (no cake this year, folks)! We take a quick roll down the hill to the entrance to Skansen, where the lovely red-headed Helene meets us. Tucked under Kaffe's arm is a copy of the Skansen guidebook. Itching to see locations, he flips the pages back and forth showing Helene exactly what he wants to see right away. "Can we go here....or here....or here?" Yes, but it soon becomes apparent that we will have to adjust to the Skansen pace; keys will need to be sent for and gloves needed to move this piece of furniture or that....this is living history after all. We load all our paraphernalia onto a handcart, and start at the

Charles Tottie Residence. Tottie's house dates from the early 1700s and was the home of a rich builder (what's new?) We are introduced to its "living guide", carefully dressed in period. Kaffe loves the chequerboard floor inside, but to photograph here we first have to remove our boots and put little socks on the feet of the tripod. No sitting on chairs or hanging a coat over anything either!

Helene navigates us and our cart over the almost impenetrable gravel outside the grand 18th century Skogaholm Manor. It is all that a tasteful manor should be: double wooden doors open into a pretty hall, painted soft grey, metal sconces on the walls, stencilled with Gustavian-style leaf garlands around them, and an elegant glass chandelier providing the finishing touch. We find many suitable locations within the manor, as the rooms have so many contrasting styles, such as a Chinese style study or a cool blue bedroom interior. In another we find a vivid green four-poster bed and rich brown lavishly gilded walls. On a nearby desk there is a whimsical letter, inked by a quill, folded and sealed with wax, and with a white soft feather. It has *never* been read as the seal is unbroken.

In another part of the manor undergoing restoration, Kaffe finds a real gem, a tiny locked room housing a quintessential and priceless Swedish collection of blue and white china, displayed in typical grey painted plate racks on every one of its walls. After permission is sought and the door unlocked, Kaffe and Brandon, plus a large wooden rake (for combing the deep gravel outside) and the chosen quilt squeeze into the tiny space. I hope you are holding your breath as much as I was while the quilt was draped, and positioned, and repositioned, and redraped - you get the picture! We are all extremely relieved when the pictures are taken, and the room is resealed fully intact, with no breakages whatsoever.

I wish I could take you through every building, as we explored almost every one of the 150 or so buildings on the 75-acre site, each one having something unique and, of course, authentic to offer. Naturally, we also enjoyed exploring the cakes layered on glass stands at Petissan and the piping hot meatballs and lingonberry relish at Stora Gungan. And who can forget the "living guide" working in the Bakehouse? She was elated to meet Kaffe, being a fan of his work: "you *must* be a beautiful person inside as you make such *beautiful* things on the outside", she says to Kaffe, as we sit at the end of our visit, warming in the glow of her wholesomeness, eating her freshly made flatbread. It is clear that the folk of Skansen were thrilled, I mean *really thrilled* to meet Kaffe, who is some kind of a demi-god in these parts whether for knitting or quilts and fabrics.

Probably something about creating living brushstrokes, I suspect.

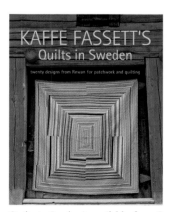

Quilts in Sweden is available from Rowan stockists from Autumn 2011

ISBN: 978-1-906007-86-7   £18.50

travel journal

words by Marie Wallin

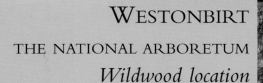

WESTONBIRT
THE NATIONAL ARBORETUM
Wildwood location

The National Arboretum at Westonbirt, Gloucestershire was the spectacular location for our wonderful *Wildwood* story. We photographed the collection at the end of October 2010 and the colours of the trees, especially the maples made it a very special and magical experience.

For most visitors Westonbirt Arboretum is synonymous with the spectacular autumn colour of the maples, however the collection has many other species that give Westonbirt all year round appeal.

Winter at Westonbirt is an amazing experience, particularly when seen on a frosty day when the deep peaceful greens of the conifers and richly coloured barks take centre stage. In Spring the arboretum comes alive with magnificent displays of rhododendrons, azaleas, magnolias and wildflowers. The Summer heralds the flowering of many grassland flowers, while the trees provide cool leafy glades to wander and relax. Autumn starts with a bang with one of the best natural firework displays in Britain as the maples in particular are ablaze in reds, oranges and yellows.

Westonbirt, The National Arboretum, Nr Tetbury, Gloucestershire GL8 8QS
Open all year 9am – 5pm
Tel: 01666 880220
www.forestry.gov.uk/westonbirt

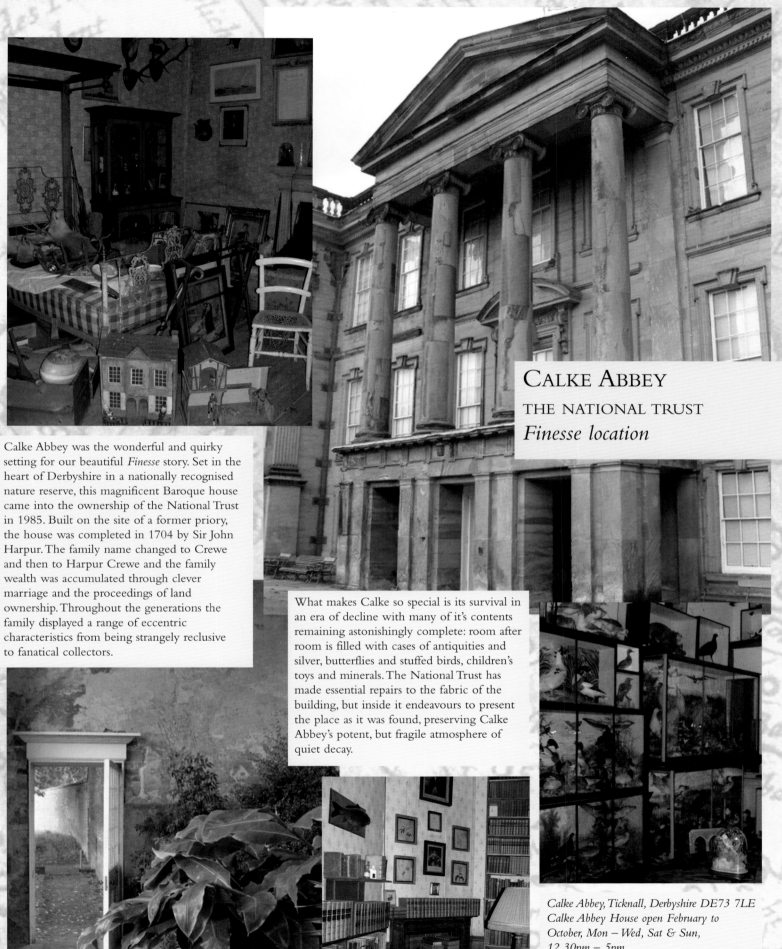

CALKE ABBEY
THE NATIONAL TRUST
Finesse location

Calke Abbey was the wonderful and quirky setting for our beautiful *Finesse* story. Set in the heart of Derbyshire in a nationally recognised nature reserve, this magnificent Baroque house came into the ownership of the National Trust in 1985. Built on the site of a former priory, the house was completed in 1704 by Sir John Harpur. The family name changed to Crewe and then to Harpur Crewe and the family wealth was accumulated through clever marriage and the proceedings of land ownership. Throughout the generations the family displayed a range of eccentric characteristics from being strangely reclusive to fanatical collectors.

What makes Calke so special is its survival in an era of decline with many of it's contents remaining astonishingly complete: room after room is filled with cases of antiquities and silver, butterflies and stuffed birds, children's toys and minerals. The National Trust has made essential repairs to the fabric of the building, but inside it endeavours to present the place as it was found, preserving Calke Abbey's potent, but fragile atmosphere of quiet decay.

Calke Abbey, Ticknall, Derbyshire DE73 7LE
Calke Abbey House open February to
October, Mon – Wed, Sat & Sun,
12.30pm – 5pm
Calke Abbey Nature Reserve open all
year round, 7.30am – 7.30pm
Tel: 01332 863822
www.nationaltrust.org.uk

117

what's new

A whole season's worth of knitting books, magazines and exhibitions covering all aspects of knitting and textile design.

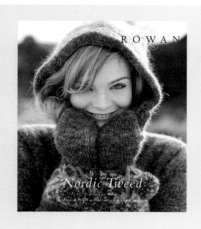

Rowan Nordic Tweed

Alpine, traditional Nordic and fairisle patterning are a strong knitwear trend for the new winter season, inspiring our lovely new *Nordic Tweed* brochure. With designs from Marie Wallin, Martin Storey, Lisa Richardson and Grace Melville, the collection showcases three of our new yarns – Colourspun, Heritage Tweed and Fine Heritage Tweed. The beautiful Colourspun yarn is used to create lovely tonal Nordic patterns as well as subtle textured stripes and cabling, whilst the rustic effects of the Heritage and Fine Heritage Tweeds are used to create the more contrasting fairisle and stitch designs. Covering the key garment shapes of the season, the *Nordic Tweed* collection showcases looks ranging from the oversized cardigan and boyfriend sweater to the more classic, vintage inspired neat and fitted styles.

Rowan Nordic Tweed is available from Rowan stockists from 1st August 2011.

Order code: ZB103

Rowan Evolution is available from Rowan stockists from 1st August 2011.

Order code: ZB104

Rowan Evolution

Evolution is a stunning collection inspired by the trend for unstructured knitwear in both shape and texture. This contemporary collection of 12 women's designs by Marie Wallin, Lisa Richardson and Grace Melville embraces new shapes and stitches whilst creating dramatic knits that are easy and desirable to wear. Some of Rowan's favourite yarns are used, including Big Wool, Cocoon, Drift and Kidsilk Haze. Using techniques such as short row shaping, pleating and partial knitting, the *Evolution* collection showcases wonderful design which is essential for the hand knitting fashionista.

Rowan Purelife Home

Knitted accessories for the home have recently seen a resurgence of interest with fashionable interior magazines promoting traditional hand knitted cushions and throws as well as more contemporary art pieces, rugs and furniture coverings. The *Purelife Home* brochure is inspired by this trend and showcases a wonderful collection of rugs, throws, table mats, and cushions designed by Marie Wallin. The collection uses a mixture of hand knit and crochet with some designs showing a dramatic sense of scale achieved by working simple motifs and knit stitches with plied up yarns. Using Purelife Renew and the Purelife British Sheep Breeds Chunky, Boucle and DK, this collection of 16 designs also introduces a new sheep breed to the Purelife range. 'Masham' is a hardy sheep which produces a soft fibre of different colours, ranging from ecru through to black. These natural shades have been blended together to create 3 lovely new additions to the Boucle range and one to the Chunky range.

Rowan Purelife Home is available from Rowan stockists from 1st August 2011.

Order code: ZB105

Rowan Winter Warmers is available from Rowan stockists from 1st August 2011.

Order code: ZCB43

Rowan Winter Warmers

Winter Warmers is a charming brochure showcasing an essential collection of 30 accessory designs by Martin Storey. Warm and cosy scarves, hats and mittens feature alongside 'snugly' shrugs, bags, cushions and tea cosies. *Winter Warmers* uses one of Rowan's most popular yarns, Lima, as well as one of the new yarns for the season, Alpaca Chunky. This beautiful, ultra soft and cuddly alpaca yarn is available in 4 delicate natural alpaca shades and is perfect for knitting Martin's fantastic accessory designs.

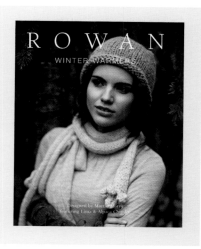

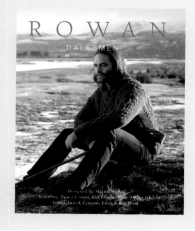

Rowan Dalesmen

Dalesmen is a men's collection of Scandinavian winter inspired knitwear designed by Martin Storey. Evoking a feeling of warmth for walking 'up and down' dale, this wonderful collection showcases beautiful snowflake designs alongside reindeer inspired knits, as well as chunky, bold and traditional cable aran designs. Using a range of Rowan's most popular yarns including Big Wool, Lima, Cocoon and Felted Tweed, this collection of 12 designs for men presents some of the most desirable knits of the winter season.

Rowan Dalesmen is available from Rowan stockists from 1st August 2011.

Order code: ZCB44

Farmhouse is available from Rowan stockists from 1st August 2011.

Order code: ZK37

Farmhouse

Farmhouse is an exciting collaboration bringing together Amy Butler and Erika Knight. Amy selected the lovely new yarn Sweet Harmony and created 10 bold and beautiful shades inspired from her fresh and vibrant fabrics. The *Farmhouse* brochure features 6 garment, 7 accessory and 7 homeware designs by renowned hand knit designer Erika Knight. The collection showcases knitted and crochet designs including throws, cushions and chair covers, accessories including a slouch beret, multi coloured scarf, gloves and cabled socks and garments including simple cables & stripes and a show stopping crochet skirt.

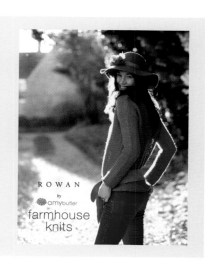

Rowan Lace

The popularity of lace goes from strength to strength, with interest ranging from heritage lace knitting to recent catwalk collections. This graceful and ethereal collection showcases our new Fine Lace yarn. This beautiful yarn is a blend of the softest suri baby alpaca and the finest merino wool and is available in 10 lovely soft & chalky shades. With designs from Marie Wallin, Martin Storey, Sharon Miller, Lisa Richardson, Jennie Atkinson and Amanda Crawford, the *Lace* collection features 14 designs including exquisite feminine knitted garments and delicate crochet and knitted accessories.

Rowan Lace is available from Rowan stockists from 1st September 2011.

Order code: ZB106

Rowan City Retreat is available from Rowan stockists from 1st August 2011.

Order code: ZB110

Rowan City Retreat

City Retreat is a stunning collection of easy to wear and simple to knit women's designs. Designed by Martin Storey, this collection of 12 designs plus accessories introduces one of Rowan's new yarns for the winter season, Creative Focus Worsted. This soft aran weight wool and mohair blended roving yarn is available in a wonderful palette of 26 rich shades. The *City Retreat* collection showcases designs ranging from a sideways knitted poncho and a slouchy sweater dress to a cable and moss stitch asymmetric cropped jacket. Accessories include a fun garter stitch stripe scarf, mittens and beanie hat.

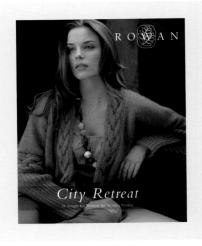

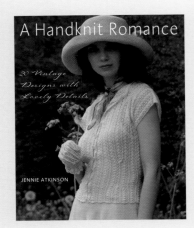

A Handknit Romance
Jennie Atkinson

Jennie needs no introduction to readers of the Rowan magazine, as her elegant designs have graced editions for many years. In this charming book, Jennie weaves her magic with a collection of lacy designs in finer yarns. Inspired by vintage patterns, the collection includes delicate little tops, a sweet jacket, a pretty lacy skirt, stockings, a shrug, two dresses and some delightful accessories.

A Handknit Romance is available from Rowan stockists from winter 2011.

ISBN: 978-1-907544-19-4
£15.99

Aran Knits is available from Rowan stockists from winter 2011.

ISBN: 978-1-907544-17-0
£15.99

Aran Knits
Martin Storey

Textural knits are ever popular with knitters. Not only do they look great, but they provide particular interest for the knitter. Aran Isle cable patterns are well known to knitters throughout the world. In this book, Martin Storey, a lifetime fan of Aran design, adds a contemporary twist, with a range of up-to-the-minute fashion garments and accessories, including shrugs, jackets, cardigans and sweaters along with a few attractive and cosy accessories.

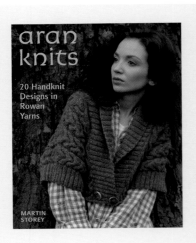

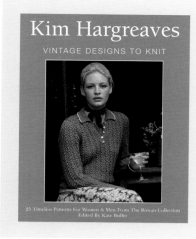

Vintage Designs to Knit

Kim Hargreaves

Edited by Kate Buller

A great collection from Rowan's archive of Kim's patterns for the Rowan Magazine, the designs for garments for women and men are all in Rowan's most popular yarns and provide a rich sourcebook of Kim's trademark design flair and Rowan's inimitable photography and styling. The chosen designs by Kate Buller include jackets, cardigans, sweaters, shrugs and sleeveless tops. Knitted in wool and cotton yarns, they offer a range of classic designs for all seasons.

Vintage Designs to Knit is available from Rowan stockists from November 2011.

ISBN: 978-1-907544-13-2
£14.99

Published by GMC

ISBN: 978-1-861088-45-1
£19.99

The Classic Collection

Sasha Kagan

Iconic knitwear designer Sasha Kagan treats us to a fascinating retrospective of her work from the past four decades in this beautifully presented book. Known best for her innovative use of the intarsia technique, striking pattern work and unique use of colour, Sasha's designs transcend fleeting fashion trends and have become classic pieces in their own right. Reworked in gorgeous new yarns, this collection of cardigans, fringed shawls, statement jackets, jumpers and waistcoats are just as wearable today as the day they were created.

My Life in Textiles

4 Decades of Classic Hand Knit by Sasha Kagan

This colourful exhibition by well-known knitwear designer, Sasha Kagan, will feature iconic designs across four decades of her career in textiles. From the early vintage inspired pieces of the late 60's to the witty and whimsical designs of the 70's, the assertive 80's, the mellow Country Inspiration garments shown at the Victoria and Albert Museum in 2000 to her most recent exploration of nature in close up.

Exhibition touring dates

6th – 9th October 2011 – The Knitting and Stitching Show, Alexandra Palace, London. Tel: 020 8693 2299

10th – 13th November 2011 – The Knitting and Stitching Show, The RDS Centre, Ballsbridge, Dublin, Ireland. Tel: 020 8693 2299

24th – 27th November 2011 – The Knitting and Stitching Show, Harrogate International Centre, Kings Road, Harrogate. Tel: 020 8693 2299

The Victoria and Albert Museum, London

www.vam.ac.uk

15th September 2011 – 26th February 2012

Free Admission

The House of Annie Lennox

Annie Lennox's success has spanned four decades and she is internationally renowned both for her music and her personal style. This exciting display will explore the image and creative vision of the artist. There will be costumes and accessories worn by Lennox, together with photographs, personal treasures and awards, ephemera from political campaigns, recorded interviews and music videos.

Photography by Mike Owen

ROWAN SIZING GUIDE

When you knit and wear a Rowan design we want you to look and feel fabulous. This all starts with the size and fit of the design you choose. To help you to achieve a great knitting experience we have looked at the sizing of our womens and menswear patterns. This has resulted in the introduction of our new sizing guide which includes the following exciting features:

Our sizing now conforms to standard clothing sizes. Therefore if you buy a standard size 12 in clothing, then our size 12 or Medium patterns will fit you perfectly.

We have extended the size range of our womenswear patterns, with over half of the designs shown being available to knit from size 8 to 26, or Small through to XXLarge, with XXLarge being equivalent to sizes 24/26.

The menswear designs are now available to knit in menswear sizes XSmall through to 2XL ie. 38" to 50" chest.

Dimensions in the charts below are body measurements, not garment dimensions, therefore please refer to the measuring guide to help you to determine which is the best size for you to knit.

STANDARD SIZING GUIDE FOR WOMEN

UK SIZE	8	10	12	14	16	18	20	22	24	26	
USA Size	6	8	10	12	14	16	18	20	22	24	
EUR Size	34	36	38	40	42	44	46	48	50	52	
To fit bust	32	34	36	38	40	42	44	46	48	50	inches
	81	86	91	97	102	107	112	117	122	127	cm
To fit waist	24	26	28	30	32	34	36	38	40	42	inches
	61	66	71	76	81	86	91	97	101	106	cm
To fit hips	34	36	38	40	42	44	46	48	50	52	inches
	86	91	97	102	107	112	117	122	127	132	cm

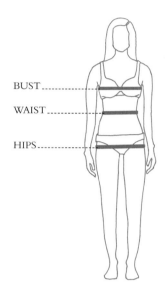

BUST
WAIST
HIPS

CASUAL SIZING GUIDE FOR WOMEN

As there are some designs that are intended to fit more generously, we have introduced our casual sizing guide. The designs that fall into this group can be recognised by the size range: Small, Medium, Large, Xlarge & XXlarge. Each of these sizes cover two sizes from the standard sizing guide, ie. Size S will fit sizes 8/10, size M will fit sizes 12/14 and so on.

The sizing within this chart is also based on the larger size within the range, ie. M will be based on size 14.

UK SIZE	S	M	L	XL	XXL	
DUAL SIZE	8/10	12/14	16/18	20/22	24/26	
To fit bust	32 – 34	36 – 38	40 – 42	44 – 46	48 – 50	inches
	81 – 86	91 – 97	102 – 107	112 – 117	122 – 127	cm
To fit waist	24 – 26	28 – 30	32 – 34	36 – 38	40 – 42	inches
	61 – 66	71 – 76	81 – 86	91 – 97	102 – 107	cm
To fit hips	34 – 36	38 – 40	42 – 44	46 – 48	50 – 52	inches
	86 – 91	97 – 102	107 – 112	117 – 122	127 – 132	cm

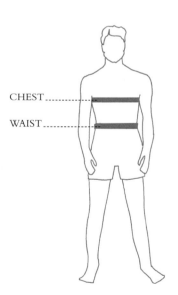

CHEST
WAIST

STANDARD SIZING GUIDE FOR MEN

UK SIZE	XS	S	M	L	XL	XXL	2XL	
EUR Size	48	50	52	54	56	58	60	
To fit chest	38	40	42	44	46	48	50	inches
	97	102	107	112	117	122	127	cm
To fit waist	30	32	34	36	38	40	42	inches
	76	81	86	91	97	102	107	cm

MEASURING GUIDE

For maximum comfort and to ensure the correct fit when choosing a size to knit, please follow the tips below when checking your size.

Measure yourself close to your body, over your underwear and don't pull the tape measure too tight!

Bust/chest – measure around the fullest part of the bust/chest and across the shoulder blades.

Waist – measure around the natural waistline, just above the hip bone.

Hips – measure around the fullest part of the bottom.

If you don't wish to measure yourself, note the size of a favourite jumper that you like the fit of. Our sizes are now comparable to the clothing sizes from the major high street retailers, so if your favourite jumper is a size Medium or size 12, then our casual size Medium and standard size 12 should be approximately the same fit.

To be extra sure, measure your favourite jumper and then compare these measurements with the Rowan size diagram given at the end of the individual instructions.

Finally, once you have decided which size is best for

you, please ensure that you achieve the tension required for the design you wish to knit.

Remember if your tension is too loose, your garment will be bigger than the pattern size and you may use more yarn. If your tension is too tight, your garment could be smaller than the pattern size and you will have yarn left over.

Furthermore if your tension is incorrect, the handle of your fabric will be too stiff or floppy and will not fit properly. It really does make sense to check your tension before starting every project.

YEW SCARF
MARTIN STOREY
Main image page 28

● ●

YARN
Rowan Felted Tweed and Cashsoft 4 ply

A	FTwd Duck Egg 173	3	x 50 g
B	4ply Forest 442	1	x 50 g
C	4ply Kiwi 443	1	x 50 g
D	4ply Pretty 460	1	x 50 g
E	4ply Quartz 446	1	x 50 g
F	4ply Loganberry 430	1	x 50 g

NEEDLES
1 pair 3¼mm (no 10) (US 3) needles

EXTRAS – Piece of velvet fabric 164 cm by 30 cm for backing

TENSION
23 sts and 32 rows to 10 cm measured over patterned st st using 3¼mm (US 3) needles.

FINISHED SIZE
Completed scarf measures 164 cm (64½ ins) long and 30 cm (12 ins) wide.

SCARF
Using 3¼mm (US 3) needles and yarn A cast on 69 sts.
Row 1 (RS): K2, *P1, K1, rep from * to last st, K1.
Row 2: K1, *P1, K1, rep from * to end.
These 2 rows form rib.
Work in rib for a further 3 rows, ending with **WS** facing for next row.
Row 6 (WS): Rib 35, M1, rib to end. 70 sts.
Using the **intarsia** technique as described on the information page, now work in patt from chart, which is worked mainly in st st beg with a K row, as folls:
Work all 64 rows of chart 7 times, then chart rows 1 to 63 again, ending with **WS** facing for next row.
Next row (WS): Patt 34 sts, work 2 tog, patt to end. 69 sts.
Break off contrasts and cont using yarn A **only**.
Beg with row 1, work in rib as given for cast-on edge for 6 rows, ending with RS facing for next row.
Cast off in rib.

MAKING UP
Press carefully as described on the information page. Lay velvet fabric against WS of knitted scarf, fold under raw edges and neatly stitch in place.

key

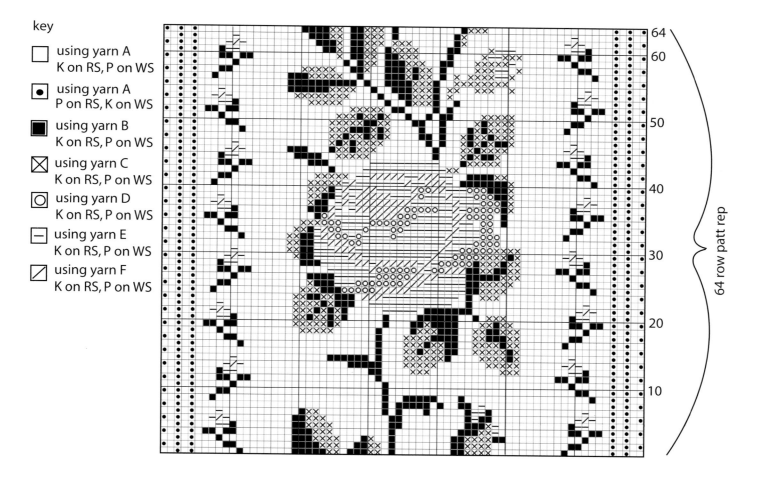

☐ using yarn A
K on RS, P on WS

☐• using yarn A
P on RS, K on WS

■ using yarn B
K on RS, P on WS

⊠ using yarn C
K on RS, P on WS

⊙ using yarn D
K on RS, P on WS

─ using yarn E
K on RS, P on WS

⧄ using yarn F
K on RS, P on WS

64 row patt rep

BEECH MITTS
ERIKA KNIGHT

Main image page 10 & 11

● ●

YARN
Rowan Felted Tweed Chunky

3   x 50 g

(photographed in Aubergine 287)

NEEDLES
Set of 4 double-pointed 8mm (no 0) (US 11)
needles

Cable needle

TENSION
11 sts and 14 rows to 10 cm measured over
rev st st using 8mm (US 11) needles.

SPECIAL ABBREVIATIONS
C6B = slip next 3 sts onto cable needle and
leave at back of work, K3, then K3 from cable
needle; **C6F** = slip next 3 sts onto cable needle
and leave at front of work, K3, then K3 from
cable needle.

MITTS (both alike)
Using double-pointed 8mm (US 11) needles
cast on 24 sts.

Distribute sts evenly over 3 of the 4 needles
and, using 4th needle and taking care not to
twist cast-on edge, cont in rounds as folls:

Round 1 (RS): *K1, P1, rep from * to end.

Rounds 2 to 11: As round 1.

Round 12: P3, K1, (M1, K2) twice, M1, K1,
P6, K1, (M1, K2) twice, M1, K1, P3. 30 sts.
Now work in cable patt as folls:

Round 13: P3, K3, C6F, P6, C6B, K3, P3.

Round 14: P3, K9, P6, K9, P3.

Rounds 15 and 16: As round 14.

Round 17: P3, C6B, K3, P6, K3, C6F, P3.

Rounds 18 to 20: As round 14.

Rounds 13 to 20 form cable patt.

Work in cable patt for a further 21 rounds.

Place marker after 15th st of last round.

Round 42: Patt to within 1 st of marker, M1P,
P2 (marker is between these 2 sts, M1P, patt to
end. 32 sts.

Work a further 3 rounds.

Round 46: As round 42. 34 sts.

Work a further 3 rounds.

Round 50: P3, (K2tog, K1) 3 times, P2, cast off
next 6 sts (for thumb opening - one st on right
needle after cast-off), P1, (K1, K2tog tbl) 3
times, P3. 22 sts.

Rounds 51 to 54: As round 1.

Cast off in rib.

MAKING UP
Press carefully as described on the information
page.

HAWTHORN
MARIE WALLIN

Main image page 10 & 11

● ● ●

YARN

	S	M	L	XL	XXL
To fit bust					
	81-86	91-97	102-107	112-117	122-127 cm
	32-34	36-38	40-42	44-46	48-50 in

Rowan Felted Tweed Aran

17   18   19   20   22   x 50 g

(photographed in Cherry 732)

NEEDLES
1 pair 5mm (no 6) (US 8) needles

Cable needle

TENSION
26 sts and 25 rows to 10 cm measured over patt
using 5mm (US 8) needles.

SPECIAL ABBREVIATIONS
C6B = slip next 3 sts onto cable needle and
leave at back of work, K3, then K3 from cable
needle; **C6F** = slip next 3 sts onto cable needle
and leave at front of work, K3, then K3 from
cable needle; **Cr4L** = slip next 3 sts onto cable
needle and leave at front of work, P1, then K3
from cable needle; **Cr4R** = slip next st onto
cable needle and leave at back of work, K3,
then P1 from cable needle; **Cr5L** = slip next 3
sts onto cable needle and leave at front of
work, P2, then K3 from cable needle; **Cr5R** =
slip next 2 sts onto cable needle and leave at
back of work, K3, then P2 from cable needle.

BACK
Using 5mm (US 8) needles cast on 189 [201:
213: 231: 249] sts.

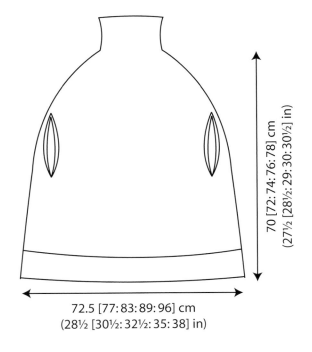

70 [72: 74: 76: 78] cm
(27½ [28½: 29: 30: 30½] in)

72.5 [77: 83: 89: 96] cm
(28½ [30½: 32½: 35: 38] in)

Row 1 (RS): K3, ★P3, K3, rep from ★ to end.
Row 2: P3, ★K3, P3, rep from ★ to end.
These 2 rows form rib.
Work in rib for a further 17 rows, dec [dec: inc: inc: inc] 1 [1: 3: 1: 1] sts evenly across last row and ending with **WS** facing for next row.
188 [200: 216: 232: 250] sts.
Working first and last 22 [28: 36: 44: 53] sts as indicated, repeating the 24 st patt rep 6 times across rows and the 52 row patt rep throughout, now work in patt from chart, noting that chart row 1 is a **WS** row, as folls:
Work 11 rows, ending with RS facing for next row.★★
Keeping patt correct, dec 1 st at each end of next and every foll 4th row to 152 [166: 184: 206: 226] sts, then on foll 35 [36: 38: 43: 44] alt rows, then on foll 7 [13: 19: 25: 33] rows, ending with RS facing for next row.
68 [68: 70: 70: 72] sts. (Back should meas 70 [72: 74: 76: 78] cm.)
Shape funnel neck
Place markers at both ends of last row to denote beg of funnel neck.
Keeping patt correct, dec 1 st at each end of next and foll alt row, then on foll 4th row.
62 [62: 64: 64: 66] sts.
Cont straight until funnel neck meas 20 cm from markers, ending with RS facing for next row.
Cast off in patt.

FRONT
Work as given for back to ★★.
Keeping patt correct, dec 1 st at each end of next and 9 [10: 11: 11: 11] foll 4th rows, then on foll 0 [0: 0: 0: 3] alt rows.
168 [178: 192: 208: 220] sts.
Work 3 [1: 1: 3: 1] rows, ending with RS facing for next row.
Divide for armhole openings
Next row (RS): (Work 2 tog) 1 [0: 0: 1: 1] times, patt 30 [34: 37: 40: 41] sts and turn, leaving rem sts on a holder.
Cont on this set of 31 [34: 37: 41: 42] sts only for left side panel.
Keeping patt correct, dec 1 st at side edge of 4th [2nd: 2nd: 2nd: 2nd] and 6 [5: 3: 0: 0] foll 4th rows, then on foll 13 [17: 22: 29: 30] alt rows, ending with **WS** facing for next row.
Break yarn and leave rem 11 sts on a 2nd holder.
With RS facing, rejoin yarn to rem sts on first holder, patt 104 [110: 118: 124: 134] sts, and turn, leaving rem sts on a holder.
Work 54 [56: 58: 60: 62] rows on this set of sts only for centre panel, ending with **WS** facing for next row.
Break yarn and leave rem sts on a 3rd holder.
With RS facing, rejoin yarn to rem sts on first holder, patt to last 2 [0: 0: 2: 2] sts, (work 2 tog) 1 [0: 0: 1: 1] times.
Cont on this set of 31 [34: 37: 41: 42] sts only

for right side panel.
Keeping patt correct, dec 1 st at side edge of 4th [2nd: 2nd: 2nd: 2nd] and 6 [5: 3: 0: 0] foll 4th rows, then on foll 13 [17: 22: 29: 30] alt rows, ending with **WS** facing for next row.
11 sts.
Join sections
Next row (WS): Patt across 11 sts of right side panel, then 104 [110: 118: 124: 134] sts of centre panel, then 11 sts of left side panel.
126 [132: 140: 146: 156] sts.
Keeping patt correct, dec 1 st at each end of next and foll 21 [18: 15: 12: 8] alt rows, then on foll 7 [13: 19: 25: 33] rows, ending with RS facing for next row. 68 [68: 70: 70: 72] sts.
Complete as given for back from beg of funnel neck shaping.

MAKING UP
Press as described on the information page.
Armhole opening borders (all 4 alike)
With RS facing and using 5mm (US 8) needles, pick up and knit 36 [37: 39: 40: 41] sts evenly along row-end edge of armhole opening.
Work in g st for 2 rows, ending with **WS** facing for next row.
Cast off knitwise (on **WS**).
Overlap armhole borders so that pick-up rows match and neatly sew row-end edges in place.
See information page for finishing instructions.

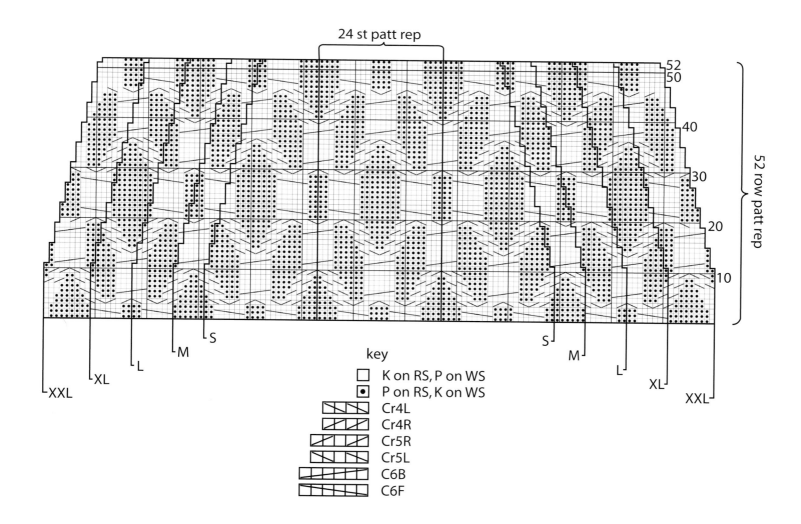

key

☐	K on RS, P on WS
⊡	P on RS, K on WS
	Cr4L
	Cr4R
	Cr5R
	Cr5L
	C6B
	C6F

OAK
ERIKA KNIGHT
Main image page 24 & 25

●●

YARN
Rowan Felted Tweed Aran

A	Plum 731	11 x 50 g
B	Heather 724	11 x 50 g

NEEDLES
1 pair 5mm (no 6) (US 8) needles
Cable needle

TENSION
21 sts and 25 rows to 10 cm measured over patt using 5mm (US 8) needles.

FINISHED SIZE
Completed wrap measures 172 cm (67½ ins) long and 72 cm (28½ ins) wide.

SPECIAL ABBREVIATION
C8B = slip next 4 sts onto cable needle and leave at back of work, K4, then K4 from cable needle.

Pattern note: Use the **intarsia** technique as described on the information page throughout.

WRAP
Using 5mm (US 8) needles cast on as folls: 5 sts using yarn A, 8 sts using yarn B, 5 sts using yarn A, ★6 sts using yarn B, 8 sts using yarn A, 5 sts using yarn B, 6 sts using yarn A, 8 sts using yarn B, 5 sts using yarn A, rep from ★ twice more, 6 sts using yarn B, 8 sts using yarn A, and 5 sts using yarn B. 151 sts in total.
Keeping colours correct as set by cast-on edge throughout, now work in patt as folls:
Row 1 (RS): K2, P3, ★C8B, P4, K1, P1, K1, P4, rep from ★ to last 13 sts, C8B, P3, K2.
8 cable panels.
Row 2: K5, P8, ★K4, P1, K1, P1, K4, P8, rep from ★ to last 5 sts, K5.
Row 3: K2, P3, ★K8, P4, K1, P1, K1, P4, rep from ★ to last 13 sts, K8, P3, K2.
Rows 4 to 9: As rows 2 and 3, 3 times.
Row 10: As row 2.
These 10 rows form patt.
Cont in patt until work meas approx 172 cm, ending after patt row 1 and with **WS** facing for next row.
Cast off in patt (on **WS**).

MAKING UP
Press carefully as described on the information page.

COMPASSION
MARTIN STOREY
Main image page 88, 90 & 91

●●

YARN

	S	M	L	XL	XXL
To fit bust					
cm	81–86	91–97	102–107	112–117	122–127
in	32–34	36–38	40–42	44–46	48–50

Rowan Cocoon

8	9	10	11	12	x100 g

(photographed in Mink 830)

NEEDLES
1 pair 6mm (no 4) (US 10) needles
1 pair 7mm (no 2) (US 10½) needles
6mm (no 4) (US 10) circular needle, 40 cm long
2 double-pointed 6mm (no 4) (US 10) needles
Cable needle

TENSION
14 sts and 16 rows to 10 cm measured over st st using 7mm (US 10½) needles.

SPECIAL ABBREVIATIONS
C6B = slip next 3 sts onto cable needle and leave at back of work, K3, then K3 from cable needle; **C6F** = slip next 3 sts onto cable needle and leave at front of work, K3, then K3 from cable needle; **C12B** = slip next 6 sts onto cable needle and leave at back of work, K6, then K6 from cable needle; **C12F** = slip next 6 sts onto cable needle and leave at front of work, K6, then K6 from cable needle.

BACK
Using 6mm (US 10) needles cast on 69 [77: 85: 93: 103] sts.
Row 1 (RS): K1 [0: 0: 0: 0], P2 [2: 1: 0: 0], ★K3, P2, rep from ★ to last 1 [0: 4: 3: 3] sts, K1 [0: 3: 3: 3], P0 [0: 1: 0: 0].
Row 2: P1 [0: 0: 0: 0], K2 [2: 1: 0: 0], ★P3, K2, rep from ★ to last 1 [0: 4: 3: 3] sts, P1 [0: 3: 3: 3], K0 [0: 1: 0: 0].
These 2 rows form rib.
Work in rib for a further 12 rows, ending with RS facing for next row.
Change to 7mm (US 10½) needles.
Beg with a K row, work in st st until back meas 27 [28: 29: 30: 31] cm, ending with RS facing

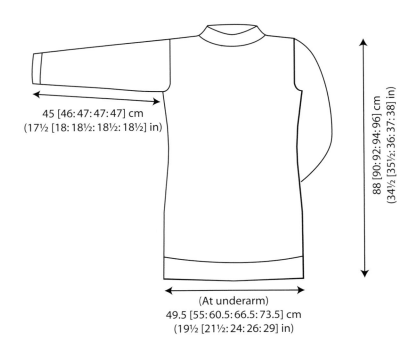

45 [46: 47: 47: 47] cm
(17½ [18: 18½: 18½: 18½] in)

88 [90: 92: 94: 96] cm
(34½ [35½: 36: 37: 38] in)

(At underarm)
49.5 [55: 60.5: 66.5: 73.5] cm
(19½ [21½: 24: 26: 29] in)

for next row.

Dec 1 st at each end of next and foll 12th row, then on foll 10th row. 63 [71: 79: 87: 97] sts.

Work 7 rows, ending with RS facing for next row.

Inc 1 st at each end of next and 2 foll 8th rows. 69 [77: 85: 93: 103] sts.

Cont straight until back meas 63 [64: 65: 66: 67] cm, ending with RS facing for next row.

Shape armholes

Cast off 3 sts at beg of next 2 rows.
63 [71: 79: 87: 97] sts.

Dec 1 st at each end of next and foll 2 alt rows.
57 [65: 73: 81: 91] sts.

Cont straight until armhole meas 21 [22: 23: 24: 25] cm, ending with RS facing for next row.

Shape shoulders and back neck

Cast off 5 [6: 7: 9: 10] sts at beg of next 2 rows.
47 [53: 59: 63: 71] sts.

Next row (RS): Cast off 5 [6: 7: 9: 10] sts, K until there are 9 [11: 12: 12: 14] sts on right needle and turn, leaving rem sts on a holder.
Work each side of neck separately.
Cast off 4 sts at beg of next row.
Cast off rem 5 [7: 8: 8: 10] sts.
With RS facing, rejoin yarn to rem sts, cast off centre 19 [19: 21: 21: 23] sts, K to end.
Complete to match first side, reversing shapings.

FRONT

Using 6mm (US 10) needles cast on 83 [91: 99: 107: 117] sts.

Row 1 (RS): K1 [0: 0: 0: 0], P2 [2: 1: 0: 0], (K3, P2) 5 [6: 7: 8: 9] times, work next 27 sts as row 1 of cable panel, (P2, K3) 5 [6: 7: 8: 9] times, P2 [2: 1: 0: 0], K1 [0: 0: 0: 0].

Row 2: P1 [0: 0: 0: 0], K2 [2: 1: 0: 0], (P3, K2) 5 [6: 7: 8: 9] times, work next 27 sts as row 2 of cable panel, (K2, P3) 5 [6: 7: 8: 9] times, K2 [2: 1: 0: 0], P1 [0: 0: 0: 0].

These 2 rows set the sts - centre 27 sts in cable patt from chart and rem sts in rib.

Working chart rows 1 to 4 **once only** and then repeating chart rows 5 to 44 **throughout**, cont as folls:

Work a further 12 rows, ending with RS facing for next row.

Change to 7mm (US 10½) needles.

Row 15 (RS): K26 [30: 34: 38: 43], P2, patt next 27 sts, P2, K to end.

Row 16: P26 [30: 34: 38: 43], K2, patt next 27 sts, K2, P to end.

These 2 rows set the sts for main section of front - centre 27 sts still in cable patt with 2 "P" sts each side, and rem sts now in st st.

Keeping sts correct as now set, cont as folls:

Work 6 rows, ending with RS facing for next row.

Row 23 (RS): K22 [26: 30: 34: 39], K2tog, yfwd, K2, P2, patt next 27 sts, P2, K2, yfwd, sl 1, K1, psso, K to end.

Last row forms eyelet holes for lacing.

Working eyelet holes as set by last row on every foll 8th row and noting that no further reference will be made to eyelet holes, cont as folls:

Cont straight until front meas 27 [28: 29: 30: 31] cm, ending with RS facing for next row.

Keeping patt correct, dec 1 st at each end of next and foll 12th row, then on foll 10th row.
77 [85: 93: 101: 111] sts.

Work 7 rows, ending with RS facing for next row.

Inc 1 st at each end of next and 2 foll 8th rows. 83 [91: 99: 107: 117] sts.

Cont straight until front matches back to beg of armhole shaping, ending with RS facing for next row.

Shape armholes

Keeping patt correct, cast off 3 sts at beg of next 2 rows. 77 [85: 93: 101: 111] sts.

Dec 1 st at each end of next and foll 2 alt rows.
71 [79: 87: 95: 105] sts.

Cont straight until 8 [8: 10: 10: 12] rows less have been worked than on back to beg of shoulder shaping, ending with RS facing for next row.

Shape front neck

Next row (RS): Patt 21 [25: 29: 33: 38] sts and turn, leaving rem sts on a holder.
Work each side of neck separately.
Keeping patt correct, dec 1 st at neck edge of next 6 rows, then on foll 0 [0: 1: 1: 2] alt rows.

15 [19: 22: 26: 30] sts.

Work 1 row, ending with RS facing for next row.

Shape shoulder

Cast off 5 [6: 7: 9: 10] sts at beg of next and foll alt row.

Work 1 row.

Cast off rem 5 [7: 8: 8: 10] sts.

With RS facing, rejoin yarn to rem sts, cast off centre 29 sts, patt to end.

Complete to match first side, reversing shapings.

SLEEVES

Using 6mm (US 10) needles cast on 33 [35: 35: 35: 37] sts.

Row 1 (RS): P0 [1: 1: 1: 2], *K3, P2, rep from * to last 3 [4: 4: 4: 5] sts, K3, P0 [1: 1: 1: 2].

Row 2: K0 [1: 1: 1: 2], *P3, K2, rep from * to last 3 [4: 4: 4: 5] sts, P3, K0 [1: 1: 1: 2].

These 2 rows form rib.

Work in rib for a further 4 rows, ending with RS facing for next row.

Change to 7mm (US 10½) needles.

Beg with a K row, work in st st, shaping sides by inc 1 st at each end of next and every foll 4th row to 53 [53: 61: 67: 69] sts, then on 3 [4: 2: 0: 0] foll 6th rows. 59 [61: 65: 67: 69] sts.

Cont straight until sleeve meas 45 [46: 47: 47: 47] cm, ending with RS facing for next row.

Shape top

Cast off 3 sts at beg of next 2 rows.
53 [55: 59: 61: 63] sts.

Dec 1 st at each end of next and foll 2 alt rows, then on foll row, ending with RS facing for next row.

Cast off rem 45 [47: 51: 53: 55] sts.

MAKING UP

Press as described on the information page.
Join both shoulder seams using back stitch, or mattress stitch if preferred.

Neckband

With RS facing and using 6mm (US 10) circular needle, pick up and knit 12 [12: 14: 14: 15] sts down left side of neck, 24 sts from front,

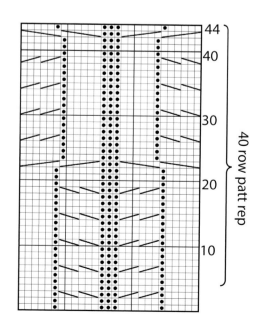

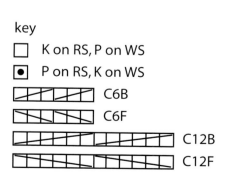

key

☐ K on RS, P on WS

⊡ P on RS, K on WS

C6B

C6F

C12B

C12F

44
40
30
20
10

40 row patt rep

12 [12: 14: 14: 15] sts up right side of neck, then 27 [27: 28: 28: 31] sts from back.
75 [75: 80: 80: 85] sts.
Round 1 (RS): ★K3, P2, rep from ★ to end.
Rep this round 9 times more.
Cast off in rib.
See information page for finishing instructions, setting in sleeves using the shallow set-in method.

Lacing cord
Using double-pointed 6mm (US 10) needles cast on 3 sts.
Row 1 (RS): K3, ★without turning slip these 3 sts to opposite end of needle and bring yarn to opposite end of work pulling it quite tightly across **WS** of work, K these 3 sts again, rep from ★ until cord is 340 cm long, K3tog and fasten off.
Using photograph as a guide, thread lacing cord through eyelet holes of front and tie ends at top of rib.

ALDER WRAP
KAFFE FASSETT
Main image page 32, 33 & 34

YARN
Rowan Kidsilk Haze

A	Hurricane	632	1	x 25 g
B	Smoke	605	1	x 25 g
C	Dewberry	600	1	x 25 g
D	Marmalade	596	1	x 25 g
E	Blood	627	1	x 25 g
F	Liqueur	595	1	x 25 g
G	Anthracite	639	1	x 25 g
H	Forest Green	651	1	x 25 g
I	Fern	629	1	x 25 g
J	Splendour	579	1	x 25 g
K	Blackcurrant	641	2	x 25 g
L	Trance	582	1	x 25 g

NEEDLES
1 pair 5mm (no 6) (US 8) needles

TENSION
18 sts and 23 rows to 10 cm measured over st st using 5mm (US 8) needles.

FINISHED SIZE
Completed wrap measures 249 cm (98 ins) long and 41 cm (16 ins) wide.

WRAP
Using 5mm (US 8) needles and yarn K cast on 73 sts.
Row 1 (RS): K1, ★P1, K1, rep from ★ to end.
Row 2: As row 1.
These 2 rows form moss st.
Work in moss st for a further 3 rows, ending with **WS** facing for next row.
Row 6 (WS): Moss st 5 sts and slip these sts onto a holder for second side border, M1, moss st 63 sts, M1, moss st rem 5 sts and slip these last 5 sts onto another holder for first side border.
Do NOT break yarn but set aside this ball of yarn for side border.
Rejoin yarn A to centre 65 sts with RS facing and, beg with a K row and joining in and breaking off colours as required, now work in st st in stripes as folls:
Rows 1 to 6: Using yarn A.
Row 7: Using yarn B.
Rows 8 and 9: Using yarn A.
Rows 10 and 11: Using yarn B.
Rows 12 and 13: Using yarn A.
Rows 14 to 19: Using yarn B.
Row 20: Using yarn C.
Rows 21 and 22: Using yarn B.
Rows 23 and 24: Using yarn C.
Row 25: Using yarn B.
Rows 26 to 31: Using yarn C.
Row 32: Using yarn D.
Rows 33 and 34: Using yarn C.
Rows 35 and 36: Using yarn D.
Row 37: Using yarn C.
Rows 38 to 43: Using yarn D.
Row 44: Using yarn E.
Rows 45 and 46: Using yarn D.
Rows 47 and 48: Using yarn E.
Row 49: Using yarn D.
Rows 50 to 55: Using yarn E.
Row 56: Using yarn F.
Rows 57 and 58: Using yarn E.
Rows 59 and 60: Using yarn F.
Row 61: Using yarn E.
Rows 62 to 67: Using yarn F.
Row 68: Using yarn G.
Rows 69 and 70: Using yarn F.
Rows 71 and 72: Using yarn G.
Row 73: Using yarn F.
Rows 74 to 79: Using yarn G.
Row 80: Using yarn H.
Rows 81 and 82: Using yarn G.
Rows 83 and 84: Using yarn H.
Row 85: Using yarn G.
Rows 86 to 91: Using yarn H.
Row 92: Using yarn I.
Rows 93 and 94: Using yarn H.
Rows 95 and 96: Using yarn I.
Row 97: Using yarn H.
Rows 98 to 103: Using yarn I.
Row 104: Using yarn J.
Rows 105 and 106: Using yarn I.
Rows 107 and 108: Using yarn J.
Row 109: Using yarn I.
Rows 110 to 115: Using yarn J.
Row 116: Using yarn K.
Rows 117 and 118: Using yarn J.
Rows 119 and 120: Using yarn K.
Row 121: Using yarn J.
Rows 122 to 127: Using yarn K.
Row 128: Using yarn F.
Rows 129 and 130: Using yarn K.
Rows 131 and 132: Using yarn F.
Row 133: Using yarn K.
Rows 134 to 139: Using yarn F.
Row 140: Using yarn A.
Rows 141 and 142: Using yarn F.
Rows 143 and 144: Using yarn A.
Row 145: Using yarn F.
Rows 146 to 151: Using yarn A.
Row 152: Using yarn L.
Rows 153 and 154: Using yarn A.
Rows 155 and 156: Using yarn L.
Row 157: Using yarn A.
Rows 158 to 163: Using yarn L.
Row 164: Using yarn C.
Rows 165 and 166: Using yarn L.
Rows 167 and 168: Using yarn C.
Row 169: Using yarn L.
Rows 170 to 175: Using yarn C.
Row 176: Using yarn E.
Rows 177 and 178: Using yarn C.
Rows 179 and 180: Using yarn E.
Row 181: Using yarn C.
Rows 182 to 187: Using yarn E.
Row 188: Using yarn J.
Rows 189 and 190: Using yarn E.
Rows 191 and 192: Using yarn J.
Row 193: Using yarn E.
Rows 194 to 199: Using yarn J.
Row 200: Using yarn H.
Rows 201 and 202: Using yarn J.
Rows 203 and 204: Using yarn H.
Row 205: Using yarn J.
Rows 206 to 211: Using yarn H.
Row 212: Using yarn A.
Rows 213 and 214: Using yarn H.
Rows 215 and 216: Using yarn A.
Row 217: Using yarn H.
Rows 218 to 223: Using yarn A.
Row 224: Using yarn K.
Rows 225 and 226: Using yarn A.
Rows 227 and 228: Using yarn K.

Row 229: Using yarn A.
Rows 230 to 235: Using yarn K.
Row 236: Using yarn F.
Rows 237 and 238: Using yarn K.
Rows 239 and 240: Using yarn F.
Row 241: Using yarn K.
Rows 242 to 247: Using yarn F.
Row 248: Using yarn E.
Rows 249 and 250: Using yarn F.
Rows 251 and 252: Using yarn E.
Row 253: Using yarn F.
Rows 254 to 259: Using yarn E.
Row 260: Using yarn D.
Rows 261 and 262: Using yarn E.
Rows 263 and 264: Using yarn D.
Row 265: Using yarn E.
Rows 266 to 272: Using yarn D.
Rows 273 and 274: Using yarn E.
Rows 275 and 276: Using yarn D.

Row 277: Using yarn E.
Rows 278 to 283: Using yarn D.
Now work second end of wrap by working stripes in reverse order by working rows 277 to row 1, ending with RS facing for next row.
Break yarn and leave sts on a holder.

First side border
Slip 5 sts of first side border back onto 5mm (US 8) needles and, using ball of yarn K set to one side with these sts, work in moss st on these 5 sts until side border, when slightly stretched, fits up side of centre striped section, ending with **WS** facing for next row.
Break yarn and slip these 5 sts back onto holder.
Slip stitch this side border in place.

Second side border
Slip 5 sts of second side border back onto 5mm (US 8) needles and join in yarn K

with RS facing.
Work in moss st on these 5 sts until side border, when slightly stretched, fits up side of centre striped section, ending with **WS** facing for next row.
Do NOT break yarn.
Slip stitch this side border in place.

Join sections
Next row (WS): Moss st 5 sts of second side border, now work across **WS** of 65 sts of centre section as folls: P2tog, P61, P2tog, then moss st across 5 sts of first side border. 73 sts.
Using yarn K, work in moss st for 6 rows, ending with RS facing for next row.
Cast off in moss st.

MAKING UP
Press carefully as described on the information page.

CHESTNUT
MARIE WALLIN
Main image page 18 & 19

●●

YARN
Rowan Kid Classic

A	Earth 872	2	x	50 g
B	Spruce 853	2	x	50 g
C	Bear 817	2	x	50 g
D	Crushed Velvet 825	2	x	50 g
E	Canard 871	1	x	50 g
F	Peat 832	1	x	50 g
G	Mellow 877	1	x	50 g
H	Straw 851	1	x	50 g

CROCHET HOOK
4.50mm (no 7) (US 7) crochet hook

TENSION
2 patt reps to 13 cm in width and 2 patt reps (8 rows) to 10 cm measured over patt using 4.50mm (US 7) crochet hook.

FINISHED SIZE
Completed scarf loop measures 170 cm (67 ins) long and 41 cm (16 ins) wide.

CROCHET ABBREVIATIONS
ss = slip stitch; **ch** = chain; **dc** = double crochet; **tr** = treble; **picot** = 3 ch, ss to top of tr just worked; **sp(s)** = space(s).

SCARF LOOP
Using 4.50mm (US 7) hook and yarn A make 74 ch.
Foundation row (RS): Using yarn A, 1 dc into 2nd ch from hook, ★5 ch, miss 3 ch, 1 dc into next ch, rep from ★ to end, turn. 18 ch sps.
Now work in patt as folls:
Row 1: Using yarn A, 5 ch (counts as 1 tr and 2 ch), ★1 dc into next ch sp, 8 tr into next ch sp, 1 dc into next ch sp★★, 5 ch, rep from ★ to end, ending last rep at ★★, 2 ch, 1 tr into last dc, turn. 6 patt reps.
Row 2: Using yarn B, 1 ch (does NOT count as st), 1 dc into tr at end of previous row, 2 ch, miss (2 ch and 1 dc), ★1 tr into each of next 8 tr, 2 ch, miss 1 dc★★, 1 dc into next ch sp, 2 ch, miss 1 dc, rep from ★ to end, ending last rep at ★★, 1 dc into 3rd of 5 ch at beg of previous row, turn.
Row 3: Using yarn C, 1 ch (does NOT count as st), 1 dc into dc at end of previous row, ★miss 2 ch, (1 tr into next tr, 1 picot) 7 times, 1 tr into next tr, miss 2 ch, 1 dc into next dc, rep from ★ to end, turn.
Row 4: Using yarn D, 8 ch (counts as 1 tr and 5 ch), miss first 2 picots, ★1 dc into next picot, 5 ch, miss 1 picot, 1 dc into next picot, 5 ch, miss 2 picot, 1 tr into next dc★★, 5 ch, miss 2 picots, rep from ★ to end, ending last rep at ★★, turn.

Row 5: Using yarn A, 5 ch (counts as 1 tr and 2 ch), ★1 dc into next ch sp, 8 tr into next ch sp, 1 dc into next ch sp★★, 5 ch, rep from ★ to end, ending last rep at ★★, 2 ch, 1 tr into 3rd of 8 ch at beg of previous row, turn.
Row 6: As row 2 but using yarn E.
Row 7: As row 3 but using yarn B.
Row 8: As row 4 but using yarn F.
Row 9: As row 5 but using yarn C.
Row 10: As row 2 but using yarn D.
Row 11: As row 3 but using yarn A.
Row 12: As row 4 but using yarn G.
Row 13: As row 5 but using yarn C.
Row 14: As row 2 but using yarn F.
Row 15: As row 3 but using yarn B.
Row 16: As row 4 but using yarn H.
Row 17: As row 5.
Rows 2 to 17 form patt and stripe sequence.
Cont in patt and stripe sequence as now set until work meas 170 cm.
Fasten off.

MAKING UP
Press as described on the information page.
Join base of foundation ch edge to top of last row to form a loop.
Edgings (both alike)
With RS facing, using 4.50mm (US 7) hook and yarn D, attach yarn to one edge of loop, 1 ch (does NOT count as st), work 1 round of dc evenly around entire loop, ss to first dc.
Next round (RS): 1 ch (does NOT count as st), 1 dc into each dc to end, ss to first dc.
Rep last round once more.
Fasten off.
See information page for finishing instructions.

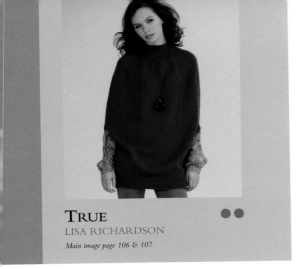

TRUE
LISA RICHARDSON

Main image page 106 & 107

● ●

YARN

S	M	L	XL	XXL

To fit bust
81-86 91-97 102-107 112-117 122-127 cm
32-34 36-38 40-42 44-46 48-50 in

Rowan Kid Classic
8   8   9   10   10   x 50 g
(photographed in Earth 872)

NEEDLES

4½mm (no 7) (US 7) circular needle,
80 cm long
5½mm (no 5) (US 9) circular needle,
one 80 cm long and one 40 cm long
1 pair 5½mm (no 5) (US 9) needles
Set of 4 double-pointed 4½mm (no 7)
(US 7) needles

TENSION

18 sts and 23 rows to 10 cm measured over st st
using 5½mm (US 9) needles.

SPECIAL ABBREVIATIONS

sL2togK = slip 2 sts as though to K2tog;
p2sso = pass 2 slipped sts over.

BODY
Using 4½mm (US 7) circular needle cast on
160 [180: 200: 220: 240] sts.
Taking care not to twist cast-on edge, now
work in rounds throughout as folls:
Round 1 (RS): *K1, P1, rep from * to end.
This round forms rib.
Place marker at end of last round to denote
beg and end of rounds.
Cont in rib until work meas 8 cm.
Change to longer 5½mm (US 9) circular needle.
Next round (RS): Knit.
This round forms st st.
Cont in st st for a further 3 rounds.
Next round: *K8 [9: 10: 11: 12], M1, rep from
* to end. 180 [200: 220: 240: 260] sts.
Work 7 rounds.
Next round: *K9 [10: 11: 12: 13], M1, rep
from * to end. 200 [220: 240: 260: 280] sts.
Work 7 rounds.
Next round: *K10 [11: 12: 13: 14], M1, rep
from * to end. 220 [240: 260: 280: 300] sts.
Work 7 rounds.
Next round: *K11 [12: 13: 14: 15], M1, rep
from * to end. 240 [260: 280: 300: 320] sts.
Cont straight until work meas 26 [27: 28:
29: 30] cm.

Divide for armhole openings
Next round: K65 [70: 75: 80: 85] and slip
these sts onto a holder, K110 [120: 130: 140:
150] and slip these sts onto another holder,
K rem 65 [70: 75: 80: 85] sts and slip these sts
onto same holder as first set of sts.
Break yarn.
Shape front
Slip 110 [120: 130: 140: 150] sts from holder
onto 5½mm (US 9) straight needles and rejoin
yarn with RS facing.
Now working in **rows**, not rounds, cont as
folls:
Row 1 (RS): K1, sl 1, K1, psso, K to last 3 sts,
K2tog, K1. 108 [118: 128: 138: 148] sts.
Beg with a P row, cont in st st until work meas
17 [18: 19: 20: 21] cm from dividing round,
ending with **WS** facing for next row.
Next row (WS): P1, M1, P to last st, M1, P1.
110 [120: 130: 140: 150] sts.
Break yarn and leave these sts on another
holder.
Shape back
Slip 130 [140: 150: 160: 170] sts from holder
onto 5½mm (US 9) straight needles and rejoin
yarn with RS facing.
Now working in **rows**, not rounds, cont as folls:
Row 1 (RS): K1, sl 1, K1, psso, K to last 3 sts,
K2tog, K1. 128 [138: 148: 158: 168] sts.
Beg with a P row, cont in st st until work meas
17 [18: 19: 20: 21] cm from dividing round,
ending with **WS** facing for next row.
Next row (WS): P1, M1, P to last st, M1, P1.
130 [140: 150: 160: 170] sts.
Break yarn.
Slip last 65 [70: 75: 80: 85] sts of last row onto
another holder.
Join sections
Using longer 5½mm (US 9) circular needle,
K 65 [70: 75: 80: 85] sts of 2nd half of back,
then K across 110 [120: 130: 140: 150] sts of
front, then K across rem 65 [70: 75: 80: 85] sts

of back left on holder.
240 [260: 280: 300: 320] sts.
Place marker at end of last round to denote
beg and end of rounds.
Now working in **rounds** of st st again, cont
as folls:
Cont straight until work meas 68 [69: 70:
71: 72] cm from cast-on edge.
Changing to shorter circular needle when
required, now shape shoulder section as folls:
Round 1: *K10 [11: 12: 13: 14], K2tog, rep
from * to end. 220 [240: 260: 280: 300] sts.
Work 9 rounds.
Round 11: *sl 1, K1, psso, K9 [10: 11: 12: 13],
rep from * to end. 200 [220: 240: 260: 280] sts.
Work 7 rounds.
Round 19: *K8 [9: 10: 11: 12], K2tog, rep
from * to end. 180 [200: 220: 240: 260] sts.
Work 5 rounds.
Round 25: *sl 1, K1, psso, K7 [8: 9: 10: 11],
rep from * to end. 160 [180: 200: 220: 240] sts.
Work 3 rounds.
Round 29: *K6 [7: 8: 9: 10], K2tog, rep from
* to end. 140 [160: 180: 200: 220] sts.
Work 1 round.
Round 31: *sl 1, K1, psso, K5 [6: 7: 8: 9], rep
from * to end. 120 [140: 160: 180: 200] sts.
Sizes M, L, XL and XXL only
Work 1 round.
Round 33: *K- [5: 6: 7: 8], K2tog, rep from *
to end. - [120: 140: 160: 180] sts.
Sizes L, XL and XXL only
Work 1 round.
Round 35: *sl 1, K1, psso, K- [-: 5: 6: 7], rep
from * to end. - [-: 120: 140: 160] sts.
Sizes XL and XXL only
Work 1 round.
Round 37: *K- [-: -: 5: 6], K2tog, rep from *
to end. - [-: -: 120: 140] sts.
Size XXL only
Work 1 round.
Round 39: *sl 1, K1, psso, K- [-: -: -: 5], rep

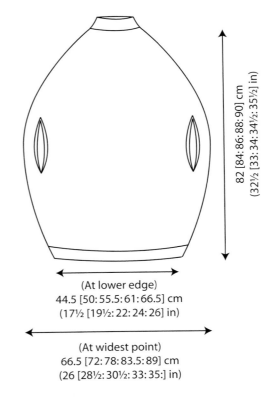

82 [84: 86: 88: 90] cm
(32½ [33: 34: 34½: 35½] in)

(At lower edge)
44.5 [50: 55.5: 61: 66.5] cm
(17½ [19½: 22: 24: 26] in)

(At widest point)
66.5 [72: 78: 83.5: 89] cm
(26 [28½: 30½: 33: 35:] in)

from ★ to end. – [-: -: -: 120] sts.
All sizes
Next round: K5, K2tog, (K10, K2tog) 9 times, K5. 110 sts.
Next round: K27.
Reposition marker after last st to denote new position of beg and end of rounds.
Shape neckband
Change to 4½mm (US 7) double-pointed needles and cont in rounds as folls:
Round 1: ★K1, (P1, K1) 27 times, rep from ★ once more.
This round sets position of rib.
Keeping rib correct as now set, cont as folls:
Work 1 round.
Round 3: ★sl 1, K1, psso, rib 23, K2tog, P1, sl

1, K1, psso, rib 23, K2tog, rep from ★ once more. 102 sts.
Work 1 round.
Round 5: ★Rib 10, sL2togK, K1, p2sso, rib 25, sL2togK, K1, p2sso, rib 10, rep from ★ once more. 94 sts.
Work 1 round.
Round 7: ★sl 1, K1, psso, rib 19, K2tog, P1, sl 1, K1, psso, rib 19, K2tog, rep from ★ once more. 86 sts.
Work 1 round.
Round 9: ★Rib 8, sL2togK, K1, p2sso, rib 21, sL2togK, K1, p2sso, rib 8, rep from ★ once more. 78 sts.
Cont in rib until neckband meas 8 cm.
Cast off **loosely** in rib.

MAKING UP
Press as described on the information page.
Armhole opening borders (both alike)
With RS facing and using set of double-pointed 4½mm (US 7) needles, beg and ending at base of armhole opening, pick up and knit 30 [32: 34: 36: 38] sts up first side of opening, then 30 [32: 34: 36: 38] sts down other side of opening. 60 [64: 68: 72: 76] sts.
Distribute sts evenly over 3 of the 4 needles and, using 4th needle, cont in rounds as folls:
Round 1: Purl.
Round 2: Knit.
Rep last 2 rows twice more.
Cast off **purlwise** (on RS).
See information page for finishing instructions.

ROBINIA
MARIE WALLIN
Main image page 8 & 9

BUTTONS – 3 x BN1368 (31mm) from Bedecked. Please see information page for contact details.

TENSION
24 sts and 32 rows to 10 cm measured over st st, 25 sts and 29 rows to 10 cm measured over patterned st st, both using 3¼mm (US 3) needles.

BACK
Using 3¼mm (US 3) needles and yarn B cast on 139 [169: 185] sts.
Row 1 (RS): K1, ★P1, K1, rep from ★ to end.
Row 2: As row 1.
These 2 rows form moss st.
Work in moss st for a further 12 rows, ending with RS facing for next row.
Break off yarn B and join in yarn A.
Beg with a K row, work in st st until back meas

YARN

	S-M	L-XL	XXL	
To fit bust				
	81–97	102–117	122–127	cm
	32–38	40–46	48–50	in

Rowan Felted Tweed

A Duck Egg 173				
	8	9	10	x 50 g
B Carbon 159				
	3	3	3	x 50 g
C Seafarer 170				
	2	2	2	x 50 g

NEEDLES
1 pair 3¼mm (no 10) (US 3) needles
3¼mm (no 10) (US 3) circular needle, 120 cm long

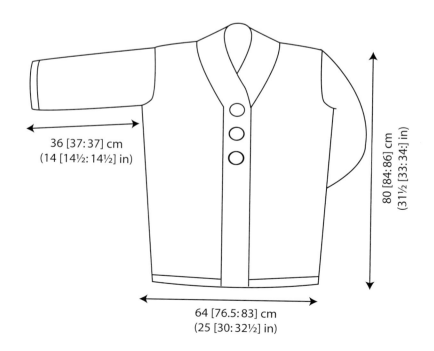

36 [37: 37] cm
(14 [14½: 14½] in)

80 [84: 86] cm
(31½ [33: 34] in)

64 [76.5: 83] cm
(25 [30: 32½] in)

11 [13: 14] cm, ending with RS facing for next row.
Inc 1 st at each end of next and 4 foll 16th rows. 149 [179: 195] sts.
Work 2 rows, ending with **WS** facing for next row.
Next row (WS): P16 [31: 39], M1, (P29, M1) 4 times, P17 [32: 40]. 154 [184: 200] sts.
Place chart
Using the **intarsia** technique as described on the information page, now place chart for body, which is worked entirely in st st beg with a K row, as folls:
Next row (RS): K3 [18: 26], work next 148 sts as row 1 of chart for body, K3 [18: 26].
Next row: P3 [18: 26], work next 148 sts as row 2 of chart for body, P3 [18: 26].
These 2 rows set the sts - central 148 sts in patt from chart with edge sts in st st using yarn A.
Cont as set, inc 1 st at each end of 11th and foll 16th row. 158 [188: 204] sts.
Cont straight until all 73 rows of chart have been completed, ending with **WS** facing for next row.
Break off yarn B and cont using yarn A only.
Next row (WS): P18 [33: 41], P2tog, (P28, P2tog) 4 times, P18 [33: 41]. 153 [183: 199] sts.
Beg with a K row, cont in st st until back meas 70 [74: 76] cm, ending with RS facing for next row.
Shape shoulders
Cast off 4 [5: 6] sts at beg of next 8 [10: 26] rows, then 5 [6: 7] sts at beg of foll 24 [22: 6] rows, ending with RS facing for next row.
Fasten off rem 1 st.

LEFT FRONT
Using 3¼mm (US 3) needles and yarn B cast on 69 [83: 91] sts.
Work in moss st as given for back for 14 rows, inc 0 [1: 1] st at end of last row and ending with RS facing for next row. 69 [84: 92] sts.
Break off yarn B and join in yarn A.
Beg with a K row, work in st st until left front meas 11 [13: 14] cm, ending with RS facing for next row.
Inc 1 st at beg of next and 4 foll 16th rows. 74 [89: 97] sts.
Work 2 rows, ending with **WS** facing for next row.
Next row (WS): P12, M1, (P24, M1) twice, P14 [29: 37]. 77 [92: 100] sts.
Place chart
Beg and ending rows as indicated, now place chart for body as folls:
Next row (RS): K3 [18: 26], work last 74 sts as row 1 of chart for body.
Next row: Work first 74 sts as row 2 of chart for body, P3 [18: 26].
These 2 rows set the sts - front opening edge 74 sts in patt from chart with edge sts in st st using yarn A.
Cont as set, inc 1 st at beg of 11th and foll 16th row. 79 [94: 102] sts.
Cont straight until all 73 rows of chart have been completed, ending with **WS** facing for next row.

Break off yarn B and cont using yarn A only.
Next row (WS): P11, P2tog, (P23, P2tog) twice, P16 [31: 39]. 76 [91: 99] sts.
Beg with a K row, cont in st st until left front matches back to beg of shoulder shaping, ending with RS facing for next row.
Shape shoulder
Cast off 4 [5: 6] sts at beg of next and foll 3 [4: 12] alt rows, then 5 [6: 7] sts at beg of foll 11 [10: 2] rows.
Work 1 row, ending with RS facing for next row.
Cast off rem 5 [6: 7] sts.

RIGHT FRONT
Using 3¼mm (US 3) needles and yarn B cast on 69 [83: 91] sts.
Work in moss st as given for back for 14 rows, inc 0 [1: 1] st at beg of last row and ending with RS facing for next row. 69 [84: 92] sts.
Break off yarn B and join in yarn A.
Beg with a K row, work in st st until right front meas 11 [13: 14] cm, ending with RS facing for next row.
Inc 1 st at end of next and 4 foll 16th rows. 74 [89: 97] sts.
Work 2 rows, ending with **WS** facing for next row.
Next row (WS): P14 [29: 37], M1, (P24, M1) twice, P12. 77 [92: 100] sts.
Place chart
Beg and ending rows as indicated, now place chart for body as folls:
Next row (RS): Work first 74 sts as row 1 of chart for body, K3 [18: 26].
Next row: P3 [18: 26], work last 74 sts as row 2 of chart for body.
These 2 rows set the sts - front opening edge 74 sts in patt from chart with edge sts in st st using yarn A.
Cont as set, inc 1 st at end of 11th and foll 16th row. 79 [94: 102] sts.
Cont straight until all 73 rows of chart have been completed, ending with **WS** facing for next row.
Break off yarn B and cont using yarn A only.
Next row (WS): P16 [31: 39], P2tog, (P23, P2tog) twice, P11. 76 [91: 99] sts.
Beg with a K row, cont in st st until right front matches back to beg of shoulder shaping, ending with **WS** facing for next row.
Shape shoulder
Cast off 4 [5: 6] sts at beg of next and foll 3 [4: 12] alt rows, then 5 [6: 7] sts at beg of foll 11 [10: 2] rows.
Work 1 row, ending with **WS** facing for next row.
Cast off rem 5 [6: 7] sts.

SLEEVES
Using 3¼mm (US 3) needles and yarn B cast on 63 [65: 67] sts.
Work in moss st as given for back for 14 rows, ending with RS facing for next row.
Break off yarn B and join in yarn A.
Beg with a K row, work in st st, shaping sides by inc 1 st at each end of 3rd and 2 [4: 4] foll

6th [4th: 4th] rows. 69 [75: 77] sts.
Work 3 [1: 1] rows, inc 1 st at centre of last row and ending with RS facing for next row. 70 [76: 78] sts.
Place chart
Beg and ending rows as indicated, now place chart for appropriate sleeve as folls:
Next row (RS): K6 [9: 10], work next 58 sts as row 1 of appropriate sleeve chart, K6 [9: 10].
Next row: P6 [9: 10], work next 58 sts as row 2 of appropriate sleeve chart, P6 [9: 10].
These 2 rows set the sts - centre 58 sts in patt from chart with edge sts in st st using yarn A.
Cont as set, inc 1 st at each end of next and 6 [1: 4] foll 6th [4th: 4th] rows, then on 3 [10: 8] foll 8th [6th: 6th] rows. 90 [100: 104] sts.
Work 6 [2: 2] rows, thereby completing all 69 rows of chart and ending with **WS** facing for next row.
Break off yarn B and cont using yarn A only.
Next row (WS): P44 [49: 51], P2tog, P44 [49: 51]. 89 [99: 103] sts.
Beg with a K row, work in st st for 8 [10: 10] rows, inc 1 st at each end of next [3rd: 3rd] row and ending with RS facing for next row. 91 [101: 105] sts.
(Sleeve should meas 36 [37: 37] cm.)
Shape top
Cast off 4 sts at beg of next 16 rows, ending with RS facing for next row.
Cast off rem 27 [37: 41] sts.

MAKING UP
Press as described on the information page. Join both shoulder seams using back stitch, or mattress stitch if preferred. (**Note:** There is no back neck edge as front shoulder edges meet at centre back neck fasten-off point.)
Front band
With RS facing, using 3¼mm (US 3) circular needle and yarn C, beg and ending at cast-on edges, pick up and knit 212 [222: 228] sts up right front opening edge to back neck fasten-off point, then 212 [222: 228] sts down left front opening edge. 424 [444: 456] sts.
Row 1 (WS): K1, P2, *K2, P2, rep from * to last st, K1.
Row 2: K3, *P2, K2, rep from * to last st, K1.
These 2 rows form rib.
Work in rib for a further 9 rows, ending with RS facing for next row.
Row 12 (RS): Rib 100 [104: 104], *cast off 3 sts (to make a buttonhole - cast on 3 sts over these cast-off sts on next row), rib until there are 14 [16: 17] sts on right needle after cast-off, rep from * once more, cast off 3 sts (to make 3rd buttonhole - cast on 3 sts over these cast-off sts on next row), rib to end.
Work in rib for a further 13 rows, ending with RS facing for next row.
Cast off in rib.
Mark points along side seam edges 20 [22: 23] cm either side of shoulder seams and sew shaped cast-off edges of sleeves to body between these points. See information page for finishing instructions.

Body Chart

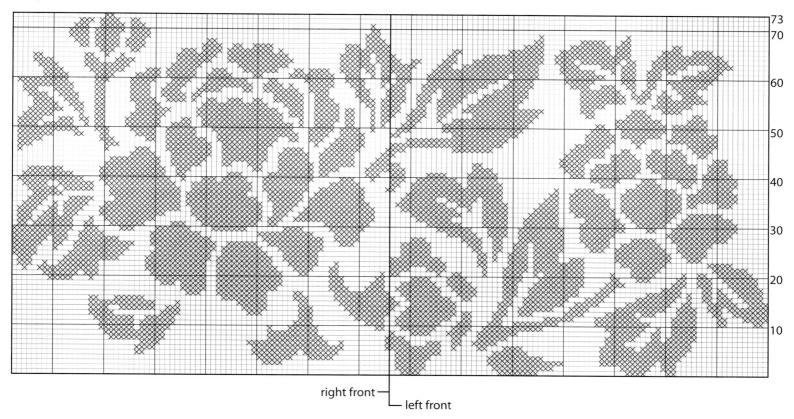

73
70

60

50

40

30

20

10

right front ⏤
└ left front

right sleeve

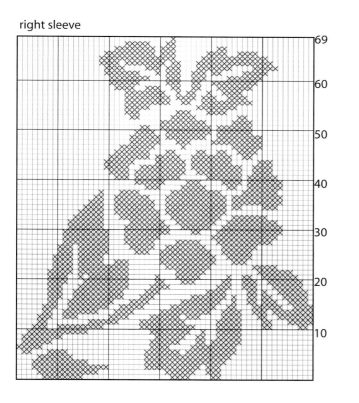

69

60

50

40

30

20

10

left sleeve

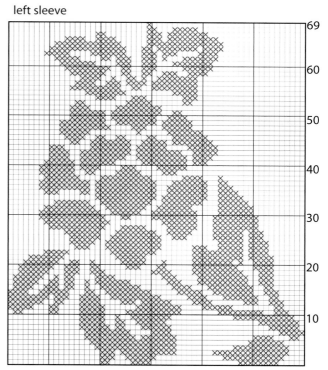

69

60

50

40

30

20

10

key
☐ A
⊠ B

PEGGY
MARIE WALLIN
Main image page 64 & 65

YARN

S	M	L	XL	XXL

To fit bust
81-86 91-97 102-107 112-117 122-127 cm
32-34 36-38 40-42 44-46 48-50 in
Rowan Cashsoft 4 ply
8   9   10   11   12   x 50 g
(photographed in Pretty 460)

NEEDLES

1 pair 2¾mm (no 12) (US 2) needles
1 pair 3¼mm (no 10) (US 3) needles
2¾mm (no 12) (US 2) circular needle,
40 cm long

TENSION

28 sts and 36 rows to 10 cm measured over rib
when slightly stretched using 3¼mm (US 3)
needles.

BACK

Using 2¾mm (US 2) needles cast on 117 [135:
147: 165: 189] sts.
Row 1 (RS): P3, *K3, P3, rep from * to end.
Row 2: K3, *P3, K3, rep from * to end.
These 2 rows form rib.
Keeping rib correct throughout, cont as folls:
Work 20 rows, ending with RS facing for
next row.
Change to 3¼mm (US 3) needles.
Next row (RS): P3, K2, sl 1, K1, psso, rib to
last 7 sts, K2tog, K2, P3.
Next row: K3, P3, rib to last 6 sts, P3, K3.
Keeping sts correct and working all decreases as
set by last 2 rows, dec 1 st at each end of 5th
and 3 foll 6th rows, then on foll 4th row.
105 [123: 135: 153: 177] sts.
Work 15 rows, ending with RS facing for
next row.
Next row (RS): P3, K3, M1, rib to last 6 sts,
M1, K3, P3.
Working all increases as set by last row and
taking inc sts into rib, inc 1 st at each end of
10th and 4 foll 10th rows.
117 [135: 147: 165: 189] sts.
Cont straight until back meas 36 [37: 38:
39: 40] cm, ending with RS facing for
next row.
Shape armholes
Keeping rib correct, cast off 6 [6: 6: 6: 12] sts at
beg of next 2 rows. 105 [123: 135: 153: 165] sts.
Next row (RS): P3, K2, sl 1, K1, psso, rib to
last 7 sts, K2tog, K2, P3.

Next row: K3, P2, P2tog, rib to last 7 sts,
P2tog tbl, P2, K3.
Rep last 2 rows 0 [1: 1: 3: 3] times more.
101 [115: 127: 137: 149] sts.
Next row (RS): P3, K2, sl 1, K1, psso, rib to
last 7 sts, K2tog, K2, P3.
Next row: K3, P3, rib to last 6 sts, P3, K3.
Rep last 2 rows 3 [7: 7: 9: 9] times more.
93 [99: 111: 117: 129] sts.
Cont straight until armhole meas 18 [19: 20:
21: 22] cm, ending with RS facing for next
row.
Shape shoulders and back neck
Next row (RS): Cast off 7 [9: 11: 11: 13] sts, rib
until there are 20 [24: 28: 28: 32] sts on right
needle and turn, leaving rem sts on a holder.
Work each side of neck separately.
Cast off 3 sts at beg of next row, 7 [9: 11:
11: 13] sts at beg of foll row, then 3 sts at beg
of next row.
Cast off rem 7 [9: 11: 11: 13] sts.
With RS facing, rejoin yarn to rem sts, cast off
centre 39 [33: 33: 39: 39] sts, rib to end.
Complete to match first side, reversing
shapings.

FRONT

Work as given for back until 24 rows less have
been worked than on back to beg of shoulder
shaping, ending with RS facing for next row.
Shape front neck
Next row (RS): Rib 33 [39: 45: 45: 51] and
turn, leaving rem sts on a holder.
Work each side of neck separately.
Next row (WS): K3, P2, P2tog, rib to end.
Next row: Rib to last 7 sts, K2tog, K2, P3.
Working all decreases as set by last 2 rows, dec
1 st at neck edge of next 4 rows, then on foll
5 alt rows, then on foll 4th row.
21 [27: 33: 33: 39] sts.
Work 3 rows, ending with RS facing for
next row.
Shape shoulder
Cast off 7 [9: 11: 11: 13] sts at beg of next and
foll alt row.

Work 1 row.
Cast off rem 7 [9: 11: 11: 13] sts.
With RS facing, slip centre 27 [21: 21: 27: 27] sts
onto a holder, rejoin yarn to rem sts, rib to
end. 33 [39: 45: 45: 51] sts.
Next row (WS): Rib to last 7 sts, P2tog tbl,
P2, K3.
Next row: P3, K2, sl 1, K1, psso, rib to end.
Complete to match first side, reversing
shapings.

SLEEVES

Using 2¾mm (US 2) needles cast on 51 [51:
57: 57: 57] sts.
Beg with row 1, work in rib as given for back
for 6 cm, ending with RS facing for next row.
Change to 3¼mm (US 3) needles.
Working all sleeve increases in same way as side
seam increases, cont in rib, inc 1 st at each end
of 5th and every foll 4th row to 77 [73: 75: 75:
111] sts, then on every foll 6th row until there
are 99 [99: 105: 105: 117] sts, taking inc sts into
rib.
Cont straight until sleeve meas 44 [45: 46: 46:
46] cm, ending with RS facing for next row.
Shape top
Keeping rib correct, cast off 6 [6: 6: 6: 12] sts at
beg of next 2 rows. 87 [87: 93: 93: 93] sts.
Working all decreases in same way as armhole
decreases, dec 1 st at each end of next 5 rows,
then on foll 18 alt rows, then on foll 7 rows,
ending with RS facing for next row. 27 [27: 33:
33: 33] sts.
Sizes L, XL and XXL only
Cast off 3 sts at beg of next 2 rows.
All sizes
Cast off rem 27 sts.

MAKING UP

Press as described on the information page.
Join both shoulder seams using back stitch, or
mattress stitch if preferred.
Collar
With RS facing and using 2¾mm (US 2)
circular needle, pick up and knit 21 [27: 27: 27:

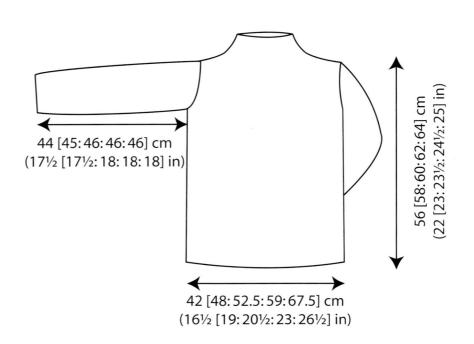

44 [45: 46: 46: 46] cm
(17½ [17½: 18: 18: 18] in)

56 [58: 60: 62: 64] cm
(22 [23: 23½: 24½: 25] in)

42 [48: 52.5: 59: 67.5] cm
(16½ [19: 20½: 23: 26½] in)

27] sts down left side of neck, rib 27 [21: 21: 27: 27] sts on front holder, pick up and knit 21 [27: 27: 27: 27] sts up right side of neck, then 51 [45: 45: 51: 51] sts from back.

120 [120: 120: 132: 132] sts.
Round 1 (RS): *P3, K3, rep from * to end. Rep this round until collar meas 11 cm from pick-up round.

Cast off in rib.
See information page for finishing instructions, setting in sleeves using the set-in method.

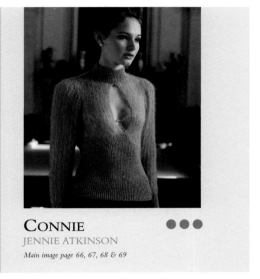

CONNIE
JENNIE ATKINSON
Main image page 66, 67, 68 & 69

YARN

	S	M	L	XL	XXL	
To fit bust						
	81-86	91-97	102-107	112-117	122-127	cm
	32-34	36-38	40-42	44-46	48-50	in

Rowan Pure Wool 4 ply and Kidsilk Haze
A 4ply Ochre 461

3	4	4	4	5	x 50 g

B KSH Mud 652

3	3	4	4	4	x 25 g

NEEDLES
1 pair 2¾mm (no 12) (US 2) needles
1 pair 3¼mm (no 10) (US 3) needles

BUTTONS – 3 x RW5019 from Bedecked. Please see information page for contact details.

TENSION
22 sts and 36 rows to 10 cm measured over patt using 3¼mm (US 3) needles and Kidsilk Haze.

BACK
Using 2¾mm (US 2) needles and yarn A cast on 123 [137: 155: 171: 191] sts.
Row 1 (RS): K1 [0: 1: 1: 1], *P1, K1, rep from * to last 0 [1: 0: 0: 0] st, P0 [1: 0: 0: 0].
Row 2: P1 [0: 1: 1: 1], *K1, P1, rep from * to last 0 [1: 0: 0: 0] st, K0 [1: 0: 0: 0].
These 2 rows form rib.
Work in rib for a further 18 rows, ending with RS facing for next row.
Change to 3¼mm (US 3) needles.
Cont in rib, shaping side seams by dec 1 st at each end of 3rd and 5 foll 8th rows.
111 [125: 143: 159: 179] sts.

Cont straight until back meas 20 cm, ending with RS facing for next row.**
Next row (RS): Rib 55 [62: 71: 79: 89], inc in next st, rib 55 [62: 71: 79: 89].
112 [126: 144: 160: 180] sts.
Divide for back opening
Break off yarn A and join in yarn B.
Next row (WS): P55 [62: 71: 79: 89], K1 and slip these sts onto a holder, K1, P to end.
56 [63: 72: 80: 90] sts.
Work each side of back separately.
Beg and ending rows as indicated and repeating the 12 row patt rep throughout, now work in patt from chart for right back as folls:
Dec 1 st at beg of 3rd and every foll 4th row until 48 [54: 61: 67: 75] sts rem.
Cont straight until right back meas 33 [34: 35: 36: 37] cm from cast-on edge, ending with RS facing for next row.
Shape armhole
Keeping patt correct, cast off 4 [5: 6: 7: 8] sts at beg of next row. 44 [49: 55: 60: 67] sts.
Work 1 row.
Dec 1 st at armhole edge of next 3 [5: 7: 9: 11] rows, then on foll 4 [4: 5: 5: 6] alt rows.
37 [40: 43: 46: 50] sts.
Cont straight until armhole meas 19 [20: 21:

22: 23] cm, ending with RS facing for next row.
Shape shoulder and back neck
Cast off 6 [7: 8: 9: 10] sts at beg of next row, 16 [16: 17: 17: 18] sts at beg of foll row, 6 [7: 8: 9: 10] sts at beg of next row, and 3 sts at beg of foll row.
Cast off rem 6 [7: 7: 8: 9] sts.
With RS facing and using 3¼mm (US 3) needles, rejoin yarn B to rem sts and cont as folls:
Beg and ending rows as indicated and repeating the 12 row patt rep throughout, now work in patt from chart for left back as folls:
Dec 1 st at end of 3rd and every foll 4th row until 48 [54: 61: 67: 75] sts rem.
Complete to match right back, reversing shapings.

FRONT
Work as given for back to **.
Using the **intarsia** technique as described on the information page, working chart rows 1 to 24 **once only** and then repeating chart rows 25 to 36 **throughout**, now work in patt from chart for front as folls:
Dec 1 st at each end of 5th and 4 foll 4th rows.
101 [115: 133: 149: 169] sts.

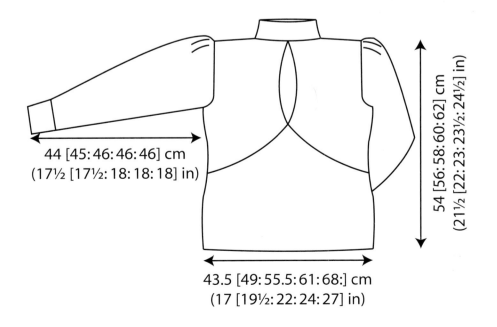

44 [45: 46: 46: 46] cm
(17½ [17½: 18: 18: 18] in)

54 [56: 58: 60: 62] cm
(21½ [22: 23: 23½: 24½] in)

43.5 [49: 55.5: 61: 68:] cm
(17 [19½: 22: 24: 27] in)

Work 2 rows, ending after chart row 23 and
with **WS** facing for next row.

Break off yarn A and cont using yarn B only.

Next row (WS): Patt 50 [57: 66: 74: 84] sts,
inc in next st, patt 50 [57: 66: 74: 84] sts.
102 [116: 134: 150: 170] sts.

Divide for front opening

Next row (RS): K2tog, patt 49 [56: 65: 73:
83] sts and turn, leaving rem sts on a holder.
50 [57: 66: 74: 84] sts.

Work each side of front separately.

Dec 1 st at beg of 4th and 1 [2: 4: 6: 8] foll 4th
rows. 48 [54: 61: 67: 75] sts rem.

Cont straight until left front matches back to
beg of armhole shaping, ending with RS facing
for next row.

Shape armhole

Keeping patt correct, cast off 4 [5: 6: 7: 8] sts at
beg of next row. 44 [49: 55: 60: 67] sts.

Work 1 row.

Dec 1 st at armhole edge of next 3 [5: 7: 9: 11]
rows, then on foll 4 [4: 5: 5: 6] alt rows.
37 [40: 43: 46: 50] sts.

Cont straight until 17 [17: 19: 19: 21] rows less
have been worked than on back to beg of
shoulder shaping, ending with **WS** facing for
next row.

Shape neck

Keeping patt correct, cast off 10 sts at beg of
next row. 27 [30: 33: 36: 40] sts.

Dec 1 st at neck edge of next 5 rows, then on
foll 3 [3: 4: 4: 5] alt rows, then on foll 4th row.
18 [21: 23: 26: 29] sts.

Work 1 row, ending with RS facing for
next row.

Shape shoulder

Cast off 6 [7: 8: 9: 10] sts at beg of next and
foll alt row.

Work 1 row.

Cast off rem 6 [7: 7: 8: 9] sts.

With RS facing and using 3¼mm (US 3)
needles, rejoin yarn B to rem sts and cont
as folls:

Next row (RS): Patt to last 2 sts, K2tog.
50 [57: 66: 74: 84] sts.

Complete to match left front, reversing
shapings.

SLEEVES

Using 2¾mm (US 2) needles and yarn A cast
on 47 [51: 53: 53: 57] sts.

Row 1 (RS): K1, *P1, K1, rep from * to end.

Row 2: P1, *K1, P1, rep from * to end.

These 2 rows form rib.

Cont in rib, shaping sides by inc 1 st at each
end of 5th and 9 [8: 9: 9: 9] foll 4th rows, then
on 0 [1: 0: 0: 0] foll 6th row, taking inc sts into
rib. 67 [71: 73: 73: 77] sts.

Work 2 [0: 2: 2: 2] rows, ending with **WS**
facing for next row.

Change to 3¼mm (US 3) needles.

Break off yarn A and join in yarn B.

Beg and ending rows as indicated, noting that
chart row 1 is a **WS** row and repeating the
12 row patt rep throughout, now work in patt
from chart for sleeve as folls:

Inc 1 st at each end of 2nd [6th: 4th: 2nd: 2nd]
and 0 [0: 0: 5: 5] foll 4th rows, then on every
foll 6th row until there are 101 [105: 109:
113: 117] sts, taking inc sts into patt.

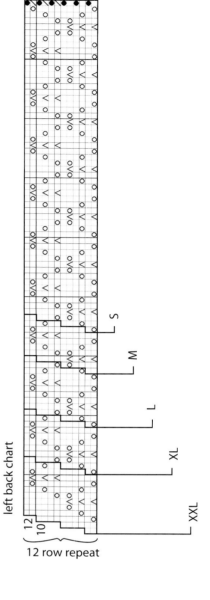

right back chart

12 row repeat

left back chart

12 row repeat

XXL

XL

L

M

S

key

using yarn B

☐ K on RS, P on WS
⬛ K on WS
◎ yfwd
⧄ sl1, K2tog, psso
⧅ K2tog
⬒ sl1, K1, psso
⬓ inc
⊠ sl1, K1, psso on left front, K2tog on right front

using yarn A

☐ K on RS, P on WS
⬛ P on RS, K on WS

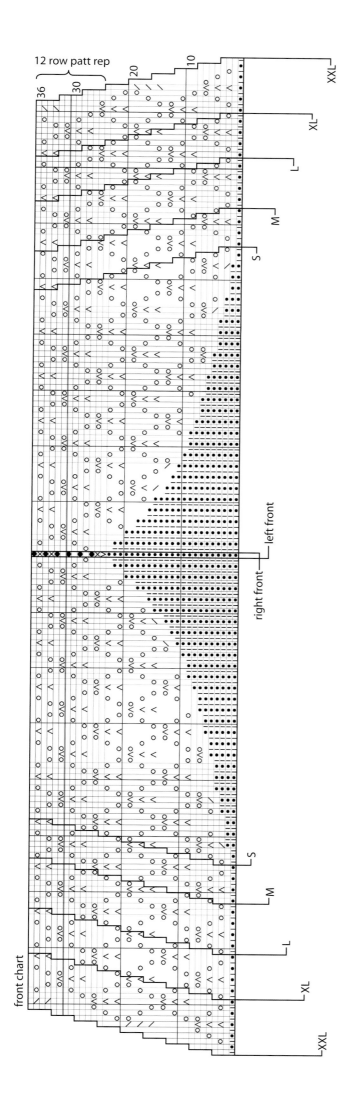

front chart

12 row patt rep

left front

right front

S

M

L

XL

XXL

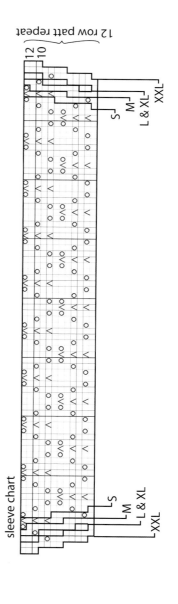

sleeve chart

12 row patt repeat

S

M

L & XL

XXL

Cont straight until sleeve meas 44 [45: 46: 46: 46] cm, ending with RS facing for next row.

Shape top

Keeping patt correct, cast off 4 [5: 6: 7: 8] sts at beg of next 2 rows. 93 [95: 97: 99: 101] sts.

Dec 1 st at each end of next 5 rows, then on foll 3 alt rows, then on 4 foll 4th rows. 69 [71: 73: 75: 77] sts.

Work 1 row, ending with RS facing for next row.

Dec 1 st at each end of next and every foll alt row to 57 sts, then on foll 8 rows, ending with **WS** facing for next row. 41 sts.

Next row (WS): P1, (P2tog) 9 times, P3tog, (P2tog tbl) 9 times, P1.

Cast off rem 21 sts.

MAKING UP

Press as described on the information page. Join both shoulder seams using back stitch, or mattress stitch if preferred. Join fronts together at neck edge.

Neckband

With RS facing, using 2¾mm (US 2) needles and yarn A, beg and ending at back opening edges, pick up and knit 24 [24: 25: 25: 26] sts from left back neck, 17 [17: 19: 19: 21] down left side of neck, 25 sts from front, 17 [17: 19: 19: 21] sts up right side of neck, then 24 [24: 25: 25: 26] sts from right back neck. 107 [107: 113: 113: 119] sts.

Row 1 (WS): K1, *P1, K1, rep from * to end.
Row 2: K2, *P1, K1, rep from * to last st, K1.

These 2 rows form rib.

Work in rib for 1 row more, ending with RS facing for next row.

Row 4 (RS): K1, (wrap yarn round right needle as though knitting a st, lift st on right needle over this loop and off right needle) 7 times (to make button loop), rib to end.

Work 7 rows.

Rep last 8 rows once more, then first of these rows (the button loop row) again.

Work a further 3 rows, ending with RS facing for next row.

Cast off in rib.

See information page for finishing instructions, setting in sleeves using the set-in method.

WARMTH
ERIKA KNIGHT
Main image page 112 & 113

YARN

	S	M	L	XL	XXL

To fit bust
81-86 91-97 102-107 112-117 122-127 cm
32-34 36-38 40-42 44-46 48-50 in

Rowan Kid Classic

	S	M	L	XL	XXL	
	8	9	9	10	10	x 50 g

(photographed in Bitter Sweet 866)

NEEDLES

1 pair 4½mm (no 7) (US 7) needles
1 pair 5mm (no 6) (US 8) needles
4½mm (no 7) (US 7) circular needle, 120 cm long

BUTTONS – 5 x RW5030 (23mm) Antique Brass from Bedecked. Please see information page for contact details.

TENSION

19 sts and 25 rows to 10 cm measured over st st using 5mm (US 8) needles.

BACK

Using 5mm (US 8) needles cast on 91 [97: 105: 113: 121] sts.

Beg with a K row, cont in st st throughout as folls:

Cont straight until back meas 26 cm, ending with RS facing for next row.

Next row (RS): K3, K2tog, K to last 5 sts, K2tog tbl, K3.

Working all decreases as set by last row, dec 1 st at each end of 8th and foll 8th row, then on 2 foll 6th rows, then on 5 [5: 4: 3: 2] foll 4th rows, then on foll 25 [28: 32: 37: 41] alt rows. 21 [21: 23: 23: 25] sts.

Work 1 row, ending with RS facing for next row.

Cast off.

LEFT FRONT

Using 5mm (US 8) needles cast on 42 [45: 49: 53: 57] sts.

Row 1 (RS): Knit.
Row 2: P to last 2 sts, K2.

These 2 rows set the sts.

Rep last 2 rows until left front meas 24 cm, ending with RS facing for next row.

Place marker at end of last row.

Beg with a K row, cont in st st throughout as folls:

Cont straight until left front meas 26 cm,

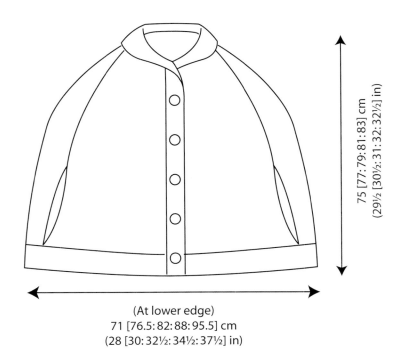

75 [77: 79: 81: 83] cm
(29½ [30½: 31: 32: 32½] in)

(At lower edge)
71 [76.5: 82: 88: 95.5] cm
(28 [30: 32½: 34½: 37½] in)

ending with RS facing for next row.
Working all decreases as set by back, dec 1 st at beg of next and 2 foll 8th rows, then on 2 foll 6th rows, then on 5 [5: 4: 3: 2] foll 4th rows, then on foll 16 [19: 22: 27: 30] alt rows.
16 [16: 18: 18: 20] sts.
Work 1 row, ending with RS facing for next row.
Shape neck
Place marker at beg of last row.
Dec 1 st at marked neck edge of next 8 [8: 8: 8: 9] rows **and at same time** dec 1 st at side edge of next and foll 3 [3: 3: 3: 4] alt rows.
4 [4: 6: 6: 6] sts.
Work 0 [0: 0: 0: 1] row, ending with RS facing for next row.
Sizes L, XL and XXL only
Next row (RS): K3, K3tog.
Next row: P4.
All sizes
Next row (RS): K1, K3tog.
Next row: P2.
Next row: K2tog and fasten off.

RIGHT FRONT
Using 5mm (US 8) needles cast on 42 [45: 49: 53: 57] sts.
Row 1 (RS): Knit.
Row 2: K2, P to end.
These 2 rows set the sts.
Rep last 2 rows until right front meas 24 cm, ending with RS facing for next row.
Place marker at beg of last row.
Beg with a K row, cont in st st throughout as folls:
Cont straight until right front meas 26 cm, ending with RS facing for next row.
Working all decreases as set by back, dec 1 st at end of next and 2 foll 8th rows, then on 2 foll 6th rows, then on 5 [5: 4: 3: 2] foll 4th rows, then on foll 16 [19: 22: 27: 30] alt rows.
16 [16: 18: 18: 20] sts.
Work 1 row, ending with RS facing for next row.
Shape neck
Place marker at end of last row.
Dec 1 st at marked neck edge of next 8 [8: 8: 8: 9] rows **and at same time** dec 1 st at side edge of next and foll 3 [3: 3: 3: 4] alt rows.
4 [4: 6: 6: 6] sts.
Work 0 [0: 0: 0: 1] row, ending with RS facing for next row.
Sizes L, XL and XXL only
Next row (RS): K3 tog tbl, K3.
Next row: P4.
All sizes
Next row (RS): K3tog tbl, K1.
Next row: P2.
Next row: K2tog and fasten off.

LEFT SIDE PANEL
Using 5mm (US 8) needles cast on 48 [52: 54: 58: 64] sts.
Row 1 (RS): Knit.
Row 2: K2, P to end.
These 2 rows set the sts.
Rep last 2 rows until left side panel meas 24 cm, ending with RS facing for next row.
Place marker at beg of last row.
Beg with a K row, cont in st st throughout

as folls:
Cont straight until left side panel meas 26 cm, ending with RS facing for next row.
Working all decreases as set by back, dec 1 st at each end of next and 2 foll 8th rows, then on 8 [7: 7: 6: 2] foll 6th rows, then on 7 [10: 11: 14: 21] foll 4th rows, ending with **WS** facing for next row. 12 sts.
Shape neck
Cast off 2 sts at beg of next and foll 3 alt rows, ending with RS facing for next row, **and at same time** dec 1 st at beg of 4th row.
Cast off rem 3 sts.

RIGHT SIDE PANEL
Using 5mm (US 8) needles cast on 48 [52: 54: 58: 64] sts.
Row 1 (RS): Knit.
Row 2: P to last 2 sts, K2.
These 2 rows set the sts.
Rep last 2 rows until right side panel meas 24 cm, ending with RS facing for next row.
Place marker at end of last row.
Beg with a K row, cont in st st throughout as folls:
Cont straight until right side panel meas 26 cm, ending with RS facing for next row.
Working all decreases as set by back, dec 1 st at each end of next and 2 foll 8th rows, then on 8 [7: 7: 6: 2] foll 6th rows, then on 6 [9: 10: 13: 20] foll 4th rows. 14 sts.
Work 3 rows, ending with RS facing for next row.
Shape neck
Cast off 3 sts at beg of next row, then 2 sts at beg of foll 3 alt rows **and at same time** dec 1 st at end of next and foll 4th row.
Work 1 row, ending with RS facing for next row.
Cast off rem 3 sts.

MAKING UP
Press as described on the information page.
Join side panels to back and fronts using back stitch, or mattress stitch if preferred and leaving front seams open below markers. Securely join fronts to side panels at cast-on edges.
Hem border
With RS facing and using 4½mm (US 7) circular needle, pick up and knit 42 [45: 49: 53: 57] sts from cast-on edge of left front, 48 [52: 54: 58: 63] sts from cast-on edge of left side panel, 90 [96: 104: 113: 120] sts from cast-on edge of back, 48 [52: 54: 58: 63] sts from cast-on edge of right side panel, then 42 [45: 49: 53: 57] sts from cast-on edge of right front.
270 [290: 310: 335: 360] sts.
Row 1 (WS): K1, *P3, K2, rep from * to last 4 sts, P3, K1.
Row 2: K4, *P2, K3, rep from * to last st, K1.
Rep last 2 rows until hem border meas 9 cm from pick-up row, ending with RS facing for next row.
Cast off in rib.
Mark positions for 5 buttonholes along right front opening edge - first to come 4 cm up from lower edge, last to come 2.5 cm below neck shaping, and rem 3 buttons evenly spaced between.

Front band and collar
Using 4½mm (US 7) needles cast on 11 sts.
Row 1 (RS): K2, (P1, K1) 4 times, K1.
Row 2: K1, (P1, K1) 5 times.
These 2 rows form rib.
Cont in rib until band meas 4 cm, ending with RS facing for next row.
Next row (buttonhole row) (RS): Rib 4, cast off 2 sts (to make a buttonhole - cast on 2 sts over these cast-off sts on next row), rib to end.
Making a further 4 buttonholes in this way to correspond with positions marked for buttonholes and noting that no further reference will be made to buttonholes, cont as folls:
Cont in rib until this band section, when slightly stretched, fits up right front opening edge from cast-off edge of hem border to just below beg of neck shaping, sewing in place as you go along and ending at outer (unattached) edge.
Next row (RS): K1, M1, rib to end. 12 sts.
Next row (RS of collar, WS of body): (K1, P1) 5 times, K2.
Next row: K1, P1, M1, rib to last st, inc in last st.
Next row: Inc in first st, rib to last 2 sts, M1, K2.
Rep last 2 rows 3 times more. 28 sts.
Next row: K1, P1, M1, rib to last st, inc in last st.
Next row: Rib to last 2 sts, K2.
Rep last 2 rows 3 times more. 36 sts.
Keeping sts correct as now set, cont as folls:
**Work 2 rows.
Next row (WS of collar): Rib 30, wrap next st (by slipping next st from left needle to right needle, taking yarn to opposite side of work between needles, then slipping same st back onto left needle - when working back across wrapped sts, work the wrapped st and the wrapping loop tog as 1 st) and turn.
Next row: Rib to end.
Next row: Rib 24, wrap next st and turn.
Next row: Rib to end.
Work 2 rows across all sts.
Rep from ** 7 [7: 9: 9: 10] times more.
Work 1 row.
Next row: K1, P2tog, rib to last 2 sts, work 2 tog.
Rep last 2 rows 3 times more. 28 sts.
Next row: Work 2 tog, rib to last 3 sts, K2tog, K1.
Next row: K1, P2tog, rib to last 2 sts, work 2 tog.
Rep last 2 rows 3 times more. 12 sts.
Next row: K1, work 2 tog, rib to end. 11 sts.
Sew last (collar) section to entire neck edge, easing in slight fullness and ending at beg of left front neck shaping.
Cont in rib as set by first section of band until this band, when slightly stretched, fits down entire left front opening edge, sewing in place as you go along and ending with RS facing for next row.
Cast off in rib.
See information page for finishing instructions.

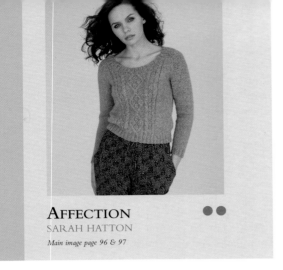

AFFECTION
SARAH HATTON

Main image page 96 & 97

● ●

YARN

8	10	12	14	16	18	20	22	

To fit bust

81	86	91	97	102	107	112	117	cm
32	34	36	38	40	42	44	46	in

Rowan Lima

8	8	9	9	10	10	11	11	x 50 g

(photographed in Ecuador 896)

NEEDLES

1 pair 4¹/₂mm (no 7) (US 7) needles
1 pair 5¹/₂mm (no 5) (US 9) needles
Cable needle

TENSION

20 sts and 26 rows to 10 cm measured over st st using 5¹/₂mm (US 9) needles.

SPECIAL ABBREVIATIONS

C4B = slip next 2 sts onto cable needle and leave at back of work, K2, then K2 from cable needle; **C4F** = slip next 2 sts onto cable needle and leave at front of work, K2, then K2 from cable needle; **C5F** = slip next 2 sts onto cable needle and leave at front of work, K3, then K2 from cable needle; **Cr3L** = slip next 2 sts onto cable needle and leave at front of work, P1, then K2 from cable needle; **Cr3R** = slip next st onto cable needle and leave at back of work, K2, then P1 from cable needle.

BACK

Using 4¹/₂mm (US 7) needles cast on 88 [92: 96: 102: 108: 114: 120: 126] sts.
Row 1 (RS): P3 [3: 3: 2: 3: 2: 3: 2], *K2, P2, rep from * to last 1 [1: 1: 0: 1: 0: 1: 0] st, P1 [1: 1: 0: 1: 0: 1: 0].
Row 2: K3 [3: 3: 2: 3: 2: 3: 2], *P2, K2, rep from * to last 1 [1: 1: 0: 1: 0: 1: 0] st, K1 [1: 1: 0: 1: 0: 1: 0].
These 2 rows form rib.
Work in rib for a further 10 rows, ending with RS facing for next row.
Change to 5¹/₂mm (US 9) needles.
Beg with a K row, work in st st until back meas 34 [34: 33: 36: 35: 37: 36: 38] cm, ending with RS facing for next row.
Shape raglan armholes
Cast off 5 sts at beg of next 2 rows. 78 [82: 86: 92: 98: 104: 110: 116] sts.
Sizes 8, 10 and 12 only
Next row (RS): K1, sl 1, K1, psso, K to last 3 sts, K2tog, K1.

Work 3 rows.
Rep last 4 rows 4 [2: 1: -: -: -: -: -] times more. 68 [76: 82: -: -: -: -: -] sts.
Sizes 14, 16, 18, 20 and 22 only
Next row (RS): K1, sl 1, K1, psso, K to last 3 sts, K2tog, K1.
Next row: P1, P2tog, P to last 3 sts, P2tog tbl, P1.
Rep last 2 rows - [-: -: 0: 1: 4: 5: 8] times more. - [-: -: 88: 90: 84: 86: 80] sts.
All sizes
Next row (RS): K1, sl 1, K1, psso, K to last 3 sts, K2tog, K1.
Work 1 row.
Rep last 2 rows 8 [12: 15: 18: 18: 15: 16: 13] times more, ending with RS facing for next row. 50 [50: 50: 50: 52: 52: 52: 52] sts.
Cast off.

Pattern note: The number of sts varies whilst working cable panel. All st counts given presume there are 51 sts in cable panel at all times.

FRONT

Using 4¹/₂mm (US 7) needles cast on 88 [92: 96: 102: 108: 114: 120: 126] sts.
Work in rib as given for back for 11 rows, ending with **WS** facing for next row.
Row 12 (WS): Rib 25 [27: 29: 32: 35: 38: 41: 44], M1, rib 8, (M1, rib 11) twice, M1, rib 8, M1, rib to end. 93 [97: 101: 107: 113: 119: 125: 131] sts.
Change to 5¹/₂mm (US 9) needles.
Row 13 (RS): K21 [23: 25: 28: 31: 34: 37: 40], work next 51 sts as row 1 of chart for cable panel, K to end.
Row 14: P21 [23: 25: 28: 31: 34: 37: 40], work next 51 sts as row 2 of chart for cable panel, P to end.
These 2 rows set the sts - centre cable panel with edge sts in st st.
Keeping sts correct as now set throughout, cont as folls:
Cont straight until front matches back to beg of armhole shaping, ending with RS facing for next row.
Shape raglan armholes

Keeping patt correct, cast off 5 sts at beg of next 2 rows.
83 [87: 91: 97: 103: 109: 115: 121] sts.
Working all raglan armhole decreases in same way as given for back, dec 1 st at each end of next 1 [1: 1: 3: 5: 10: 12: 12] rows, then on 1 [1: 2: 2: 2: 0: 0: 0] foll 4th [4th: 4th: alt: alt: 0: 0: 0] rows. 79 [83: 85: 87: 89: 89: 91: 97] sts.
Work 3 [3: 1: 1: 1: 0: 0: 0] rows, ending with RS facing for next row.
Shape front neck
Next row (RS): K1, sl 1, K1, psso, patt 29 [31: 32: 34: 34: 34: 36: 39] sts and turn, leaving rem sts on a holder.
Work each side of neck separately.
Keeping patt and raglan armhole decreases correct, dec 1 st at neck edge of next 10 rows, then on foll 8 [8: 8: 9: 9: 9: 10: 10] alt rows **and at same time** dec 1 st at raglan armhole edge of 4th [4th: 2nd: 2nd: 2nd: 2nd: next] and foll 0 [0: 0: 0: 0: 0: 0: 5] rows, then on 2 [0: 0: 0: 0: 0: 0: 0] foll 4th rows, then on foll 7 [11: 12: 13: 13: 13: 14: 12] alt rows. 3 sts.
Work 1 row, ending with RS facing for next row.
Next row (RS): K1, sl 1, K1, psso.
Next row: P2.
Next row: K2tog and fasten off.
Shape shoulder
With RS facing, rejoin yarn to rem sts, cast off centre 15 [15: 15: 13: 15: 15: 13: 13] sts, patt to last 3 sts, K2tog, K1.
Complete to match first side, reversing shapings.

SLEEVES

Using 4¹/₂mm (US 7) needles cast on 42 [42: 44: 44: 46: 46: 48: 48] sts.
Row 1 (RS): P0 [0: 1: 1: 0: 0: 1: 1], *K2, P2, rep from * to last 2 [2: 3: 3: 2: 2: 3: 3] sts, K2, P0 [0: 1: 1: 0: 0: 1: 1].
Row 2: K0 [0: 1: 1: 0: 0: 1: 1], *P2, K2, rep from * to last 2 [2: 3: 3: 2: 2: 3: 3] sts, P2, K0 [0: 1: 1: 0: 0: 1: 1].
These 2 rows form rib.
Work in rib for a further 8 rows, ending with RS facing for next row.
Change to 5¹/₂mm (US 9) needles.
Beg with a K row, work in st st, shaping sides by inc 1 st at each end of 5th and every foll 6th

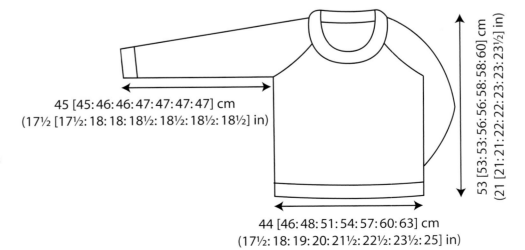

45 [45: 46: 46: 47: 47: 47: 47] cm
(17½ [17½: 18: 18: 18½: 18½: 18½: 18½] in)

53 [53: 53: 56: 56: 58: 58: 60] cm
(21 [21: 21: 22: 22: 23: 23: 23½] in)

44 [46: 48: 51: 54: 57: 60: 63] cm
(17½ [18: 19: 20: 21½: 22½: 23½: 25] in)

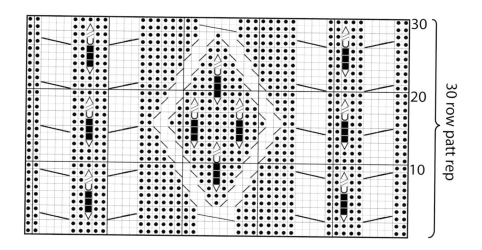

30 row patt rep

key

☐ K on RS, P on WS

⊡ P on RS, K on WS

■ K5 on RS, P5 on WS

▽ (K1, yfwd, K1, yfwd, K1) all into next st

⊔ sl1, K1, psso, K1, K2tog

▱ P3

◺ sl1, K2tog, psso

⬚⬚⬚ C4B

⬚⬚⬚ C4F

⬚⬚⬚⬚ C5F

▱▱ Cr3R

◣◣ Cr3L

row to 46 [52: 52: 60: 58: 66: 68: 76] sts, then on every foll 8th row until there are 66 [68: 70: 72: 74: 76: 78: 80] sts.
Cont straight until sleeve meas 45 [45: 46: 46: 47: 47: 47: 47] cm, ending with RS facing for next row.

Shape raglan
Cast off 5 sts at beg of next 2 rows.
56 [58: 60: 62: 64: 66: 68: 70] sts.

Sizes 10, 12, 14, 16, 18, 20 and 22 only
Next row (RS): K1, sl 1, K1, psso, K to last 3 sts, K2tog, K1.
Next row: P1, P2tog, P to last 3 sts, P2tog tbl, P1.
Rep last 2 rows - [0: 0: 1: 1: 2: 1: 2] times more.
- [54: 56: 54: 56: 54: 60: 58] sts.

All sizes
Next row (RS): K1, sl 1, K1, psso, K to last 3 sts, K2tog, K1.
Work 1 row.
Rep last 2 rows 18 [17: 18: 17: 18: 17: 20: 19] times more, ending with RS facing for next row. 18 sts.
Cast off.

MAKING UP
Press as described on the information page.
Join both front and right back raglan seams using back stitch, or mattress stitch if preferred.
Neckband
With RS facing and using 4¹/₂mm (US 7)

needles, pick up and knit 16 sts from top of left sleeve, 25 [25: 25: 28: 28: 28: 29: 29] sts down left side of neck, 15 [15: 15: 13: 15: 15: 13: 13] sts from front, 25 [25: 25: 28: 28: 28: 29: 29] sts up right side of neck, 16 sts from top of right sleeve, then 49 [49: 49: 49: 51: 51: 51: 51] sts from back. 146 [146: 146: 150: 154: 154: 154: 154] sts.
Row 1 (WS): P2, *K2, P2, rep from * to end.
Row 2: K2, *P2, K2, rep from * to end.
These 2 rows form rib.
Work in rib for a further 7 rows, ending with RS facing for next row.
Cast off in rib.
See information page for finishing instructions.

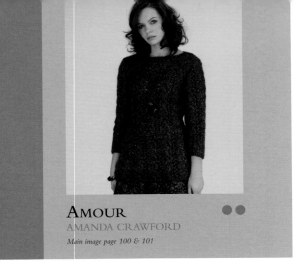

AMOUR

AMANDA CRAWFORD

Main image page 100 & 101

●●

YARN

S	M	L	XL	XXL

To fit bust
81–86 91–97 102–107 112–117 122–127 cm
32–34 36–38 40–42 44–46 48–50 in

Rowan Silk Twist

12	13	14	16	17	x 50 g

(photographed in Mahogany 669)

NEEDLES

1 pair 5mm (no 6) (US 8) needles
1 pair 6mm (no 4) (US 10) needles
Cable needle

TENSION

18 sts and 21 rows to 10 cm measured over patt
using 6mm (US 10) needles.

SPECIAL ABBREVIATIONS

C4B = slip next 2 sts onto cable needle and
leave at back of work, K2, then K2 from cable
needle; **C4F** = slip next 2 sts onto cable needle
and leave at front of work, K2, then K2 from
cable needle.

BACK

Using 6mm (US 10) needles cast on 90 [98:
108: 120: 132] sts.
Row 1 (RS): P2 [3: 2: 2: 2], (yon, K2tog, P1)
1 [0: 0: 0: 0] times, *K8, P1, yon, K2tog, P1, rep
from * to last 13 [11: 10: 10: 10] sts, K8, (P1,
yon, K2tog) 1 [0: 0: 0: 0] times, P2 [3: 2: 2: 2].
Row 2 and every foll alt row: K2 [3: 2: 2:
2], (P2, K1) 1 [0: 0: 0: 0] times, *P8, K1, P2,
K1, rep from * to last 13 [11: 10: 10: 10] sts, P8,
(K1, P2) 1 [0: 0: 0: 0] times, K2 [3: 2: 2: 2].
Row 3: P2 [3: 2: 2: 2], (K2tog, yfrn, P1) 1 [0:
0: 0: 0] times, *C4F, C4B, P1, K2tog, yfrn, P1,
rep from * to last 13 [11: 10: 10: 10] sts, C4F,
C4B, (P1, K2tog, yfrn) 1 [0: 0: 0: 0] times,
P2 [3: 2: 2: 2].
Row 5: As row 1.
Row 7: P2 [3: 2: 2: 2], (K2tog, yfrn, P1) 1 [0:
0: 0: 0] times, *K8, P1, K2tog, yfrn, P1, rep
from * to last 13 [11: 10: 10: 10] sts, K8, (P1,
K2tog, yfrn) 1 [0: 0: 0: 0] times, P2 [3: 2: 2: 2].
Row 8: As row 2.
These 8 rows form patt.
Cont in patt until back meas 7 [8: 9: 10: 11] cm,
ending with RS facing for next row.
Keeping patt correct, dec 1 st at each end of
next and 4 foll 6th rows, then on 4 foll 4th
rows. 72 [80: 90: 102: 114] sts.

Work 11 rows, ending with RS facing for next
row.
Inc 1 st at each end of next and 4 foll 6th rows,
taking inc sts into patt.
82 [90: 100: 112: 124] sts.
Cont straight until back meas 49 [50: 51: 52:
53] cm, ending with RS facing for next row.
Shape armholes
Keeping patt correct, cast off 3 [4: 5: 6: 7] sts at
beg of next 2 rows. 76 [82: 90: 100: 110] sts.
Dec 1 st at each end of next 3 [5: 5: 7: 7] rows,
then on foll 4 [4: 5: 5: 7] alt rows. 62 [64: 70:
76: 82] sts.
Cont straight until armhole meas 19 [20: 21:
22: 23] cm, ending with RS facing for next
row.
Shape shoulders and back neck
Next row (RS): Cast off 4 [5: 6: 7: 8] sts, patt
until there are 8 [8: 9: 11: 12] sts on right
needle and turn, leaving rem sts on a holder.
Work each side of neck separately.
Cast off 3 sts at beg of next row.
Cast off rem 5 [5: 6: 8: 9] sts.
With RS facing, rejoin yarn to rem sts, cast off
centre 38 [38: 40: 40: 42] sts, patt to end.
Complete to match first side, reversing
shapings.

FRONT

Work as given for back until 10 [10: 12: 12: 14]
rows less have been worked than on back to
beg of shoulder shaping, ending with RS facing
for next row.
Shape front neck
Next row (RS): Patt 16 [17: 20: 23: 26] sts
and turn, leaving rem sts on a holder.
Work each side of neck separately.
Keeping patt correct, dec 1 st at neck edge of
next 6 rows, then on foll 1 [1: 2: 2: 3] alt rows.
9 [10: 12: 15: 17] sts.
Work 1 row, ending with RS facing for next row.
Shape shoulder
Cast off 4 [5: 6: 7: 8] sts at beg of next row.
Work 1 row.

Cast off rem 5 [5: 6: 8: 9] sts.
With RS facing, rejoin yarn to rem sts, cast off
centre 30 sts, patt to end.
Complete to match first side, reversing
shapings.

SLEEVES

Using 5mm (US 8) needles cast on 46 [48: 50:
50: 52] sts.
Row 1 (RS): K0 [1: 2: 2: 0], *P1, K2, rep from
* to last 1 [2: 0: 0: 1] sts, P1 [1: 0: 0: 1], K0 [1:
0: 0: 0].
Row 2: P0 [1: 2: 2: 0], *K1, P2, rep from * to
last 1 [2: 0: 0: 1] sts, K1 [1: 0: 0: 1], P0 [1: 0: 0:
0].
These 2 rows form rib.
Cont in rib, shaping sides by inc 1 st at each
end of 3rd [3rd: 3rd: next: next] and 2 [2: 2: 4:
4] foll 6th [6th: 6th: 4th: 4th] rows. 52 [54: 56:
60: 62] sts.
Work 5 [5: 5: 3: 3] rows, ending with RS facing
for next row. (22 rows of rib completed.)
Change to 6mm (US 10) needles.
Now work in patt as folls:
Row 1 (RS): (Inc in first st) 1 [1: 1: 0: 1]
times, K0 [0: 1: 4: 4], P0 [1: 1: 1: 1], *yon,
K2tog, P1, K8, P1, rep from * to last 3 [4: 5: 7:
8] sts, yon, K2tog, P0 [1: 1: 1: 1], K0 [0: 1: 4: 4],
(inc in last st) 1 [1: 1: 0: 1] times.
54 [56: 58: 60: 64] sts.
Row 2: P1 [2: 3: 4: 6], K1, P2, *K1, P8, K1,
P2, rep from * to last 2 [3: 4: 5: 7] sts, K1,
P1 [2: 3: 4: 6].
Row 3: (Inc in first st) 0 [0: 0: 1: 0] times,
K1 [2: 3: 3: 2], (C4B) 0 [0: 0: 0: 1] times, P1,
*K2tog, yfrn, P1, C4F, C4B, P1, rep from * to
last 4 [5: 6: 7: 9] sts, K2tog, yfrn, P1, (C4F) 0 [0:
0: 0: 1] times, K1 [2: 3: 3: 2], (inc in last st) 0 [0:
0: 1: 0] times. 54 [56: 58: 62: 64] sts.
Row 4: P1 [2: 3: 5: 6], K1, P2, *K1, P8, K1,
P2, rep from * to last 2 [3: 4: 6: 7] sts, K1,
P1 [2: 3: 5: 6].
Row 5: (Inc in first st) 0 [0: 0: 0: 1] times,
K1 [2: 3: 5: 5], P1, *yon, K2tog, P1, K8, P1, rep

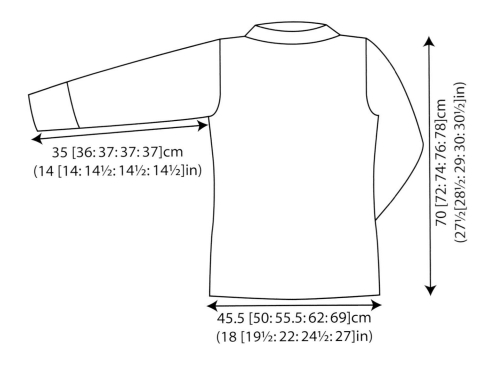

35 [36: 37: 37: 37]cm
(14 [14: 14½: 14½: 14½]in)

70 [72: 74: 76: 78]cm
(27½ [28½: 29: 30: 30½]in)

45.5 [50: 55.5: 62: 69]cm
(18 [19½: 22: 24½: 27]in)

from ★ to last 4 [5: 6: 8: 9] sts, yon, K2tog, P1, K1 [2: 3: 5: 5], (inc in last st) 0 [0: 0: 0: 1] times. 54 [56: 58: 62: 66] sts.

Row 6: P1 [2: 3: 5: 7], K1, P2, ★K1, P8, K1, P2, rep from ★ to last 2 [3: 4: 6: 8] sts, K1, P1 [2: 3: 5: 7].

Row 7: (Inc in first st) 0 [1: 1: 0: 0] times, K1 [1: 2: 5: 7], P1, ★K2tog, yfrn, P1, K8, P1, rep from ★ to last 4 [5: 6: 8: 10] sts, K2tog, yfrn, P1, K1 [1: 2: 5: 7], (inc in last st) 0 [1: 1: 0: 0] times. 54 [58: 60: 62: 66] sts.

Row 8: P1 [3: 4: 5: 7], K1, P2, ★K1, P8, K1, P2, rep from ★ to last 2 [4: 5: 6: 8] sts, K1, P1 [3: 4: 5: 7].

These 8 rows form patt and cont sleeve shaping.

Cont in patt, inc 1 st at each end of next [5th:

5th: next: next] and every foll 8th [6th: 6th: 6th: 6th] row to 64 [62: 70: 76: 80] sts, then on every foll - [8th: 8th: -: -] row until there are - [68: 72: -: -] sts, taking inc sts into patt.
Cont straight until sleeve meas 35 [36: 37: 37: 37] cm, ending with RS facing for next row.

Shape top
Keeping patt correct, cast off 3 [4: 5: 6: 7] sts at beg of next 2 rows. 58 [60: 62: 64: 66] sts.
Dec 1 st at each end of next 5 rows, then on every foll alt row to 34 sts, then on foll 5 rows, ending with RS facing for next row. 24 sts.
Cast off 4 sts at beg of next 2 rows.
Cast off rem 16 sts.

MAKING UP
Press as described on the information page.

Join right shoulder seam using back stitch, or mattress stitch if preferred.

Neckband
With RS facing and using 5mm (US 8) needles, pick up and knit 10 [10: 12: 12: 14] sts down left side of neck, 30 sts from front, 10 [10: 12: 12: 14] sts up right side of neck, then 44 [44: 46: 46: 48] sts from back. 94 [94: 100: 100: 106] sts.
Row 1 (WS): K1, ★P2, K1, rep from ★ to end.
Row 2: P1, ★K2, P1, rep from ★ to end.
These 2 rows form rib.
Work in rib for a further 3 rows, ending with RS facing for next row.
Cast off in rib.
See information page for finishing instructions, setting in sleeves using the set-in method.

GENEROUS
GRACE MELVILLE
Main image page 102 & 103

●●

YARN

S	M	L	XL	XXL
To fit bust				
81-86	91-97	102-107	112-117	122-127 cm
32-34	36-38	40-42	44-46	48-50 in

Rowan Silk Twist

| 17 | 18 | 20 | 21 | 23 | x 50 g |

(photographed in Aged 672)

NEEDLES
1 pair 4½mm (no 7) (US 7) needles
1 pair 5mm (no 6) (US 8) needles

BUTTONS – 5 x BN5030 Aged Silver from Bedecked. Please see information page for contact details.

TENSION
17 sts and 36 rows to 10 cm measured over patt using 5mm (US 8) needles.

SPECIAL ABBREVIATION
ytf = bring yarn to front of work - this is RS on RS rows, and WS on WS rows.

BACK
Using 4½mm (US 7) needles cast on 92 [100: 112: 120: 132] sts.
Row 1 (RS): K3, ★P2, K2, rep from ★ to last st, K1.
Row 2: K1, P2, ★K2, P2, rep from ★ to last st, K1.

These 2 rows form rib.
Work in rib for a further 12 rows, ending with RS facing for next row.
Change to 5mm (US 8) needles.
Row 15 (RS): K1, ★K2, ytf, (sl 1 purlwise) twice, yon, rep from ★ to last 3 sts, K3.
Now work in patt as folls:
Row 1 (WS): K1, ytf, (sl 1 purlwise) twice, yon, ★(K tog next st with yon of previous row) twice, ytf, (sl 1 purlwise) twice, yon, rep from ★ to last st, K1.

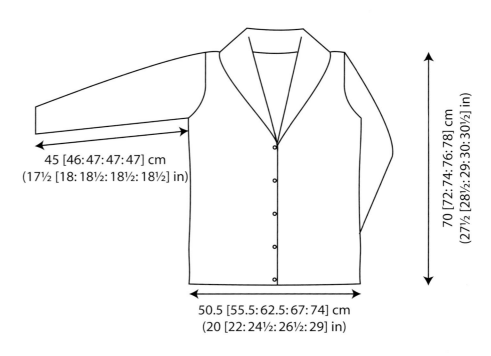

45 [46: 47: 47: 47] cm
(17½ [18: 18½: 18½: 18½] in)

50.5 [55.5: 62.5: 67: 74] cm
(20 [22: 24½: 26½: 29] in)

70 [72: 74: 76: 78] cm
(27½ [28½: 29: 30: 30½] in)

Row 2: K1, (K tog next st with yon of previous row) twice, *ytf, (sl 1 purlwise) twice, yon, (K tog next st with yon of previous row) twice, rep from * to last st, K1.
These 2 rows form patt.
Cont in patt until back meas 23 [24: 25: 26: 27] cm, ending with RS facing for next row.
Keeping patt correct, dec 1 st at each end of next and 2 foll 26th rows.
86 [94: 106: 114: 126] sts.
Work 29 rows, ending with RS facing for next row. (Back should meas 46 [47: 48: 49: 50] cm.)

Shape armholes
Keeping patt correct, cast off 4 [5: 6: 7: 8] sts at beg of next 2 rows. 78 [84: 94: 100: 110] sts.
Dec 1 st at each end of next 3 [5: 7: 9: 11] rows, then on foll 4 [4: 6: 6: 8] alt rows.
64 [66: 68: 70: 72] sts.
Cont straight until armhole meas 22 [23: 24: 25: 26] cm, ending with RS facing for next row.

Shape shoulders and back neck
Cast off 5 [5: 5: 6: 6] sts at beg of next 2 rows. 54 [56: 58: 58: 60] sts.
Next row (RS): Cast off 5 [5: 5: 6: 6] sts, patt until there are 8 [9: 9: 8: 8] sts on right needle and turn, leaving rem sts on a holder.
Work each side of neck separately.
Cast off 3 sts at beg of next row.
Cast off rem 5 [6: 6: 5: 5] sts.
With RS facing, rejoin yarn to rem sts, cast off centre 28 [28: 30: 30: 32] sts, patt to end.
Complete to match first side, reversing shapings.

LEFT FRONT
Using 4¹/₂mm (US 7) needles cast on 44 [48: 56: 60: 64] sts.
Work in rib as given for back for 14 rows, ending with RS facing for next row.
Change to 5mm (US 8) needles.
Row 15 (RS): K1, *K2, ytf, (sl 1 purlwise) twice, yon, rep from * to last 3 sts, K3.
Now work in patt as given for back as folls:
Cont in patt until left front meas 16 [17: 18: 19: 20] cm, ending with RS facing for next row.
Keeping patt correct, dec 1 st at beg of next and 2 foll 26th rows. 41 [45: 53: 57: 61] sts.
Work 9 rows, ending with RS facing for next row.

Shape front slope
Keeping patt correct, dec 1 st at end of next and 0 [0: 4: 2: 0] foll 6th rows, then on 5 [5: 2: 4: 5] foll 8th rows **and at same time** dec 1 st at beg of 17th row. 34 [38: 45: 49: 54] sts.
Work 5 [5: 5: 1: 5] rows, ending with RS facing for next row.

Shape armhole
Keeping patt correct, cast off 4 [5: 6: 7: 8] sts at beg of next row. 30 [33: 39: 42: 46] sts.
Work 1 row.
Dec 1 st at armhole edge of next 3 [5: 7: 9: 11] rows, then on foll 4 [4: 6: 6: 8] alt rows **and at same time** dec 1 st at front slope edge of next [next: next: 5th: next] and 1 [1: 2: 2: 3] foll 8th rows. 21 [22: 23: 24: 23] sts.
Dec 1 st at front slope edge **only** on 6th [6th: 6th: 8th: 6th] and 0 [0: 6: 6: 1] foll 8th rows, then on 5 [5: 0: 0: 4] foll 10th rows.
15 [16: 16: 17: 17] sts.
Cont straight until left front matches back to beg of shoulder shaping, ending with RS facing for next row.

Shape shoulder
Cast off 5 [5: 5: 6: 6] sts at beg of next and foll alt row.
Work 1 row.
Cast off rem 5 [6: 6: 5: 5] sts.

RIGHT FRONT
Work as given for left front, reversing all shapings.

SLEEVES
Using 4¹/₂mm (US 7) needles cast on 36 [36: 40: 40: 40] sts.
Work in rib as given for back for 8 rows, ending with RS facing for next row.
Change to 5mm (US 8) needles.
Row 9 (RS): K1, *K2, ytf, (sl 1 purlwise) twice, yon, rep from * to last 3 sts, K3.
Now work in patt as given for back, shaping sides by inc 1 st at each end of 8th [6th: 6th: 6th: 6th] and every foll 10th [8th: 8th: 8th: 8th] row to 62 [42: 44: 54: 74] sts, then on every foll - [10th: 10th: 10th: -] row until there are - [64: 68: 70: -] sts, taking inc sts into patt.
Cont straight until sleeve meas 45 [46: 47: 47: 47] cm, ending with RS facing for next row.

Shape top
Keeping patt correct, cast off 4 [5: 6: 7: 8] sts at beg of next 2 rows. 54 [54: 56: 56: 58] sts.
Dec 1 st at each end of next 3 rows, then on foll 2 alt rows, then on 6 foll 4th rows.
32 [32: 34: 34: 36] sts.
Work 1 row.
Dec 1 st at each end of next and every foll alt row to 20 sts, then on foll 5 rows, ending with RS facing for next row.
Cast off rem 10 sts.

MAKING UP
Press as described on the information page.
Join both shoulder seams using back stitch, or mattress stitch if preferred.

Button band and left collar
Using 4¹/₂mm (US 7) needles cast on 8 sts.
Row 1 (RS): K3, P2, K3.
Row 2: K1, P2, K2, P2, K1.
These 2 rows form rib.
Cont in rib until this button band section fits up left front opening edge from cast-on edge to beg of front slope shaping, ending with RS facing for next row.

Shape for collar
Inc 1 st at each end of next row, then at beg of foll row, taking inc sts into rib. 11 sts.
Inc 1 st at beg of next and foll 27 alt rows, then on 3 foll 4th rows, taking inc sts into rib. 42 sts.
Work 2 rows, ending with **WS** facing for next row.
Next row (WS): Rib 32, wrap next st (by slipping next st from left needle to right needle, taking yarn to opposite side of work between needles, then slipping same st back onto left needle - when working back across wrapped sts, work the wrapped st and the wrapping loop tog as 1 st) and turn.
Next row: Rib to end.
Next row: Rib 16, wrap next st and turn.
Next row: Rib to end.
Work 4 rows across all sts.
Rep from ** until shorter (shaped) row-end edge, unstretched, fits up left front slope and across to centre back neck, ending with **WS** facing (RS of collar) for next row.
Cast off in rib.
Slip st band and collar in place.
Mark positions for 5 buttons along button band section - first button to come in row 5, last button to come just below beg of collar shaping, and rem 3 buttons evenly spaced between.

Buttonhole band and right collar
Using 4¹/₂mm (US 7) needles cast on 8 sts.
Work in rib as given for button band for 4 rows, ending with RS facing for next row.
Row 5 (buttonhole row) (RS): K3, P2tog, yon (to make a buttonhole, K3.
Making a further 4 buttonholes in this way to correspond with positions marked for buttons on button band and reversing all shaping, complete to match button band and left collar.
See information page for finishing instructions, setting in sleeves using the set-in method.

Belt
Using 4¹/₂mm (US 7) needles cast on 8 sts.
Work in rib as given for button band for 130 [140: 150: 160: 170] cm, ending with RS facing for next row.
Cast off.

LORETTA

MARIE WALLIN

Main image page 46 & 47

YARN

S	M	L	XL	XXL

To fit bust
81-86 91-97102-107112-117122-127 cm
32-34 36-38 40-42 44-46 48-50 in

Rowan Pure Wool DK

7 8 10 11 12 x 50 g

(photographed in Raspberry 028)

NEEDLES

1 pair 3¼mm (no 10) (US 3) needles
1 pair 3¾mm (no 9) (US 5) needles

TENSION

24 sts and 30 rows to 10 cm measured over st st using 3¾mm (US 5) needles.

Pattern note: The number of sts varies whilst working patt. All st counts given presume there are 5 sts in each side patt panel repeat at all times.

BACK

Using 3¼mm (US 3) needles cast on 113 [125: 139: 153: 171] sts.
Row 1 (RS): K1, *P1, K1, rep from * to end.
Row 2: As row 1.
These 2 rows form moss st.
Work in moss st for a further 13 rows, ending with **WS** facing for next row.
Change to 3¾mm (US 5) needles.
Now work in patt as folls:
Row 1 (WS): K1, P1 tbl, K1, (P2, K1, P1 tbl, K1) 6 times, place marker on right needle, P to last 33 sts, place marker on right needle, (K1, P1 tbl, K1, P2) 6 times, K1, P1 tbl, K1.
Row 2: P1, K1 tbl, P1, (K1, yfwd, K1, P1, K1 tbl, P1) 6 times, slip marker to right needle, K to next marker, slip marker onto right needle, (P1, K1 tbl, P1, K1, yfwd, K1) 6 times, P1, K1 tbl, P1.
Row 3: K1, P1 tbl, K1, (P3, K1, P1 tbl, K1) 6 times, slip marker onto right needle, P to next marker, slip marker onto right needle, (K1, P1 tbl, K1, P3) 6 times, K1, P1 tbl, K1.
Row 4: P1, K1 tbl, P1, (K3, lift 3rd st on right needle over 1st and 2nd sts and off right needle, P1, K1 tbl, P1) 6 times, slip marker to right needle, K to next marker, slip marker onto right needle, (P1, K1 tbl, P1, K3, lift 3rd st on right needle over 1st and 2nd sts and off right needle) 6 times, P1, K1 tbl, P1.
These 4 rows form patt.
Keeping patt correct throughout (see pattern note), cont as folls:
Work 1 row, ending with RS facing for next row.
Next row (RS): Patt to marker, slip marker onto right needle, K2, sl 1, K1, psso, K to within 4 sts of next marker, K2tog, K2, slip marker onto right needle, patt to end.
111 [123: 137: 151: 169] sts.
Working all decreases as set by last row, dec 1 st at each end of 4th and 5 foll 4th rows.
99 [111: 125: 139: 157] sts.
Cont straight until back meas 18 [19: 20: 21: 22] cm, ending with RS facing for next row.
Next row (RS): Patt to marker, slip marker onto right needle, K3, M1, K to within 3 sts of next marker, M1, K3, slip marker onto right needle, patt to end. 101 [113: 127: 141: 159] sts.
Working all increases as set by last row, inc 1 st at each end of 12th and 3 foll 12th rows, ending with **WS** facing for next row.
109 [121: 135: 149: 167] sts.
Shape for cap sleeves
Inc 1 st at beg and end (rather than next to markers) of next 5 rows, taking inc sts into patt.
119 [131: 145: 159: 177] sts.
Mark both ends of last row to denote base of armhole openings.
Next row (RS): Patt to marker, slip marker onto right needle, K to next marker, slip marker onto right needle, patt to end.
Next row: Patt to marker, slip marker onto right needle, P to next marker, slip marker onto right needle, patt to end.
These 2 rows set the sts.★★
Now working all increases next to markers again, inc 1 st at each end of 5th and 2 [2: 2: 3: 3] foll 12th rows.
125 [137: 151: 167: 185] sts.
Work 11 [15: 17: 9: 11] rows, ending with RS facing for next row. (Work should meas 14 [15: 16: 17: 18] cm from markers.)
Shape shoulders and back neck
Cast off 7 [8: 9: 10: 12] sts at beg of next 8 rows. 69 [73: 79: 87: 89] sts.

Next row (RS): Cast off 7 [8: 9: 11: 11] sts, K until there are 10 [11: 12: 14: 14] sts on right needle and turn, leaving rem sts on a holder.
Work each side of neck separately.
Cast off 3 sts at beg of next row.
Cast off rem 7 [8: 9: 11: 11] sts.
With RS facing, rejoin yarn to rem sts, cast off centre 35 [35: 37: 37: 39] sts, K to end.
Complete to match first side, reversing shapings.

FRONT

Work as given for back to ★★.
Now working all increases next to markers again, inc 1 st at each end of 5th and 0 [0: 0: 1: 1] foll 12th row. 121 [133: 147: 163: 181] sts.
Work 4 [8: 8: 0: 0] rows, ending with **WS** facing for next row.
Divide for front opening
Next row (WS): Patt 60 [66: 73: 81: 90] sts and slip these sts onto a holder, cast off 1 st, patt to end. 60 [66: 73: 81: 90] sts.
Work each side of neck separately.
Work 17 rows, inc 1 st at armhole edge of 7th [3rd: 3rd: 11th: 11th] and foll – [12th: 12th: –: –] of these rows and ending with **WS** facing for next row. 61 [68: 75: 82: 91] sts.
Shape neck
Keeping patt correct, cast off 9 sts at beg of next row. 52 [59: 66: 73: 82] sts.
Dec 1 st at neck edge of next 7 rows, then on foll 2 [2: 3: 3: 4] alt rows **and at same time** inc 1 [0: 0: 1: 1] st at armhole edge of next [0: 0: 5th: 5th] row. 44 [50: 56: 64: 72] sts.
Work 1 row, ending with RS facing for next row.
Shape shoulder
Cast off 7 [8: 9: 10: 12] sts at beg of next and foll 3 alt rows, then 7 [8: 9: 11: 11] sts at beg of foll alt row **and at same time** dec 1 st at neck edge of next and foll 4th row.
Work 1 row.
Cast off rem 7 [8: 9: 11: 11] sts.
With RS facing, rejoin yarn to rem sts, patt to end.
Complete to match first side, reversing shapings.

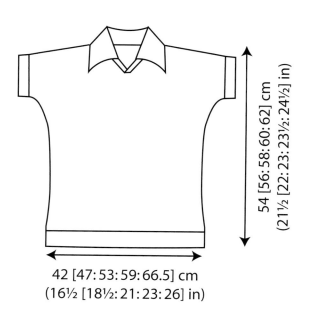

54 [56:58:60:62] cm
(21½ [22: 23: 23½: 24½] in)

42 [47: 53: 59: 66.5] cm
(16½ [18½: 21: 23: 26] in)

MAKING UP

Press as described on the information page.

Front bands (both alike)

With RS facing and using 3¼mm (US 3) needles, pick up and knit 15 sts evenly along one side of front opening, between base of opening and neck shaping.

Work in moss st as given for back for 2 rows, ending with **WS** facing for next row.

Cast off in moss st (on **WS**).

Lay right front band over left front band and sew row-end edges to base of opening.

Join both shoulder seams using back stitch, or mattress stitch if preferred.

Collar

With RS facing and using 3¼mm (US 3) needles, beg and ending at edge of front bands, pick up and knit 31 [31: 33: 33: 35] sts up right side of neck, 41 [41: 43: 43: 45] sts from back, then 31 [31: 33: 33: 35] sts down left side of neck. 103 [103: 109: 109: 115] sts.

Work in moss st as given for back for 2 rows.

Next row: Moss st 2 sts, inc twice in next st, moss st to last 3 sts, inc twice in next st, moss st 2 sts. 107 [107: 113: 113: 119] sts.

Work 3 rows.

Rep last 4 rows until collar meas approx 10 cm, ending after 3 rows without shaping.

Cast off in moss st.

Armhole borders (both alike)

With RS facing and using 3¼mm (US 3) needles, pick up and knit 67 [73: 77: 81: 87] sts evenly along armhole opening edges between marked points.

Work in moss st as given for back for 7 rows, ending with RS facing for next row.

Cast off in moss st.

See information page for finishing instructions.

PASSION
AMANDA CRAWFORD

Main image page 108 & 109

● ●

YARN

	S	M	L	XL	XXL

To fit bust

81-86 91-97 102-107 112-117 122-127 cm
32-34 36-38 40-42 44-46 48-50 in

Rowan Cocoon

10   11   12   13   14   x 100 g

(photographed in Tundra 808)

NEEDLES

1 pair 6mm (no 4) (US 10) needles
1 pair 7mm (no 2) (US 10½) needles
6mm (no 4) (US 10) circular needle, 40 cm long
7mm (no 2) (US 10½) circular needle, 60 cm long
Cable needle

TENSION

19 sts and 18 rows to 10 cm measured over patt using 7mm (US 10½) needles.

SPECIAL ABBREVIATIONS

C4B = slip next 2 sts onto cable needle and leave at back of work, K2, then K2 from cable needle; **C4F** = slip next 2 sts onto cable needle and leave at front of work, K2, then K2 from cable needle.

BACK

Using 7mm (US 10½) needles cast on 92 [100: 112: 124: 136] sts.

Beg and ending rows as indicated and repeating the 20 row patt rep throughout, now work in patt from chart as folls:

Cont straight until back meas 36 [37: 38: 39: 40] cm, ending with RS facing for next row.

Shape armholes

Keeping patt correct, cast off 4 [5: 6: 7: 8] sts at beg of next 2 rows. 84 [90: 100: 110: 120] sts.

Dec 1 st at each end of next 5 [5: 7: 7: 9] rows, then on foll 5 [6: 6: 8: 8] alt rows.

64 [68: 74: 80: 86] sts.

Cont straight until armhole meas 20 [21: 22: 23: 24] cm, ending with RS facing for next row.

Shape shoulders

Cast off 6 [7: 8: 10: 11] sts at beg of next 2 rows, then 7 [8: 9: 10: 11] sts at beg of foll 2 rows.

Cast off rem 38 [38: 40: 40: 42] sts.

FRONT

Work as given for back until 8 [8: 10: 10: 12] rows less have been worked than on back to beg of shoulder shaping, ending with RS facing for next row.

Shape front neck

Next row (RS): Patt 19 [21: 24: 27: 30] sts and turn, leaving rem sts on a holder.

Work each side of neck separately.

Keeping patt correct, dec 1 st at neck edge of next 6 rows, then on foll 0 [0: 1: 1: 2] alt rows.

13 [15: 17: 20: 22] sts.

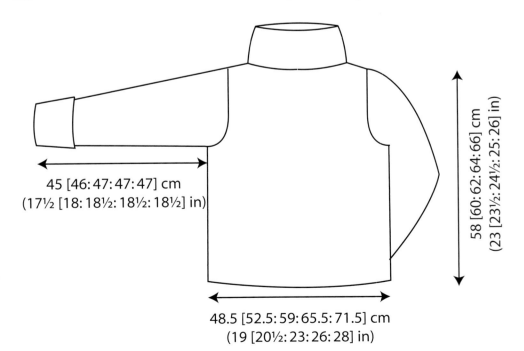

45 [46: 47: 47: 47] cm
(17½ [18: 18½: 18½: 18½] in)

48.5 [52.5: 59: 65.5: 71.5] cm
(19 [20½: 23: 26: 28] in)

58 [60: 62: 64: 66] cm
(23 [23½: 24½: 25: 26] in)

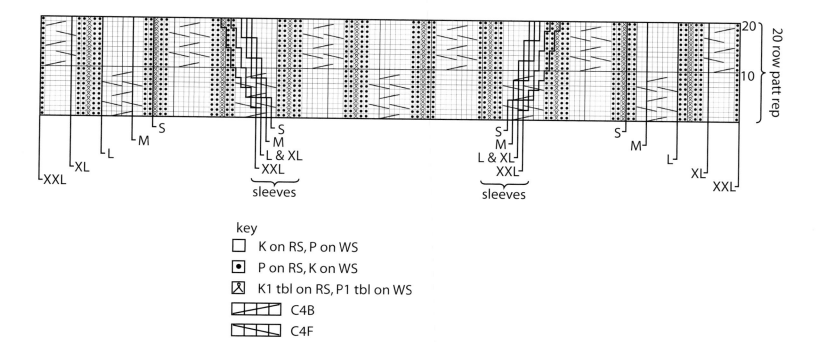

20 row patt rep

20

10

XXL, XL, L, M, S

S, M, L & XL, XXL (sleeves)

S, M, L & XL, XXL (sleeves)

S, M, L, XL, XXL

key

☐ K on RS, P on WS

▣ P on RS, K on WS

⊠ K1 tbl on RS, P1 tbl on WS

⬜ C4B

⬜ C4F

Work 1 row, ending with RS facing for next row.

Shape shoulder

Cast off 6 [7: 8: 10: 11] sts at beg of next row.
Work 1 row.
Cast off rem 7 [8: 9: 10: 11] sts.
With RS facing, rejoin yarn to rem sts, cast off centre 26 sts, patt to end.
Complete to match first side, reversing shapings.

SLEEVES

Using 7mm (US 10½) needles cast on 47 [49: 51: 51: 53] sts.

Row 1 (RS): K1 [2: 3: 3: 1], *P3, K3, rep from * to last 4 [5: 0: 0: 4] sts, P3 [3: 0: 0: 3], K1 [2: 0: 0: 1].

Row 2: P1 [2: 3: 3: 1], *K3, P3, rep from * to last 4 [5: 0: 0: 4] sts, K3 [3: 0: 0: 3], P1 [2: 0: 0: 1].

These 2 rows form rib.
Cont in rib until sleeve meas 12 cm, ending with RS facing for next row.
Change to 6mm (US 10) needles.
Cont in rib until sleeve meas 18 cm, dec 1 st at end of last row and ending with RS facing for

next row. 46 [48: 50: 50: 52] sts.
Change to 7mm (US 10½) needles.
Beg and ending rows as indicated and repeating the 20 row patt rep throughout, now work in patt from chart as folls:
Inc 1 st at each end of 5th [5th: 5th: 3rd: 3rd] and every foll 4th [4th: 4th: alt: alt] row to 66 [72: 78: 56: 62] sts, then on every foll 6th [6th: 6th: 4th: 4th] row until there are 72 [76: 80: 84: 88] sts, taking inc sts into patt.
Cont straight until sleeve meas 55 [56: 57: 57: 57] cm, ending with RS facing for next row.

Shape top

Keeping patt correct, cast off 4 [5: 6: 7: 8] sts at beg of next 2 rows. 64 [66: 68: 70: 72] sts.
Dec 1 st at each end of next 5 rows, then on every foll alt row to 40 sts, then on foll 7 rows, ending with RS facing for next row. 26 sts.
Cast off 4 sts at beg of next 2 rows.
Cast off rem 18 sts.

MAKING UP

Press as described on the information page.
Join both shoulder seams using back stitch, or

mattress stitch if preferred.

Collar

With RS facing and using 6mm (US 10) circular needle, pick up and knit 8 [8: 9: 11: 12] sts down left side of neck, 20 sts from front, 8 [8: 9: 11: 12] sts up right side of neck, then 28 [28: 30: 30: 32] sts from back. 64 [64: 68: 72: 76] sts.

Rounds 1 to 8 (RS): *K2, P2, rep from * to end.

Round 9: *K1, M1, K1, P2, rep from * to end. 80 [80: 85: 90: 95] sts.

Rounds 10 to 17: *K3, P2, rep from * to end.

Round 18: *K3, P1, M1, P1, rep from * to end. 96 [96: 102: 108: 114] sts.

Round 19: *K3, P3, rep from * to end.
Rep last round until collar meas 15 cm from pick-up round.
Change to 7mm (US 10½) circular needle.
Cont as set until collar meas 40 cm from pick-up round.
Cast off **very loosely** in rib.
See information page for finishing instructions, setting in sleeves using the set-in method and reversing sleeve seam for first 12 cm for turn-back cuff. Fold 10 cm cuff to RS.

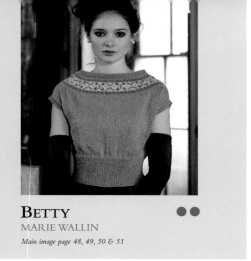

BETTY
MARIE WALLIN

Main image page 48, 49, 50 & 51

YARN

	S	M	L	XL	XXL	
To fit bust						
	81-86	91-97	102-107	112-117	122-127	cm
	32-34	36-38	40-42	44-46	48-50	in

Rowan Pure Wool 4 ply

A	Eau de Nil 450					
	4	5	6	7	8	x 50 g
B	Porcelaine 451					
	1	1	1	1	1	x 50 g
C	Ochre 461					
	1	1	1	1	1	x 50 g
D	Avocado 419					
	1	1	1	1	1	x 50 g
E	Raspberry 428					
	1	1	1	1	1	x 50 g
F	Blue Iris 455					
	1	1	1	1	1	x 50 g

NEEDLES

1 pair 2³⁄₄mm (no 12) (US 2) needles
1 pair 3¹⁄₄mm (no 10) (US 3) needles
2³⁄₄mm (no 12) (US 2) circular needle,
40 cm long
3¹⁄₄mm (no 10) (US 3) circular needle, one
60 cm long and one 40 cm long

TENSION

28 sts and 36 rows to 10 cm measured over st st
using 3¹⁄₄mm (US 3) needles.

BACK and FRONT (both alike)

Using 2³⁄₄mm (US 2) needles and yarn A cast
on 117 [131: 149: 165: 185] sts.
Row 1 (RS): K1, *P1, K1, rep from * to end.
Row 2: P1, *K1, P1, rep from * to end.
These 2 rows form rib.
Cont in rib, dec 1 st at each end of 3rd and
2 foll 4th rows, then on foll 2 alt rows.
107 [121: 139: 155: 175] sts.
Work 23 rows, ending with RS facing for
next row.
Inc 1 st at each end of next row.
109 [123: 141: 157: 177] sts.
Work 3 rows, ending with RS facing for
next row.
Change to 3¹⁄₄mm (US 3) needles.
Beg with a K row, now work in st st as folls:
Inc 1 st at each end of 7th [9th: 11th: 11th:
13th] and foll 10th [12th: 14th: 14th: 16th] row,
then on foll 10th [10th: 10th: 14th: 14th] row,
then on foll 6th row, then on foll 4th row, then
on foll 3 alt rows, then on foll 4 rows, ending

with **WS** facing for next row.
133 [147: 165: 181: 201] sts.
Place markers at both ends of last row to
denote base of armhole openings.
Cont straight until work meas 9 [10: 11: 12:
13] cm from markers, ending with RS facing
for next row.
Shape neck
Next row (RS): K43 [52: 64: 74: 83] and
turn, leaving rem sts on a holder.
Work each side of neck separately.
Cast off 5 sts at beg of next and foll alt row,
4 sts at beg of foll 2 alt rows, then 3 sts at beg
of foll alt row. 22 [31: 43: 53: 62] sts.
Dec 1 st at neck edge of next 8 rows, ending
with RS facing for next row.
14 [23: 35: 45: 54] sts.
Shape shoulder
Dec 1 st at neck edge of next 6 [8: 12: 14: 14]
rows, ending with RS facing for next row, **and
at same time** cast off 2 [3: 3: 4: 5] sts at beg of
next and foll 2 [3: 2: 6: 6] alt rows, then - [-: 4:
-: -] sts at beg of foll - [-: 3: -: -] alt rows.
Cast off rem 2 [3: 2: 3: 5] sts.
With RS facing, rejoin yarn to rem sts, cast off
centre 47 [43: 37: 33: 35] sts placing marker on
centre cast-off st (this denotes centre back or
front neck), K to end.

Complete to match first side, reversing
shapings.

MAKING UP
Press as described on the information page.
Join both shoulder seams using back stitch, or
mattress stitch if preferred.
Yoke and neckband
With RS facing, using longer 3¹⁄₄mm (US 3)
circular needle and yarn A, beg and ending at
centre back neck st, pick up and knit 24 [22:
19: 17: 17] sts from left side of back, 36 [38: 41:
43: 43] sts up left side of back neck, 37 [39: 42:
44: 43] sts down left side of front neck, 47 [43:
37: 33: 35] sts from front, 37 [39: 42: 44: 43] sts
up right side of front neck, 36 [38: 41: 43: 43] sts
down right side of back neck, then 23 [21: 18:
16: 16] sts from right side of back. 240 sts.
Joining in and breaking off colours as required,
using the **fairisle** technique as described on the
information page and repeating the 24 st patt
rep 10 times around each round, now work in
patt from chart for yoke, which is worked
entirely in st st (K every round) as folls:
Work chart rounds 1 to 20.
Round 21 (RS): (K2tog, patt 10 sts) 20 times.
220 sts.
All 21 rounds of chart now completed.

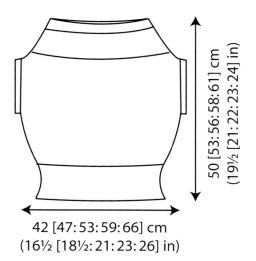

50 [53:56:58:61] cm
(19½ [21:22:23:24] in)

42 [47:53:59:66] cm
(16½ [18½:21:23:26] in)

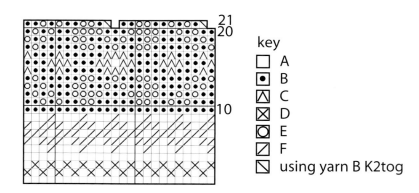

21
20

10

key

☐	A
⊡	B
◩	C
⊠	D
⊙	E
▨	F
◩	using yarn B K2tog

Changing to shorter circular needle when required, cont as folls:

Round 22: Using yarn B (K5, K2tog, K4) 20 times. 200 sts.
Break off yarn B and join in yarns A and F.
Round 23: ★Using yarn A K2, using yarn F K1, using yarn A K1, rep from ★ to end.
Round 24: ★Using yarn A K1, using yarn F K3, rep from ★ to end.
Round 25: ★Using yarn A K1, using yarn F K1, rep from ★ to end.
Round 26: ★Using yarn F K2, using yarn A K1, using yarn F K1, rep from ★ to end.

Round 27: Using yarn F K1, using yarn A K3, rep from ★ to end.
Break off yarn F.
Round 28: Using yarn A (K8, K2tog) 20 times. 180 sts.
Join in yarn D.
Round 29: ★Using yarn A K1, using yarn D K1, rep from ★ to end.
Round 30: ★Using yarn D K1, using yarn A K1, rep from ★ to end.
Break off yarn D and complete work using yarn A only.
Round 31: (K4, K2tog, K3) 20 times. 160 sts.

Change to 2¾mm (US 2) circular needle.
Round 32: ★K1, P1, rep from ★ to end.
Rep last round 5 times more.
Cast off in rib.
Armhole borders (both alike)
With RS facing, using 2¾mm (US 2) needles and yarn A, pick up and knit 79 [87: 97: 105: 113] sts evenly along armhole opening edge between markers.
Work in rib as given for back and front for 7 rows, ending with RS facing for next row.
Cast off in rib.
See information page for finishing instructions.

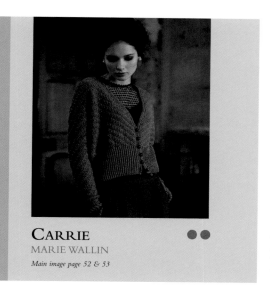

CARRIE
MARIE WALLIN
Main image page 52 & 53

YARN
S M L XL XXL
To fit bust
81–86 91–97 102–107 112–117 122–127 cm
32–34 36–38 40–42 44–46 48–50 in
Rowan Wool Cotton
11 11 15 17 20 x 50 g
(photographed in Grand 954)

NEEDLES
1 pair 3¼mm (no 10) (US 3) needles
1 pair 3¾mm (no 9) (US 5) needles
3¾mm (no 9) (US 5) circular needle, 80 cm long

BUTTONS – 6 x RW5019 from Bedecked. Please see information page for contact details.

DETACHABLE COLLAR – Narrow fake fur collar ref - 9136 - brown from MacCulloch & Wallis. Please see information page for contact details.

TENSION
24 sts and 32 rows to 10 cm measured over patt using 3¾mm (US 5) needles.
BACK
Using 3¼mm (US 3) needles cast on 101 [113: 129: 143: 159] sts.
Row 1 (RS): P1, ★K1 tbl, P1, rep from ★ to end.
Row 2: K1, ★P1 tbl, K1, rep from ★ to end.
These 2 rows form rib.
Cont in rib until back meas 12 cm, ending with **WS** facing for next row.
Next row (WS): Rib 5 [4: 4: 4: 4], M1, (rib 6 [7: 8: 9: 10], M1) 15 times, rib 6 [4: 5: 4: 5]. 117 [129: 145: 159: 175] sts.
Change to 3¾mm (US 5) needles.

Beg and ending rows as indicated and repeating the 8 row patt rep throughout, now work in patt from chart as folls:
Work 22 [26: 28: 32: 36] rows, ending with RS facing for next row.
Shape for sleeves
Changing to circular needle when there are too many sts to fit on straight needles, cont as folls:
Inc 1 st at each end of next and 2 foll 4th rows, then on foll 6 [3: 5: 7: 7] alt rows, then on foll 11 [17: 17: 15: 15] rows, taking inc sts into patt. 157 [175: 195: 209: 225] sts.
Cast on 3 sts at beg of next 4 rows, 4 sts at beg of foll 4 rows, 5 sts at beg of next 4 rows, 6 sts at beg of foll 4 rows, 7 sts at beg of next 4 rows, then 8 sts at beg of foll 4 rows, taking inc

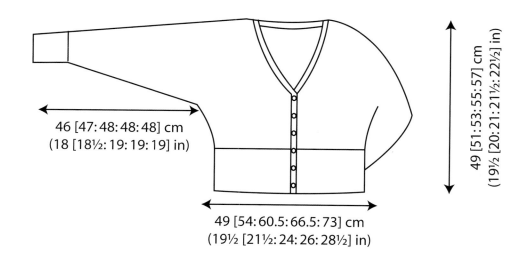

46 [47: 48: 48: 48] cm
(18 [18½: 19: 19: 19] in)

49 [54: 60.5: 66.5: 73] cm
(19½ [21½: 24: 26: 28½] in)

49 [51: 53: 55: 57] cm
(19½ [20: 21: 21½: 22½] in)

sts into patt. 289 [307: 327: 341: 357] sts.
Work 28 [30: 32: 32: 34] rows, ending with RS facing for next row.

Shape shoulders
Keeping patt correct, cast off 21 [22: 23: 24: 26] sts at beg of next 6 [6: 4: 2: 6] rows, then - [-: 24: 25: -] sts at beg of foll - [-: 2: 4: -] rows.
163 [175: 187: 193: 201] sts.

Shape back neck
Next row (RS): Cast off 21 [22: 24: 25: 26] sts, patt until there are 46 [51: 54: 56: 58] sts on right needle and turn, leaving rem sts on a holder.
Work each side of neck separately.
Cast off 3 sts at beg of next row, 20 [22: 24: 25: 26] sts at beg of foll row, then 3 sts at beg of next row.
Cast off rem 20 [23: 24: 25: 26] sts.
With RS facing, rejoin yarn to rem sts, cast off centre 29 [29: 31: 31: 33] sts, patt to end.
Complete to match first side, reversing shapings.

LEFT FRONT
Using 3¼mm (US 3) needles cast on 51 [57: 65: 71: 79] sts.
Work in rib as given for back for 12 cm, ending with **WS** facing for next row.
Next row (WS): Rib 4 [4: 4: 3: 3], M1, (rib 6 [7: 8: 8: 9], M1) 7 [7: 7: 8: 8] times, rib 5 [4: 5: 4: 4]. 59 [65: 73: 80: 88] sts.
Change to 3¾mm (US 5) needles.
Beg and ending rows as indicated and repeating the 8 row patt rep throughout, now work in patt from chart as folls:
Work 22 [26: 28: 32: 36] rows, ending with RS facing for next row.

Shape for sleeve
Inc 1 st at beg of next and foll 4th row, taking inc sts into patt. 61 [67: 75: 82: 90] sts.
Work 1 row, ending with RS facing for next row.

Shape front slope
Inc 1 st at shaped sleeve edge of 3rd and foll 6 [3: 5: 7: 7] alt rows, then on foll 11 [17: 17: 15: 15] rows, taking inc sts into patt and ending with RS facing for next row, **and at same time** dec 1 st at end of next and 6 [6: 7: 7: 7] foll 4th rows. 72 [81: 90: 97: 105] sts.
Cast on 3 sts at beg of next and foll alt row, 4 sts at beg of foll 2 alt rows, 5 sts at beg of foll 2 alt rows, 6 sts at beg of foll 2 alt rows, 7 sts at beg of foll 2 alt rows, then 8 sts at beg of foll 2 alt rows, taking inc sts into patt, **and at same time** dec 1 st at end of 3rd [3rd: 3rd: next: next] and 5 foll 4th rows.
132 [141: 150: 157: 165] sts.
Dec 1 st at front slope edge **only** on 4th [4th: 4th: 2nd: 2nd] and 6 [6: 5: 4: 6] foll 4th rows, then on 0 [0: 1: 2: 1] foll 6th row.
125 [134: 143: 150: 157] sts.
Work 1 [3: 3: 3: 3] rows, ending with RS facing for next row.

Shape shoulder
Keeping patt correct, cast off 21 [22: 23: 24: 26] sts

at beg of next and foll 3 [4: 1: 0: 4] alt rows, then 20 [-: 24: 25: -] sts at beg of foll 1 [-: 3: 4: -] alt rows **and at same time** dec 1 st at front slope edge of 3rd row.
Work 1 row.
Cast off rem 20 [23: 24: 25: 26] sts.

RIGHT FRONT
Using 3¼mm (US 3) needles cast on 51 [57: 65: 71: 79] sts.
Work in rib as given for back for 12 cm, ending with **WS** facing for next row.
Next row (WS): Rib 5 [4: 5: 4: 4], M1, (rib 6 [7: 8: 8: 9], M1) 7 [7: 7: 8: 8] times, rib 4 [4: 4: 3: 3]. 59 [65: 73: 80: 88] sts.
Change to 3¾mm (US 5) needles.
Beg and ending rows as indicated and repeating the 8 row patt rep throughout, now work in patt from chart as folls:
Work 22 [26: 28: 32: 36] rows, ending with RS facing for next row.

Shape for sleeve
Inc 1 st at end of next and foll 4th row, taking inc sts into patt. 61 [67: 75: 82: 90] sts.
Complete to match left front, reversing shapings.

MAKING UP
Press as described on the information page.
Join both shoulder/overarm seams using back stitch, or mattress stitch if preferred.

Front band
Using 3¼mm (US 3) needles cast on 5 sts.
Row 1 (RS): K1, K1 tbl, P1, K1 tbl, K1.
Row 2: K1, (P1 tbl, K1) twice.
These 2 rows form rib.
Cont in rib until front band, when slightly stretched, fits up left front opening edge, from cast-on edge to beg of front slope shaping and sewing in place as you go along.
Mark positions for 6 buttons on this section of band - first button to come 1.5 cm up from cast-on edge, last button to come just below beg of front slope shaping, and rem 4 buttons evenly spaced between.
Cont in rib until band, when slightly stretched, fits up left front slope, across back neck, down right front slope, then down right front opening edge to cast-on edge, sewing in place as you go along and with the addition of 6 buttonholes in last section of band worked to correspond with positions marked for buttons as folls:
Buttonhole row (RS): K1, K2tog tbl, yfwd, K1 tbl, K1.
When band is complete, ending with RS facing for next row, cast off in rib.

Cuffs (both alike)
With RS facing and using 3¼mm (US 3) needles, pick up and knit 45 [49: 51: 51: 55] sts evenly along straight row-end edge of sleeve section.
Beg with row 2, work in rib as given for back for 10 cm, ending with RS facing for next row.
Cast off in rib.
See information page for finishing instructions.

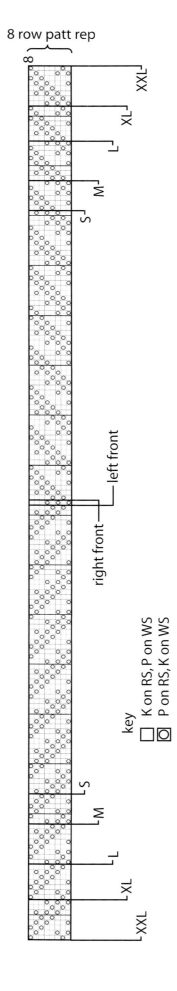

8 row patt rep

8

XXL
XL
L
M
S

left front

right front

S
M
L
XL
XXL

key
☐ K on RS, P on WS
◉ P on RS, K on WS

GLENDA
AMANDA CRAWFORD
Main image page 60 & 61

YARN

	S	M	L	XL	XXL
To fit bust					

81-86 91-97 102-107 112-117 122-127 cm
32-34 36-38 40-42 44-46 48-50 in

Rowan Wool Cotton

8 9 10 11 12 x 50 g
(photographed in Cypress 968)

NEEDLES

1 pair 3¼mm (no 10) (US 3) needles
1 pair 3¾mm (no 9) (US 5) needles
Cable needle

TENSION

30 sts and 34 rows to 10 cm measured over patt
using 3¾mm (US 5) needles.

SPECIAL ABBREVIATIONS

C2B = slip next st onto cable needle and leave
at back of work, K1, then K1 from cable
needle; **C2F** = slip next st onto cable needle
and leave at front of work, K1, then K1 from
cable needle.

BACK

Using 3¼mm (US 3) needles cast on 146 [160:
178: 196: 218] sts.
Row 1 (RS): (K1 tbl) 2 [1: 2: 1: 2] times, *P2,
(K1 tbl) twice, rep from * to last 0 [3: 0: 3: 0] sts,
(P2, K1 tbl) 0 [1: 0: 1: 0] times.
Row 2: (P1 tbl) 2 [1: 2: 1: 2] times, *K2, (P1
tbl) twice, rep from * to last 0 [3: 0: 3: 0] sts,
(K2, P1 tbl) 0 [1: 0: 1: 0] times.
These 2 rows form rib.
Cont in rib, dec 1 st at each end of 5th and
foll 6th row. 142 [156: 174: 192: 214] sts.
Work 1 row, ending with RS facing for
next row.
Change to 3¾mm (US 5) needles.
Now work in patt as folls:
Row 1 (RS): K1 [2: 1: 2: 1], (C2F) 0 [1: 0:
1: 0] times, *C2B, C2F, rep from * to last 1 [4:
1: 4: 1] sts, (C2B) 0 [1: 0: 1: 0] times, K1 [2: 1:
2: 1].
Row 2: Purl.
Row 3: K1 [2: 1: 2: 1], (C2B) 0 [1: 0: 1: 0]
times, *C2F, C2B, rep from * to last 1 [4: 1:
4: 1] sts, (C2F) 0 [1: 0: 1: 0] times, K1 [2: 1:
2: 1].
Row 4: Purl.
These 4 rows form patt.
Cont in patt, shaping side seams by dec 1 st at

each end of next and foll 6th row, then on 2
foll 4th rows, then on 6 foll 3rd rows.
122 [136: 154: 172: 194] sts.
Work 13 rows, ending with RS facing for
next row.
Inc 1 st at each end of next and 6 foll 8th rows,
taking inc sts into st st until there are sufficient
to work in patt. 136 [150: 168: 186: 208] sts.
Cont straight until back meas 37 [38: 39: 40:
41] cm, ending with RS facing for next row.

Shape armholes

Keeping patt correct, cast off 6 [7: 8: 9: 10] sts
at beg of next 2 rows.
124 [136: 152: 168: 188] sts.★★
Dec 1 st at each end of next 5 [7: 9: 11: 13]
rows, then on foll 6 [7: 8: 10: 13] alt rows.
102 [108: 118: 126: 136] sts.
Cont straight until armhole meas 19 [20: 21:
22: 23] cm, ending with RS facing for next
row.

Shape shoulders and back neck

Next row (RS): Cast off 7 [8: 9: 10: 12] sts,
patt until there are 20 [22: 24: 27: 29] sts on
right needle and turn, leaving rem sts on a
holder.
Work each side of neck separately.
Cast off 3 sts at beg of next row, 7 [8: 9:
10: 12] sts at beg of foll row, then 3 sts at beg
of next row.
Cast off rem 7 [8: 9: 11: 11] sts.
With RS facing, rejoin yarn to rem sts, cast off
centre 48 [48: 52: 52: 54] sts, patt to end.
Complete to match first side, reversing
shapings.

FRONT

Work as given for back to ★★.
Dec 1 st at each end of next 5 [7: 9: 11: 13]
rows, then on foll 5 [5: 4: 4: 3] alt rows.
104 [112: 126: 138: 156] sts.
Work 1 row, ending with RS facing for
next row.

Shape front neck

Next row (RS): Work 2 tog, patt 40 [44: 49:
55: 63] sts and turn, leaving rem sts on a holder.

Work each side of neck separately.
Keeping patt correct, cast off 3 sts at beg of
next and foll alt row **and at same time** dec
- [1: 1: 1: 1] st at armhole edge of - [2nd: 2nd:
2nd: 2nd] row. 35 [38: 43: 49: 57] sts.
Dec 1 st at neck edge of next 9 rows, then on
foll 3 alt rows, then on foll 4th row, then on foll
6th row **and at same time** dec - [-: 1: 1: 1] st
at armhole edge of - [-: next: next: next] and
foll - [-: 1: 3: 7] alt rows. 21 [24: 27: 31: 35] sts.
Cont straight until front matches back to beg
of shoulder shaping, ending with RS facing for
next row.

Shape shoulder

Cast off 7 [8: 9: 10: 12] sts at beg of next and
foll alt row.
Work 1 row.
Cast off rem 7 [8: 9: 11: 11] sts.
With RS facing, rejoin yarn to rem sts, cast off
centre 20 [20: 24: 24: 26] sts, patt to last 2 sts,
work 2 tog.
Complete to match first side, reversing shapings.

SLEEVES

Using 3¼mm (US 3) needles cast on 66 [70:
72: 72: 76] sts.
Row 1 (RS): (K1 tbl) 2 [2: 1: 1: 1] times,
*P2, (K1 tbl) twice, rep from * to last 0 [0: 3:
3: 3] sts, (P2, K1 tbl) 0 [0: 1: 1: 1] times.
Row 2: (P1 tbl) 2 [2: 1: 1: 1] times, *K2, (P1
tbl) twice, rep from * to last 0 [0: 3: 3: 3] sts,
(K2, P1 tbl) 0 [0: 1: 1: 1] times.
These 2 rows form rib.
Work in rib for a further 8 rows, ending with
RS facing for next row.
Change to 3¾mm (US 5) needles.
Now work in patt as folls:
Row 1 (RS): K1 [1: 2: 2: 2], (C2F) 0 [0: 1:
1: 1] times, *C2B, C2F, rep from * to last 1 [1:
4: 4: 4] sts, (C2B) 0 [0: 1: 1: 1] times, K1 [1: 2:
2: 2].
Row 2: Purl.
Row 3: K1 [1: 2: 2: 2], (C2B) 0 [0: 1: 1: 1]
times, *C2F, C2B, rep from * to last 1 [1: 4: 4:
4] sts, (C2F) 0 [0: 1: 1: 1] times, K1 [1: 2: 2: 2].

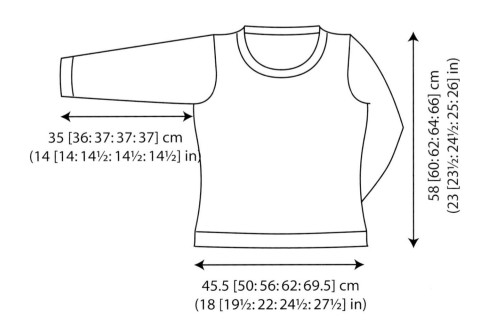

35 [36: 37: 37: 37] cm
(14 [14: 14½: 14½: 14½] in)

58 [60: 62: 64: 66] cm
(23 [23½: 24½: 25: 26] in)

45.5 [50: 56: 62: 69.5] cm
(18 [19½: 22: 24½: 27½] in)

Row 4: Purl.

These 4 rows form patt.

Cont in patt, shaping sides by inc 1 st at each end of next and every foll 4th row to 96 [98: 102: 114: 118] sts, then on every foll 6th row until there are 108 [112: 116: 120: 124] sts, taking inc sts into st st until there are sufficient to work in patt.

Cont straight until sleeve meas 35 [36: 37: 37: 37] cm, ending with RS facing for next row.

Shape top

Keeping patt correct, cast off 6 [7: 8: 9: 10] sts at beg of next 2 rows.
96 [98: 100: 102: 104] sts.

Dec 1 st at each end of next 9 rows, then on every foll alt row to 66 sts, then on foll 11 rows, ending with RS facing for next row. 44 sts.
Cast off 4 sts at beg of next 6 rows.
Cast off rem 20 sts.

MAKING UP

Press as described on the information page. Join right shoulder seam using back stitch, or mattress stitch if preferred.

Neckband

With RS facing and using 3¼mm (US 3) needles, pick up and knit 39 [39: 43: 43: 47] sts

down left side of neck, 20 [20: 24: 24: 26] sts from front, 39 [39: 43: 43: 47] sts up right side of neck, then 60 [60: 64: 64: 66] sts from back. 158 [158: 174: 174: 186] sts.

Row 1 (WS): K2, ★(P1 tbl) twice, K2, rep from ★ to end.

Row 2: P2, ★(K1 tbl) twice, P2, rep from ★ to end.

These 2 rows form rib.

Work in rib for a further 3 rows, ending with RS facing for next row.

Cast off in rib.

See information page for finishing instructions, setting in sleeves using the set-in method.

CINDY
LISA RICHARDSON
Main image page 54, 55, 56 & 57

YARN

8	10	12	14	16	18	20	22	

To fit bust

81	86	91	97	102	107	112	117	cm
32	34	36	38	40	42	44	46	in

Rowan Cashsoft 4 ply

7	7	7	8	9	9	10	10	x 50 g

(photographed in Elite 451)

NEEDLES

1 pair 2¾mm (no 12) (US 2) needles
1 pair 3¼mm (no 10) (US 3) needles
2¾mm (no 12) (US 2) circular needle, 80 cm long

TENSION

28 sts and 36 rows to 10 cm measured over st st using 3¼mm (US 3) needles.

BACK

Using 2¾mm (US 2) needles cast on 122 [128: 134: 142: 150: 158: 168: 176] sts.
Work in g st for 4 rows, ending with RS facing for next row.
Change to 3¼mm (US 3) needles.
Beg with a K row, work in st st until back meas

3 [3: 2: 5: 4: 6: 5: 7] cm, ending with RS facing for next row.★★
Dec 1 st at each end of next and 6 foll 6th rows.
108 [114: 120: 128: 136: 144: 154: 162] sts.
Work 15 rows, ending with RS facing for next row.
Inc 1 st at each end of next and 5 foll 10th rows.
120 [126: 132: 140: 148: 156: 166: 174] sts.
Work 11 rows, ending with RS facing for next row. (Back should meas 35 [35: 34: 37: 36: 38: 37: 39] cm.)

Shape armholes

Cast off 5 [6: 6: 7: 7: 8: 8: 9] sts at beg of next 2 rows.
110 [114: 120: 126: 134: 140: 150: 156] sts.
Dec 1 st at each end of next 3 [3: 5: 5: 7: 7: 9: 9] rows, then on foll 7 [8: 7: 8: 8: 9: 10: 11] alt rows. 90 [92: 96: 100: 104: 108: 112: 116] sts.

Cont straight until armhole meas 19 [19: 20: 20: 21: 21: 22: 22] cm, ending with RS facing for next row.

Shape shoulders and back neck

Cast off 5 [5: 6: 6: 6: 7: 7: 8] sts at beg of next 2 rows. 80 [82: 84: 88: 92: 94: 98: 100] sts.

Next row (RS): Cast off 5 [5: 6: 6: 7: 7: 8: 8] sts, K until there are 17 [18: 18: 20: 20: 21: 22: 23] sts on right needle and turn, leaving rem sts on a holder.
Work each side of neck separately.
Cast off 3 sts at beg of next row, 5 [6: 6: 7: 7: 7: 8: 8] sts at beg of foll row, then 3 sts at beg of next row.
Cast off rem 6 [6: 6: 7: 7: 8: 8: 9] sts.
With RS facing, rejoin yarn to rem sts, cast off centre 36 [36: 36: 36: 38: 38: 38: 38] sts, K to end.
Complete to match first side, reversing shapings.

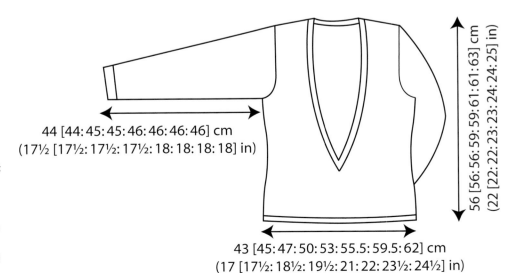

44 [44: 45: 45: 46: 46: 46: 46] cm
(17½ [17½: 17½: 17½: 18: 18: 18: 18] in)

56 [56: 56: 59: 59: 61: 61: 63] cm
(22 [22: 22: 23: 23: 24: 24: 25] in)

43 [45: 47: 50: 53: 55.5: 59.5: 62] cm
(17 [17½: 18½: 19½: 21: 22: 23½: 24½] in)

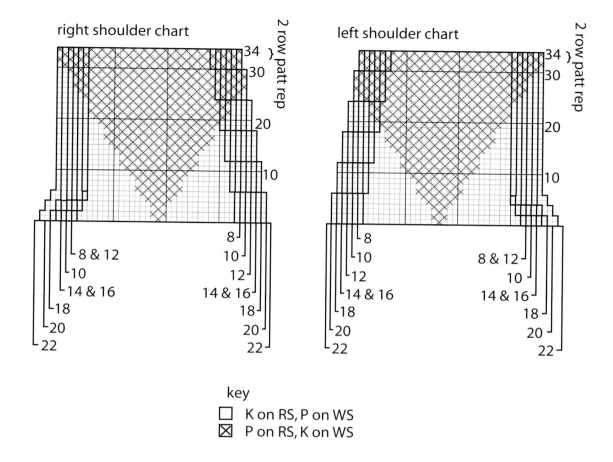

right shoulder chart

left shoulder chart

2 row patt rep

2 row patt rep

key

☐ K on RS, P on WS

⊠ P on RS, K on WS

FRONT

Work as given for back to ★★.

Dec 1 st at each end of next and 5 foll 6th rows.

110 [116: 122: 130: 138: 146: 156: 164] sts.

Work 3 rows, ending with RS facing for next row.

Divide for neck

Next row (RS): K55 [58: 61: 65: 69: 73: 78: 82] and turn, leaving rem sts on a holder.

Work each side of neck separately.

Work 1 row.

Dec 1 st at each end of next row.

53 [56: 59: 63: 67: 71: 76: 80] sts.

Dec 1 st at neck edge of 8th and 3 [3: 1: 1: 2: 2: 0: 0] foll 4th rows, then on 9 [9: 10: 10: 10: 10: 11: 11] foll 6th rows **and at same time** inc 1 st at side seam edge of 16th and 5 foll 10th rows. 46 [49: 53: 57: 60: 64: 70: 74] sts.

Work 3 [3: 5: 5: 1: 1: 3: 3] rows, ending with RS facing for next row.

Shape armhole

Cast off 5 [6: 6: 7: 7: 8: 8: 9] sts at beg and dec 0 [0: 1: 1: 0: 0: 0: 0] st at end of next row.

41 [43: 46: 49: 53: 56: 62: 65] sts.

Work 1 row.

Dec 1 st at armhole edge of next 3 [3: 5: 5: 7: 7: 9: 9] rows, then on foll 4 [4: 5: 5: 6: 6: 7: 7] alt rows **and at same time** dec 1 st at neck edge of next [next: 5th: 5th: 3rd: 3rd: next: next] and 1 [1: 1: 1: 2: 2: 3: 3] foll 6th rows.

32 [34: 34: 37: 37: 40: 42: 45] sts.

Work 1 row, ending with RS facing for next row.

Beg and ending rows as indicated, working rows 1 to 32 **once only** and then repeating

rows 33 and 34 **throughout**, now work in patt from chart for left shoulder as folls:

Dec 1 st at neck edge of next and 7 foll 6th rows **and at same time** dec 1 st at armhole edge of next and foll 2 [3: 1: 2: 1: 2: 2: 3] alt rows. 21 [22: 24: 26: 27: 29: 31: 33] sts.

Cont straight until front matches back to beg of shoulder shaping, ending with RS facing for next row.

Shape shoulder

Cast off 5 [5: 6: 6: 6: 7: 7: 8] sts at beg of next row, 5 [5: 6: 6: 7: 7: 8: 8] sts at beg of foll alt row, then 5 [6: 6: 7: 7: 7: 8: 8] sts at beg of foll alt row.

Work 1 row.

Cast off rem 6 [6: 6: 7: 7: 8: 8: 9] sts.

With RS facing, rejoin yarn to rem sts, K to end.

Complete to match first side, reversing shapings and foll chart for right shoulder.

SLEEVES

Using 2¾mm (US 2) needles cast on 51 [51: 53: 53: 57: 57: 59: 59] sts.

Work in g st for 4 rows, ending with RS facing for next row.

Change to 3¼mm (US 3) needles.

Beg with a K row, work in st st, shaping sides by inc 1 st at each end of 9th [9th: 9th: 7th: 9th: 7th: 7th: 7th] and every foll 10th [10th: 10th: 8th: 10th: 10th: 10th: 8th] row to 67 [79: 77: 59: 77: 87: 89: 71] sts, then on every foll 12th [–: 12th: 10th: 12th: –: –: 10th] row until there are 77 [–: 81: 83: 85: –: –: 91] sts.

Cont straight until sleeve meas 44 [44: 45: 45: 46: 46: 46: 46] cm, ending with RS facing for

next row.

Shape top

Cast off 5 [6: 6: 7: 7: 8: 8: 9] sts at beg of next 2 rows. 67 [67: 69: 69: 71: 71: 73: 73] sts.

Dec 1 st at each end of next 5 rows, then on foll 4 alt rows, then on 3 foll 4th rows. 43 [43: 45: 45: 47: 47: 49: 49] sts.

Work 1 row, ending with RS facing for next row.

Dec 1 st at each end of next and every foll alt row to 33 sts, then on foll 7 rows, ending with RS facing for next row. 19 sts.

Cast off 3 sts at beg of next 2 rows.

Cast off rem 13 sts.

MAKING UP

Press as described on the information page.

Join right shoulder seam using back stitch, or mattress stitch if preferred.

Neckband

With RS facing and using 2¾mm (US 2) circular needle, pick up and knit 114 [114: 117: 117: 120: 120: 124: 124] sts down left side of neck, place marker on needle, pick up and knit 114 [114: 117: 117: 120: 120: 124: 124] sts up right side of neck, then 48 [48: 48: 48: 50: 50: 50: 50] sts from back.

276 [276: 282: 282: 290: 290: 298: 298] sts.

Row 1 (WS): K to within 2 sts of marker, K2tog, slip marker onto right needle, K2tog tbl, K to end.

Row 2: As row 1.

Cast off knitwise (on **WS**), still dec 1 st either side of marker as before.

See information page for finishing instructions, setting in sleeves using the set-in method.

CORDIAL
SARAH HATTON
Main image page 98 & 99

●●

YARN

S	M	L	XL	XXL

To fit bust
81-86 91-97 102-107 112-117 122-127 cm
32-34 36-38 40-42 44-46 48-50 in

Rowan Big Wool

7 7 8 9 10 x100 g

(photographed in Eternal 055)

NEEDLES

1 pair 10mm (no 000) (US 15) needles
Cable needle

BUTTONS – 1 x BN1368 (31mm) from
Bedecked. Please see information page for
contact details.

TENSION

9½ sts and 14 rows to 10 cm measured over
moss st using 10mm (US 15) needles.

SPECIAL ABBREVIATIONS

C3B = slip next st onto cable needle and leave
at back of work, K2, then K1 from cable
needle; **C3F** = slip next 2 sts onto cable needle
and leave at front of work, K1, then K2 from
cable needle; **C4B** = slip next 2 sts onto cable
needle and leave at back of work, K2, then K2
from cable needle; **C4F** = slip next 2 sts onto
cable needle and leave at front of work, K2,
then K2 from cable needle; **Cr3L** = slip next 2
sts onto cable needle and leave at front of
work, P1, then K2 from cable needle; **Cr3R** =
slip next st onto cable needle and leave at back
of work, K2, then P1 from cable needle.

BODY (worked in one piece)
Right front
Using 10mm (US 15) needles cast on 27 [29:
32: 35: 38] sts.
Row 1 (RS): Purl.
Row 2: Purl.
Now work in patt as folls:
Row 3: P1, (K1, P1) 5 [6: 6: 7: 7] times, work
next 12 sts as row 1 of cable panel, (P1, K1)
2 [2: 3: 4: 5] times, P0 [0: 1: 0: 1].
Row 4: P0 [0: 1: 0: 1], (K1, P1) 2 [2: 3: 4: 5]
times, work next 12 sts as row 2 of cable panel,
P1, (K1, P1) 5 [6: 6: 7: 7] times.
These 2 rows set the sts – cable panel with
moss st at each side.
Keeping sts correct throughout as now set,
cont as folls:

Work 28 [30: 30: 32: 34] rows, ending with RS
facing for next row.
Shape for sleeve
Keeping patt correct, inc 1 st at end of next
row and at same edge on foll 3 rows, taking inc
sts into moss st. 31 [33: 36: 39: 42] sts.
Work 1 row.
Cast on 9 sts at beg of next row, then 10 [11:
12: 12: 12] sts at beg of foll alt row, taking cast-
on sts into moss st. 50 [53: 57: 60: 63] sts.
Work 2 rows, ending with RS facing for next row.
Next row (RS): Patt 2 sts, yrn, work 2 tog
(to make a buttonhole), patt to end.
Work 1 row, ending with RS facing for
next row.
Shape front slope
Next row (RS): Patt 2 sts, work 3 tog, patt to
end. 48 [51: 55: 58: 61] sts.
Working all front slope decreases as set by last
row and keeping patt correct, dec 2 sts at beg
of 2nd [2nd: 4th: 4th: 4th] and 3 [3: 2: 2: 1] foll
4th rows, then on 0 [0: 1: 1: 2] foll 6th rows.
40 [43: 47: 50: 53] sts.
Work 5 rows, ending with RS facing for

next row.
Next row (RS): Patt 2 sts, (P1, K1, P1) all
into next st, patt to end. 42 [45: 49: 52: 55] sts.
Work 1 row, ending with RS facing for
next row.
Break yarn and leave sts on a holder.
Left front
Using 10mm (US 15) needles cast on 27 [29:
32: 35: 38] sts.
Row 1 (RS): Purl.
Row 2: Purl.
Now work in patt as folls:
Row 3: P0 [0: 1: 0: 1], (K1, P1) 2 [2: 3: 4: 5]
times, work next 12 sts as row 1 of cable panel,
P1, (K1, P1) 5 [6: 6: 7: 7] times.
Row 4: P1, (K1, P1) 5 [6: 6: 7: 7] times, work
next 12 sts as row 2 of cable panel, (P1, K1)
2 [2: 3: 4: 5] times, P0 [0: 1: 0: 1].
These 2 rows set the sts – cable panel with
moss st at each side.
Keeping sts correct throughout as now set, cont
as folls:
Work 28 [30: 30: 32: 34] rows, ending with RS
facing for next row.

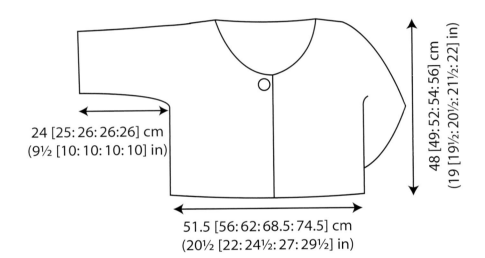

24 [25: 26: 26: 26] cm
(9½ [10: 10: 10: 10] in)

51.5 [56: 62: 68.5: 74.5] cm
(20½ [22: 24½: 27: 29½] in)

48 [49: 52: 54: 56] cm
(19 [19½: 20½: 21½: 22] in)

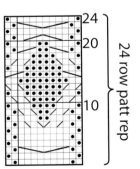

24 row patt rep

24
20
10

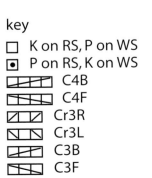

key

☐	K on RS, P on WS
⊡	P on RS, K on WS
	C4B
	C4F
	Cr3R
	Cr3L
	C3B
	C3F

Shape for sleeve

Keeping patt correct, inc 1 st at beg of next row and at same edge on foll 3 rows, taking inc sts into moss st. 31 [33: 36: 39: 42] sts.
Cast on 9 sts at beg of next row, then 10 [11: 12: 12: 12] sts at beg of foll alt row, taking cast-on sts into moss st. 50 [53: 57: 60: 63] sts.
Work 5 rows, ending with RS facing for next row.

Shape front slope

Next row (RS): Patt to last 5 sts, work 3 tog, patt 2 sts. 48 [51: 55: 58: 61] sts.
Working all front slope decreases as set by last row and keeping patt correct, dec 2 sts at end of 2nd [2nd: 4th: 4th: 4th] and 3 [3: 2: 2: 1] foll 4th rows, then on 0 [0: 1: 1: 2] foll 6th rows. 40 [43: 47: 50: 53] sts.
Work 5 rows, ending with RS facing for next row.
Next row (RS): Patt to last 3 sts, (P1, K1, P1) all into next st, patt 2 sts. 42 [45: 49: 52: 55] sts.
Work 1 row, ending with RS facing for next row.
Do NOT break yarn.

Join sections

Next row (RS): Patt 42 [45: 49: 52: 55] sts of left front, turn and cast on 11 sts, turn and patt across 42 [45: 49: 52: 55] sts of right front. 95 [101: 109: 115: 121] sts.
Work 27 [27: 31: 31: 33] rows, ending with RS facing for next row.

Shape for sleeves

Keeping patt correct, cast off 10 [11: 12: 12: 12] sts at beg of next 2 rows, then 9 sts at beg of foll 2 rows. 57 [61: 67: 73: 79] sts.
Dec 1 st at each end of next 4 rows. 49 [53: 59: 65: 71] sts.
Work 31 [33: 33: 35: 37] rows, ending with **WS** facing for next row.
Next row (WS): Purl.
Cast off purlwise (on RS).

MAKING UP

Press as described on the information page.
See information page for finishing instructions.

NANCY
ERIKA KNIGHT

Main image page 70 & 71

YARN

8 10 12 14 16 18 20 22
To fit bust
81 86 91 97 102 107 112 117 cm
32 34 36 38 40 42 44 46 in
Rowan Cashsoft 4 ply
6 7 7 7 8 8 9 9 x 50 g
(photographed in Jewel 461)

NEEDLES

1 pair 2¾mm (no 12) (US 2) needles
1 pair 3¼mm (no 10) (US 3) needles

BUTTONS – 7 x BN1365 from Bedecked.
Please see information page for contact details.

TENSION

28 sts and 36 rows to 10 cm measured over st st using 3¼mm (US 3) needles.

BACK

Using 2¾mm (US 2) needles cast on 118 [122: 130: 138: 146: 154: 162: 170] sts.
Row 1 (RS): K2, *P2, K2, rep from * to end.
Row 2: P2, *K2, P2, rep from * to end.
These 2 rows form rib.
Work in rib for a further 16 rows, ending with RS facing for next row.

Row 19 (RS): K2, P1, P2tog, rib to last 5 sts, P2tog tbl, P1, K2.
Row 20: P2, K2, rib to last 4 sts, K2, P2.
Working decreases as set by row 19 and keeping sts correct as set by last 2 rows, dec 1 st at each end of 5th and 4 foll 6th rows. 106 [110: 118: 126: 134: 142: 150: 158] sts.
Work 1 row, dec [inc: dec: dec: dec: inc: inc: inc] 1 st at end of last row and ending with RS facing for next row.
105 [111: 117: 125: 133: 143: 151: 159] sts.
Change to 3¼mm (US 3) needles.
Beg with a K row, work in st st as folls:
Work 16 rows, ending with RS facing for next row.
Next row (RS): K3, M1, K to last 3 sts, M1, K3.
Working all increases as set by last row, inc 1 st at each end of 10th and 4 foll 10th rows. 117 [123: 129: 137: 145: 155: 163: 171] sts.
Cont straight until back meas 37 [37: 36: 39: 38: 40: 39: 41] cm, ending with RS facing for next row.

Shape raglan armholes

Cast off 3 sts at beg of next 2 rows. 111 [117: 123: 131: 139: 149: 157: 165] sts.
Next row (RS): K3, K2tog, K to last 5 sts, K2tog tbl, K3.
Next row: P3, P2tog tbl, P to last 5 sts, P2tog, P3.
Rep last 2 rows 0 [3: 4: 8: 9: 14: 16: 20] times more. 107 [101: 103: 95: 99: 89: 89: 81] sts.
Next row (RS): K3, K2tog, K to last 5 sts, K2tog tbl, K3.
Next row: Purl.
Rep last 2 rows 31 [28: 29: 25: 26: 21: 21: 17] times more, ending with RS facing for next row.
Cast off rem 43 [43: 43: 43: 45: 45: 45: 45] sts.

LEFT FRONT

Using 2¾mm (US 2) needles cast on 63 [67: 67: 71: 75: 83: 87: 91] sts.
Row 1 (RS): K2, *P2, K2, rep from * to last 5 sts, P1, K1, P1, K2.
Row 2: (K1, P1) twice, K1, P2, *K2, P2, rep

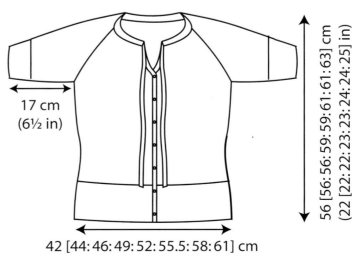

17 cm
(6½ in)

56 [56: 56: 59: 59: 61: 61: 63] cm
(22 [22: 22: 23: 23: 24: 24: 25] in)

42 [44: 46: 49: 52: 55.5: 58: 61] cm
(16½ [17½: 18: 19½: 20½: 22: 23: 24] in)

from * to end.

These 2 rows form rib.

Working side seam decreases as given for back, cont in rib, dec 1 st at beg of 17th and 5 foll 6th rows. 57 [61: 61: 65: 69: 77: 81: 85] sts.

Work one row, dec [dec: inc: inc: inc: dec: dec: dec] 1 [2: 1: 1: 1: 2: 2: 2] sts evenly across this row and ending with RS facing for next row. 56 [59: 62: 66: 70: 75: 79: 83] sts. (**Note**: Do **not** work inc or decs within front opening edge 5 sts.)

Change to 3¼mm (US 3) needles.

Next row (RS): K to last 5 sts, P1, K1, P1, K2.

Next row: (K1, P1) twice, K1, P to end.

These 2 rows set the sts - front opening edge 5 sts still in rib with all other sts now in st st. Working all increases as set by back, inc 1 st at beg of 15th and 5 foll 10th rows. 62 [65: 68: 72: 76: 81: 85: 89] sts.

Cont straight until left front matches back to beg of raglan armhole shaping, ending with RS facing for next row.

Shape raglan armhole

Cast off 3 sts at beg of next row. 59 [62: 65: 69: 73: 78: 82: 86] sts.

Work 1 row.

Next row (RS): K3, K2tog, K to last 10 sts, K2tog tbl, patt to end. 57 [60: 63: 67: 71: 76: 80: 84] sts.

Working front opening decreases as set by last row and raglan armhole decreases as set by back, dec 1 st at raglan armhole edge of next 2 [8: 10: 18: 20: 29: 31: 31] rows, then on foll 10 [7: 8: 3: 4: 0: 0: 0] alt rows **and at same time** dec 1 st at front opening edge of 6th row. 44 [44: 44: 45: 46: 46: 48: 52] sts.

Work 1 [1: 1: 1: 1: 0: 0: 0] row, ending with RS facing for next row.

Next row (RS): K3, K2tog, K to last 8 sts, M1, patt to end. 44 [44: 44: 45: 46: 46: 48: 52] sts.

Working front opening increases as set by last row and raglan armhole decreases as set, dec 1 st at raglan armhole edge of 2nd [2nd: 2nd: 2nd: 2nd: next: next] and foll 0 [0: 0: 0: 0: 0: 1: 6] rows, then on foll 2 [2: 2: 2: 2: 2: 2: 0] alt rows **and at same time** inc 1 st at front opening edge of 6th row. 42 [42: 42: 43: 44: 44: 45: 46] sts.

Work 1 [1: 1: 1: 1: 1: 1: 0] row, ending with RS facing for next row.

Shape neck

Next row (RS): K3, K2tog, K to last 11 [11: 11: 10: 11: 11: 10: 10] sts and turn, leaving rem sts on a holder. 30 [30: 30: 32: 32: 32: 34: 35] sts.

Working neck and raglan armhole decreases as set by raglan armhole decreases, dec 1 st at neck edge of next 12 rows, then on foll 2 [2: 2: 3: 3: 3: 4: 4] alt rows **and at same time** dec 1 st at raglan armhole edge of 2nd [2nd: 2nd: 2nd: 2nd: 2nd: next] and foll 0 [0: 0: 0: 0: 0: 1] row, then on foll 7 [7: 7: 8: 8: 8: 9: 9] alt rows. 8 sts.

Work 1 row, ending with RS facing for next row.

Next row (RS): K3, K3tog, K2.

Next row: P6.

Next row: K3, K3tog.

Next row: P4.

Next row: K1, sl 1, K2tog, psso.

Next row: P2.

Next row: K2tog and fasten off.

Mark positions for 7 buttons along left front opening edge - first button to come in row 5, last button to come just below beg of raglan armhole shaping, and rem 5 buttons evenly spaced between.

RIGHT FRONT

Using 2¾mm (US 2) needles cast on 63 [67: 67: 71: 75: 83: 87: 91] sts.

Row 1 (RS): K2, P1, K1, P1, *K2, P2, rep from * to last 2 sts, K2.

Row 2: *P2, K2, rep from * to last 7 sts, P2, (K1, P1) twice, K1.

These 2 rows form rib.

Work 2 rows, ending with RS facing for next row.

Row 5 (buttonhole row) (RS): K2, cast off 2 sts (to make a buttonhole - cast on 2 sts over these cast off sts on next row), patt to end.

Working a further 6 buttonholes in this way to correspond with positions marked for buttons on left front and noting that no further reference will be made to buttonholes, cont as folls:

Working side seam decreases as given for back, cont in rib, dec 1 st at end of 14th and 5 foll 6th rows. 57 [61: 61: 65: 69: 77: 81: 85] sts.

Work one row, dec [dec: inc: inc: inc: dec: dec: dec] 1 [2: 1: 1: 1: 2: 2: 2] sts evenly across this row and ending with RS facing for next row. 56 [59: 62: 66: 70: 75: 79: 83] sts. (**Note**: Do **not** work inc or decs within front opening edge 5 sts.)

Change to 3¼mm (US 3) needles.

Next row (RS): K2, P1, K1, P1, K to end.

Next row: P to last 5 sts, (K1, P1) twice, K1.

These 2 rows set the sts - front opening edge 5 sts still in rib with all other sts now in st st. Working all increases as set by back, inc 1 st at end of 15th and 5 foll 10th rows. 62 [65: 68: 72: 76: 81: 85: 89] sts.

Complete to match left front, reversing shapings and working first row of neck shaping as folls:

Shape neck

Next row (RS): Patt 11 [11: 11: 10: 11: 11: 10: 10] sts and slip these sts onto another holder, K to last 5 sts, K2tog tbl, K3. 30 [30: 30: 32: 32: 32: 34: 35] sts.

SLEEVES

Using 2¾mm (US 2) needles cast on 70 [70: 74: 74: 78: 78: 82: 82] sts.

Work in rib as given for back for 6 cm, inc 3 sts evenly across last row and ending with RS facing for next row. 73 [73: 77: 77: 81: 81: 85: 85] sts.

Change to 3¼mm (US 3) needles.

Beg with a K row, work in st st as folls:

Cont straight until sleeve meas 17 cm, ending with RS facing for next row.

Shape raglan

Cast off 3 sts at beg of next 2 rows.

67 [67: 71: 71: 75: 75: 79: 79] sts.

Working all raglan decreases as set by back raglan armholes, dec 1 st at each end of next and 3 foll 4th rows, then on every foll alt row until 17 sts rem.

Work 1 row, ending with RS facing for next row.

Left sleeve only

Place marker at beg of last row - this matches to fasten-off point of left front.

Working all decreases as set, dec 1 st at front (marked) edge of next 6 rows **and at same time** dec 1 st at back (unmarked) edge of next and foll 2 alt rows, ending with RS facing for next row. 8 sts.

Next row (RS): K3, K3tog, K2.

Next row: P1, P2tog, P3.

Next row: K2, K3tog tbl.

Next row: P2tog, P1.

Right sleeve only

Place marker at end of last row - this matches to fasten-off point of right front.

Working all decreases as set, dec 1 st at front (marked) edge of next 6 rows **and at same time** dec 1 st at back (unmarked) edge of next and foll 2 alt rows, ending with RS facing for next row. 8 sts.

Next row (RS): K2, K3tog tbl, K3.

Next row: P3, P2tog tbl, P1.

Next row: K3tog, K2.

Next row: P1, P2tog tbl.

Both sleeves

Next row: K2tog and fasten off.

MAKING UP

Press as described on the information page.

Join all raglan seams using back stitch, or mattress stitch if preferred.

Neckband

With RS facing and using 2¾mm (US 2) needles, slip 11 [11: 11: 10: 11: 11: 10: 10] sts from right front holder onto right needle, pick up and knit 23 [23: 23: 25: 25: 25: 27: 27] sts up right side of neck, 10 sts from top of right sleeve, 43 [43: 43: 43: 45: 45: 45: 45] sts from back, 10 sts from top of left sleeve, and 23 [23: 23: 25: 25: 25: 27: 27] sts down left side of neck, then patt across 11 [11: 11: 10: 11: 11: 10: 10] sts on left front holder. 131 [131: 131: 133: 137: 137: 139: 139] sts.

Row 1 (WS): K1, *P1, K1, rep from * to end.

Row 2: K2, *P1, K1, rep from * to last st, K1.

These 2 rows form rib.

Work in rib for a further 3 rows, ending with RS facing for next row.

Cast off in rib.

Ties (both alike)

With RS facing and using 2¾mm (US 2) needles, pick up and knit 5 sts along row-end edge of neckband.

Row 1 (WS): K1, (P1, K1) twice.

Row 2: K2, P1, K2.

These 2 rows form rib.

Cont in rib until tie meas 40 cm, ending with RS facing for next row.

Cast off in rib.

See information page for finishing instructions.

HOLLY
KAFFE FASSETT

Main image page 5, 6 & 7

● ● ●

YARN

	S–M	L–XL	XXL	
To fit bust				
	81–97	102–117	122–127	cm
	32–38	40–46	48–50	in

Rowan Felted Tweed

	S–M	L–XL	XXL	
A Seafarer 170	2	2	2	x 50 g
B Phantom 153	2	2	2	x 50 g
C Rage 150	3	3	4	x 50 g
D Ginger 154	2	2	3	x 50 g
E Cinnamon 175	1	2	2	x 50 g
F Watery 152	1	2	2	x 50 g
G Avocado 161	1	1	2	x 50 g
H Carbon 159	1	1	2	x 50 g
I Gilt 160	1	1	1	x 50 g
J Camel 157	1	1	1	x 50 g
K Bilberry 151	1	1	1	x 50 g
L Paisley 171	1	1	1	x 50 g
M Pine 158	1	1	1	x 50 g
N Duck Egg 173	1	1	1	x 50 g

NEEDLES

1 pair 3¼mm (no 10) (US 3) needles
1 pair 3¾mm (no 9) (US 5) needles
3¼mm (no 10) (US 3) circular needle,
100 cm long

TENSION

25 sts and 29 rows to 10 cm measured over
patterned st st using 3¾mm (US 5) needles.

BACK

Using 3¾mm (US 5) needles and yarn A cast
on 75 [105: 121] sts.
Beg and ending rows as indicated and using the
intarsia technique as described on the
information page, now work in patt from chart,
which is worked entirely in st st beg with a K
row, as folls:

Work 1 row, ending with **WS** facing for
next row.
Cast on 4 sts at beg of next 6 rows, then 3 sts at
beg of foll 2 rows, ending with **WS** facing for
next row. 105 [135: 151] sts.
Inc 1 st at each end of next 12 rows, then on
foll 2 alt rows, then on 2 foll 4th rows, then on
2 foll 6th rows. 141 [171: 187] sts.
Cont straight until chart row 182 [194: 200]
has been completed, ending with RS facing
for next row.
Shape shoulders
Keeping patt correct, cast off 3 [3: 4] sts at beg
of next 24 [2: 18] rows, then - [4: 5] sts at beg
of foll - [22: 6] rows, ending with RS facing for
next row. 69 [77: 85] sts.
Shape back neck
Next row (RS): Cast off 3 [4: 5] sts, patt until
there are 12 [14: 16] sts on right needle and
turn, leaving rem sts on a holder.
Work each side of neck separately.
Cast off 3 sts at beg of next row, 3 [4: 5] sts at
beg of foll row, then 3 sts at beg of next row.
Cast off rem 3 [4: 5] sts.
With RS facing, rejoin yarns to rem sts, cast off
centre 39 [41: 43] sts, patt to end.
Complete to match first side, reversing
shapings.

FRONT

Work as given for back to beg of shoulder
shaping, ending with RS facing for next row.
Shape shoulders
Size S–M and L–XL only
Keeping patt correct, cast off 3 sts at beg of
next 4 [2: -] rows. 129 [165: -] sts.
All sizes
Shape front neck
Next row (RS): Cast off 3 [4: 4] sts, patt until
there are 47 [64: 75] sts on right needle and
turn, leaving rem sts on a holder.
Work each side of neck separately. (**Note:** Front
neck shaping is NOT shown on chart.)
Keeping patt correct, dec 1 st at neck edge of
next 6 rows, then on foll 4 [5: 6] alt rows, then
on foll 4th row **and at same time** cast off 3
[4: 4] sts at beg of 2nd and foll 8 [9: 7] alt rows,
then - [: 5] sts at beg of foll - [-: 3] alt rows.
9 [12: 15] sts.
Work 1 row, ending with RS facing for
next row.
Cast off 3 [4: 5] sts at beg of next and foll
alt row.
Work 1 row.
Cast off rem 3 [4: 5] sts.
With RS facing, rejoin yarns to rem sts, cast off
centre 29 sts, patt to end.
Complete to match first side, reversing
shapings.

MAKING UP

Press as described on the information page.
Side and lower borders (both alike)
With RS facing, using 3¼mm (US 3) circular
needle and yarn E, beg and ending at beg of
shoulder shaping, pick up and knit 132 [143:
149] sts down first row-end edge to last inc,
61 sts down shaped row-end edge to original
cast-on edge, 75 [105: 121] sts from original
cast-on edge, 61 sts up shaped row-end edge
to last inc, then 132 [143: 149] sts up second
row-end edge.
461 [513: 541] sts.
Row 1 (WS): K1, *P1, K1, rep from * to end.
Row 2: K1, sl 1, K1, psso, K1, *P1, K1, rep
from * to last 3 sts, K2tog, K1.
459 [511: 539] sts.
These 2 rows set the sts.
Keeping sts correct as now set, cont as folls:
Row 3: Using yarn D, K1, P1, rib to last 2 sts,

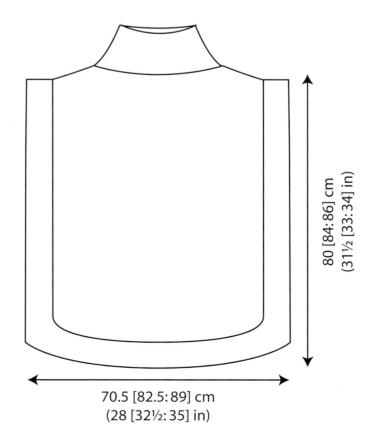

80 [84:86] cm
(31½ [33: 34] in)

70.5 [82.5:89] cm
(28 [32½: 35] in)

P1, K1.

Row 4: Using yarn D, K1, sl 1, K1, psso, rib to last 3 sts, K2tog, K1.

Rep last 2 rows 8 times more, and then row 3 again **and at same time**, joining in and breaking off colours as required, work in stripes as folls:

Row 5: Using yarn E.

Rows 6 to 8: Using yarn D. K1.

453 [505: 533] sts.

Rows 9 and 10: Using yarn C.

Row 11: Using yarn D.

Rows 12 to 14: Using yarn C.

447 [499: 527] sts.

Rows 15 and 16: Using yarn B.

Row 17: Using yarn C.

Rows 18 and 19: Using yarn B.

443 [495: 523] sts.

Rows 20 and 21: Using yarn A.

441 [493: 521] sts.

Using yarn A, cast off **loosely** in rib, still decreasing at each end of row as before.

Join right shoulder/overarm seam using back stitch, or mattress stitch if preferred.

Collar

With RS facing, using 3¼mm (US 3) needles and yarn G, pick up and knit 24 [26: 28] sts down left side of neck, 29 sts from front, 24 [26: 28] sts up right side of neck, then 54 [56: 58] sts from back. 131 [137: 143] sts.

Row 1 (WS): P1, ★K1, P1, rep from ★ to end.

Row 2: K1, ★P1, K1, rep from ★ to end.

These 2 rows form rib.

Joining in and breaking off colours as required, cont in rib in stripes as folls:

Rows 3 and 4: Using yarn F.

Row 5: Using yarn G.

Rows 6 to 8: Using yarn F.

Rows 9 and 10: Using yarn E.

Row 11: Using yarn F.

Rows 12 to 14: Using yarn E.

Rows 15 and 16: Using yarn D.

Row 17: Using yarn E.

Rows 18 to 20: Using yarn D.

Rows 21 and 22: Using yarn C.

Row 23: Using yarn D.

Rows 24 to 26: Using yarn C.

Rows 27 and 28: Using yarn B.

Row 29: Using yarn C.

Rows 30 and 31: Using yarn B.

Rows 32 and 33: Using yarn A.

Using yarn A, cast off **loosely** in rib.

See information page for finishing instructions.

Lay garment flat, folding it along shoulder/overarm seams, and mark points along side edges 26 [28: 29] cm down from shoulder seams. Now stitch through both layers across borders at these points (to join sections to denote base of armhole openings), stitching from pick-up row to cast-off edge.

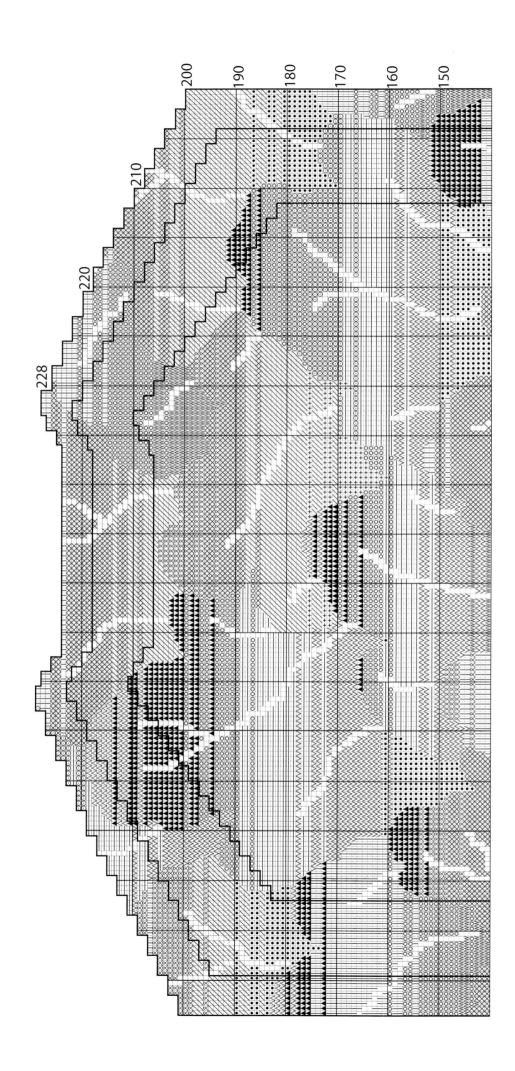

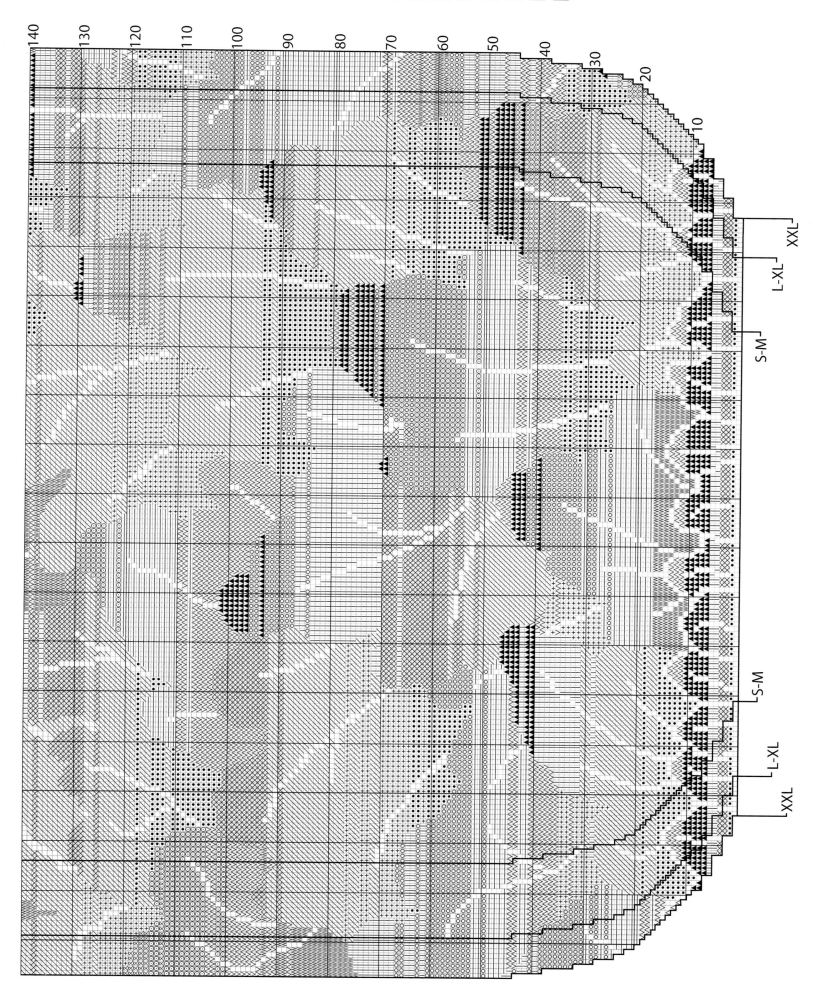

key
A B C D E F G H I J K L M N

140 130 120 110 100 90 80 70 60 50 40 30 20 10

XXL
L-XL
S-M
S-M
L-XL
XXL

MARTHA
SARAH DALLAS
Main image page 42, 44 & 45

●●

YARN

S	M	L	XL	XXL
To fit bust
81-86 91-97 102-107 112-117 122-127 cm
32-34 36-38 40-42 44-46 48-50 in

Rowan Pure Wool DK

| 12 | 12 | 14 | 16 | 17 | x 50 g |

(photographed in Shale 002)

NEEDLES

1 pair 4mm (no 8) (US 6) needles
3.50mm (no 9) (US E4) crochet hook - optional

BUTTONS – 3 x RW5021 (18mm) from Bedecked. Please see information page for contact details.

TENSION

24 sts and 31 rows to 10 cm measured over patt using 4mm (US 6) needles.

BACK

Using 4mm (US 6) needles cast on 134 [146: 160: 176: 192] sts.
Work in patt as folls:
Row 1 (RS): Knit.
Row 2: *P2tog leaving sts on left needle, now K same 2 sts tog and slip both sts off left needle at same time, rep from * to end.
Row 3: Knit.
Row 4: P1, *P2tog leaving sts on left needle, now K same 2 sts tog and slip both sts off left needle at same time, rep from * to last st, P1.
These 4 rows form patt.
Cont in patt, dec 1 st at each end of 9th and 5 foll 12th rows. 122 [134: 148: 164: 180] sts.
Cont straight until back meas 28 [29: 30: 31: 32] cm, ending with RS facing for next row.
Shape armholes
Keeping patt correct, cast off 2 sts at beg of next 2 rows. 118 [130: 144: 160: 176] sts.
Dec 1 st at each end of next and foll 3 alt rows. 110 [122: 136: 152: 168] sts.
Cont straight until armhole meas 21 [22: 23: 24: 25] cm, ending with RS facing for next row.
Shape shoulders and back neck
Cast off 11 [13: 15: 18: 20] sts at beg of next 2 rows. 88 [96: 106: 116: 128] sts.
Next row (RS): Cast off 11 [13: 15: 18: 20] sts, patt until there are 14 [16: 18: 20: 23] sts on right needle and turn, leaving rem sts on a holder.

Work each side of neck separately.
Cast off 3 sts at beg of next row.
Cast off rem 11 [13: 15: 17: 20] sts.
With RS facing, rejoin yarn to rem sts, cast off centre 38 [38: 40: 40: 42] sts, patt to end.
Complete to match first side, reversing shapings.

LEFT FRONT

Using 4mm (US 6) needles cast on 72 [78: 85: 93: 101] sts.
Work in patt as folls:
Row 1 (RS): Knit.
Row 2: K1, P1 [1: 0: 0: 0], *P2tog leaving sts on left needle, now K same 2 sts tog and slip both sts off left needle at same time, rep from * to end.
Row 3: Knit.
Row 4: K1, P0 [0: 1: 1: 1], *P2tog leaving sts on left needle, now K same 2 sts tog and slip both sts off left needle at same time, rep from * to last st, P1.
These 4 rows form patt.
Cont in patt, dec 1 st at beg of 9th and 5 foll 12th rows. 66 [72: 79: 87: 95] sts.
Cont straight until left front matches back to beg of armhole shaping, ending with RS facing for next row.
Shape armhole
Keeping patt correct, cast off 2 sts at beg of next row. 64 [70: 77: 85: 93] sts.
Work 1 row.
Dec 1 st at armhole edge of next and foll 3 alt rows. 60 [66: 73: 81: 89] sts.
Cont straight until 17 [17: 19: 19: 21] rows less have been worked than on back to beg of shoulder shaping, ending with **WS** facing for next row.
Shape neck
Keeping patt correct, cast off 15 sts at beg of next row. 45 [51: 58: 66: 74] sts.
Dec 1 st at neck edge of next 9 rows, then on foll 3 [3: 4: 4: 5] alt rows. 33 [39: 45: 53: 60] sts.
Work 1 row, ending with RS facing for next row.
Shape shoulder
Cast off 11 [13: 15: 18: 20] sts at beg of next and foll alt row.

Work 1 row.
Cast off rem 11 [13: 15: 17: 20] sts.
Mark positions for 3 buttons along left front opening edge - first button to come 8 rows below beg of armhole shaping, last button to come 2 cm below neck shaping, and rem button evenly spaced between.

RIGHT FRONT

Using 4mm (US 6) needles cast on 72 [78: 85: 93: 101] sts.
Work in patt as folls:
Row 1 (RS): Knit.
Row 2: *P2tog leaving sts on left needle, now K same 2 sts tog and slip both sts off left needle at same time, rep from * to last 2 [2: 1: 1: 1] sts, P1 [1: 0: 0: 0], K1.
Row 3: Knit.
Row 4: P1, *P2tog leaving sts on left needle, now K same 2 sts tog and slip both sts off left needle at same time, rep from * to last 1 [1: 2: 2: 2] sts, P0 [0: 1: 1: 1], K1.
These 4 rows form patt.
Cont in patt, dec 1 st at end of 9th and 5 foll 12th rows. 66 [72: 79: 87: 95] sts.
Cont straight until 8 rows less have been worked than on back to beg of armhole shaping, ending with RS facing for next row.
Next row (buttonhole row) (RS): K4, cast off 2 sts (to make a buttonhole - cast on 2 sts over these cast-off sts on next row), K to end.
Working a further 2 buttonholes in this way to correspond with positions marked for buttons on left front and noting that no further reference will be made to buttonholes, complete to match left front, reversing shapings.

SLEEVES

Using 4mm (US 6) needles cast on 72 [74: 76: 76: 78] sts.
Beg with row 1, work in patt as given for back, shaping sides by inc 1 st at each end of 7th [5th: 5th: 5th: 5th] and every foll 6th [4th: 4th: 4th: 4th] row to 98 [80: 84: 102: 110] sts, then on every foll 8th [6th: 6th: 6th: 6th] row until there are 100 [106: 110: 116: 120] sts, taking inc

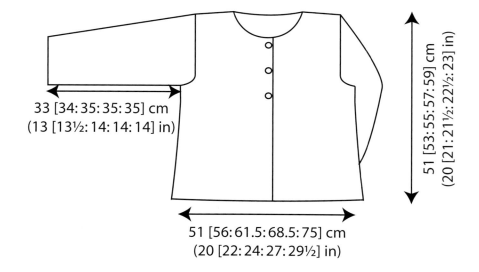

33 [34: 35: 35: 35] cm
(13 [13½: 14: 14: 14] in)

51 [56: 61.5: 68.5: 75] cm
(20 [22: 24: 27: 29½] in)

51 [53: 55: 57: 59] cm
(20 [21: 21½: 22½: 23] in)

sts into patt.

Cont straight until sleeve meas 33 [34: 35: 35: 35] cm, ending with RS facing for next row.

Shape top

Keeping patt correct, cast off 2 sts at beg of next 2 rows. 96 [102: 106: 112: 116] sts.

Dec 1 st at each end of next and foll 2 alt rows, then on foll row, ending with RS facing for

next row.

Cast off rem 88 [94: 98: 104: 108] sts.

MAKING UP

Press as described on the information page. Join both shoulder seams using back stitch, or mattress stitch if preferred.

See information page for finishing instructions,

setting in sleeves using the shallow set-in method.

Neck edging (optional)

Using 3.50mm (US E4) crochet hook, attach yarn at top of right front opening edge and work one row of double crochet around entire neck edge, to top of left front opening edge. Fasten off.

SINCERE
MARIE WALLIN
Main image page 92 & 93

● ● ●

YARN

	S	M	L	XL	XXL

To fit bust

81-86 91-97 102-107 112-117 122-127 cm

32-34 36-38 40-42 44-46 48-50 in

Rowan Kid Classic

10 11 12 13 14 x 50 g

(photographed in Straw 851)

NEEDLES

1 pair 4mm (no 8) (US 6) needles
1 pair 5mm (no 6) (US 8) needles
2 cable needles

TENSION

26 sts and 30 rows to 10 cm measured over patt using 5mm (US 8) needles.

SPECIAL ABBREVIATIONS

C5B = slip next 3 sts onto cable needle and leave at back of work, K2, then P1, K2 from cable needle; **C5F** = slip next 2 sts onto first cable needle and leave at front of work, slip next st onto 2nd cable needle and leave at back of work, K2, then P1 from 2nd cable needle and K2 from first cable needle; **C6B** = slip next 3 sts onto cable needle and leave at back of work, K3, then K3 from cable needle; **C6F** = slip next 3 sts onto cable needle and leave at

front of work, K3, then K3 from cable needle; **Cr5L** = slip next 3 sts onto cable needle and leave at front of work, P2, then K3 from cable needle; **Cr5R** = slip next 2 sts onto cable needle and leave at back of work, K3, then P2 from cable needle.

Pattern note: When working patt from chart, on WS rows work the st above the yfwd or yrn as "K1 tbl" to avoid holes forming.

BACK

Using 4mm (US 6) needles cast on 138 [150: 166: 182: 202] sts.

Row 1 (RS): K2, *P2, K2, rep from * to end.

Row 2: P2, *K2, P2, rep from * to end.

These 2 rows form rib.

Work in rib for a further 25 rows, inc 3 [3: 3: 3: 1] sts evenly across last row and ending with

WS facing for next row.

141 [153: 169: 185: 203] sts.

Change to 5mm (US 8) needles.

Beg and ending rows as indicated, noting that chart row 1 is a **WS** row and repeating the 20 and 24 row patt reps throughout, now work in patt from chart (see pattern note) as folls:

Cont straight until back meas 42 [43: 44: 45: 46] cm, ending with RS facing for next row.

Shape armholes

Keeping patt correct, cast off 6 [7: 8: 9: 10] sts at beg of next 2 rows.

129 [139: 153: 167: 183] sts.

Dec 1 st at each end of next 7 [9: 11: 13: 15] rows, then on foll 5 [6: 7: 8: 10] alt rows.

105 [109: 117: 125: 133] sts.

Cont straight until armhole meas 20 [21: 22: 23: 24] cm, ending with RS facing for next row.

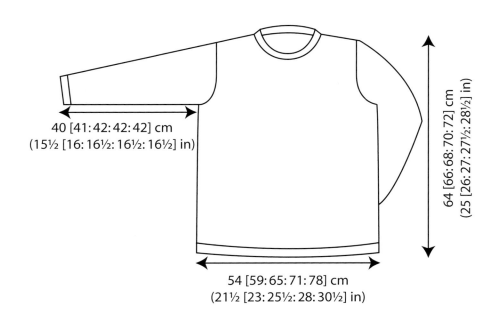

40 [41: 42: 42: 42] cm
(15½ [16: 16½: 16½: 16½] in)

64 [66: 68: 70: 72] cm
(25 [26: 27: 27½: 28½] in)

54 [59: 65: 71: 78] cm
(21½ [23: 25½: 28: 30½] in)

Shape shoulders and back neck

Next row (RS): Cast off 10 [11: 12: 13: 14] sts, patt until there are 26 [27: 29: 32: 34] sts on right needle and turn, leaving rem sts on a holder.

Work each side of neck separately.

Cast off 3 sts at beg of next row, 10 [11: 12: 13: 14] sts at beg of foll row, then 3 sts at beg of next row.

Cast off rem 10 [10: 11: 13: 14] sts.

With RS facing, rejoin yarn to rem sts, cast off centre 33 [33: 35: 35: 37] sts, patt to end.

Complete to match first side, reversing shapings.

FRONT

Work as given for back until 20 [20: 22: 22: 24] rows less have been worked than on back to beg of shoulder shaping, ending with RS facing for next row.

Shape front neck

Next row (RS): Patt 42 [44: 48: 52: 56] sts and turn, leaving rem sts on a holder.

Work each side of neck separately.

Keeping patt correct, dec 1 st at neck edge of next 8 rows, then on foll 4 [4: 5: 5: 6] alt rows. 30 [32: 35: 39: 42] sts.

Work 3 rows, ending with RS facing for next row.

Shape shoulder

Cast off 10 [11: 12: 13: 14] sts at beg of next and foll alt row.

Work 1 row.

Cast off rem 10 [10: 11: 13: 14] sts.

With RS facing, rejoin yarn to rem sts, cast off centre 21 sts, patt to end.

Complete to match first side, reversing shapings.

SLEEVES

Using 4mm (US 6) needles cast on 50 [54: 54: 54: 58] sts.

Work in rib as given for back for 15 rows, inc 3 [1: 3: 3: 1] sts evenly across last row and ending with **WS** facing for next row. 53 [55: 57: 57: 59] sts.

Change to 5mm (US 8) needles.

Beg and ending rows as indicated, noting that chart row 1 is a **WS** row and repeating the 20 and 24 row patt reps throughout, now work in patt from chart (see pattern note) as folls: Inc 1 st at each end of 2nd and foll 1 [2: 2: 6: 8] alt rows, then on every foll 4th row until there are 99 [103: 107: 111: 115] sts, taking inc sts into patt.

Cont straight until sleeve meas 40 [41: 42: 42: 42] cm, ending with RS facing for next row.

Shape top

Keeping patt correct, cast off 6 [7: 8: 9: 10] sts at beg of next 2 rows. 87 [89: 91: 93: 95] sts.

Dec 1 st at each end of next 7 rows, then on every foll alt row to 63 sts, then on foll 11 rows, ending with RS facing for next row. 41 sts.

Cast off 3 sts at beg of next 6 rows.

Cast off rem 23 sts.

MAKING UP

Press as described on the information page.

Join right shoulder seam using back stitch, or mattress stitch if preferred.

Neckband

With RS facing and using 4mm (US 6) needles, pick up and knit 21 [21: 22: 22: 23] sts down left side of neck, 18 sts from front, 21 [21: 22: 22: 23] sts up right side of neck, then 34 [34: 36: 36: 38] sts from back.

94 [94: 98: 98: 102] sts.

Beg with row 2, work in rib as given for back for 5 rows, ending with RS facing for next row.

Cast off in rib.

See information page for finishing instructions, setting in sleeves using the set-in method.

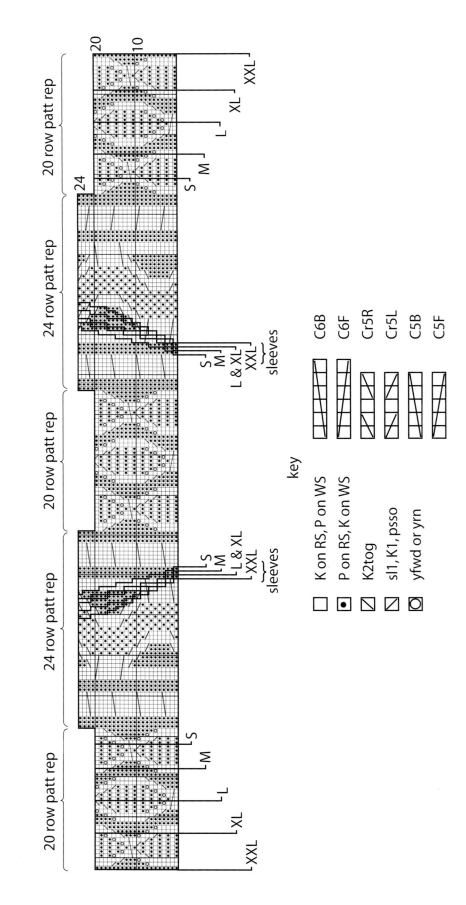

key

□ K on RS, P on WS
☐• P on RS, K on WS
◪ K2tog
◨ sl1, K1, psso
⊘ yfwd or yrn

C6B
C6F
Cr5R
Cr5L
C5B
C5F

LAUREL
MARIE WALLIN
Main image page 22 & 23

●●●

YARN

S	M	L	XL	XXL

To fit bust
81-86 91-97102-107112-117122-127 cm
32-34 36-38 40-42 44-46 48-50 in
Rowan Kid Classic
11   12   13   14   16   x 50 g
(photographed in Mellow 877)

NEEDLES

1 pair 4½mm (no 7) (US 7) needles
Cable needle

TENSION

24 sts and 27 rows to 10 cm measured over patt
using 4½mm (US 7) needles.

SPECIAL ABBREVIATIONS

C7F = slip next 4 sts onto cable needle and
leave at front of work, K3, slip centre of these
7 sts back onto left needle and K this st, then
K3 from cable needle; **Cr4L** = slip next 3 sts
onto cable needle and leave at front of work,
P1, then K3 from cable needle; **Cr4R** = slip
next st onto cable needle and leave at back
of work, K3, then P1 from cable needle;
Cr5L = slip next 3 sts onto cable needle and
leave at front of work, P2, then K3 from cable
needle; **inc 2** = (K1 tbl, K1) into next st, insert
left needle point behind vertical strand that
runs downward from between 2 sts just made
and K tbl into this strand - 2 sts increased.

Pattern note: The number of sts varies whilst
working patt panel. All st counts given presume
there are 21 sts in patt panel at all times.

BACK

Using 4½mm (US 7) needles cast on 135 [147:
159: 177: 189] sts.
Row 1 (RS): K3, *P3, K3, rep from * to end.
Row 2: P3, *K3, P3, rep from * to end.
These 2 rows form rib.
Work in rib for a further 25 rows, dec [dec:
inc: dec: inc] 1 [1: 1: 1: 3] sts evenly across last
row and ending with **WS** facing for next row.
134 [146: 160: 176: 192] sts.
Row 28 (WS): K4 [10: 17: 4: 12], (K9, P3, K9)
6 [6: 6: 8: 8] times, K4 [10: 17: 4: 12].
Work in patt as folls:
Row 1 (RS): P4 [10: 17: 4: 12], (work next
21 sts as row 1 of patt panel) 6 [6: 6: 8: 8]
times, P4 [10: 17: 4: 12].

Row 2: K4 [10: 17: 4: 12], (work row 2 of patt
panel) 6 [6: 6: 8: 8] times, K4 [10: 17: 4: 12].
These 2 rows set the sts - 6 [6: 6: 8: 8] patt
panels with rev st st at sides.
Cont as set until back meas 40 [41: 42: 43:
44] cm, ending with RS facing for next row.
Shape armholes
Keeping patt correct, cast off 2 [3: 3: 2: 3] sts at
beg of next 2 rows. 130 [140: 154: 172: 186] sts.
Dec 1 st at each end of next and foll 1 [3: 3:
1: 3] alt rows. 126 [132: 146: 168: 178] sts.
Cont straight until armhole meas 18 [19: 20:
21: 22] cm, ending with RS facing for next row.
Shape shoulders
Keeping patt correct, cast off 7 [8: 9: 10: 11] sts
at beg of next 2 [12: 14: 8: 14] rows, then 8 [9:
10: 11: 12] sts at beg of foll 13 [3: 1: 7: 1] rows,
ending with **WS** facing for next row.
Cast off rem 8 [9: 10: 11: 12] sts.

FRONT

Work as given for back until 4 rows less have
been worked than on back to beg of armhole
shaping, ending with RS facing for next row.
Divide for neck opening
Next row (RS): Patt 67 [73: 80: 88: 96] sts
and turn, leaving rem sts on a holder.
Work each side of neck separately.
Work 3 rows, ending with RS facing for
next row.
Shape armhole
Keeping patt correct, cast off 2 [3: 3: 2: 3] sts at
beg of next row. 65 [70: 77: 86: 93] sts.
Work 1 row.
Dec 1 st at armhole edge of next and foll 1 [3:
3: 1: 3] alt rows. 63 [66: 73: 84: 89] sts.
Cont straight until front matches back to beg
of shoulder shaping, ending with RS facing for
next row.
Shape shoulder
Keeping patt correct, cast off 7 [8: 9: 10: 11] sts
at beg of next and foll 0 [5: 6: 3: 6] alt rows,
then 8 [9: -: 11: -] sts at beg of foll 6 [1: -: 3: -]
alt rows.

Work 1 row.
Cast off rem 8 [9: 10: 11: 12] sts.
With RS facing, rejoin yarn to rem sts, patt
to end.
Complete to match first side, reversing
shapings.

SLEEVES

Using 4½mm (US 7) needles cast on 52 [54:
56: 56: 58] sts.
Row 1 (WS): K5 [6: 7: 7: 8], (K9, P3, K9)
twice, K5 [6: 7: 7: 8].
Work in patt as folls:
Row 1 (RS): P5 [6: 7: 7: 8], (work next 21 sts
as row 1 of patt panel) twice, P5 [6: 7: 7: 8].
Row 2: K5 [6: 7: 7: 8], (work row 2 of patt
panel) twice, K5 [6: 7: 7: 8].
These 2 rows set the sts - 2 patt panels with
rev st st at sides.
Cont in patt, shaping sides by inc 1 st at each
end of 3rd [3rd: next: next: next] and every foll
6th [6th: 6th: 4th: 4th] row to 78 [84: 90: 70:
78] sts, then on every foll 8th [8th: -: 6th: 6th]
row until there are 82 [86: -: 94: 98] sts, taking
inc sts into rev st st until there are sufficient to
work as patt panel.
Cont straight until sleeve meas 40 [41: 42: 42:
42] cm, ending with RS facing for next row.
Shape top
Keeping patt correct, cast off 2 [3: 3: 2: 3] sts at
beg of next 2 rows. 78 [80: 84: 90: 92] sts.
Dec 1 st at each end of next and foll 0 [2: 2: 0:
2] alt rows, then on foll row, ending with RS
facing for next row.
Cast off rem 74 [72: 76: 86: 84] sts.

MAKING UP

Press as described on the information page.
Neck edging
With RS facing and using 4½mm (US 7)
needles, pick up and knit 52 [54: 56: 58: 60] sts
down left side of neck opening, then 52 [54:
56: 58: 60] sts up right side of neck opening.
104 [108: 112: 116: 120] sts.

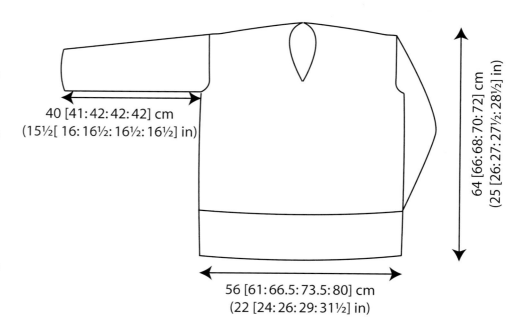

40 [41: 42: 42: 42] cm
(15½[16: 16½: 16½: 16½] in)

64 [66: 68: 70: 72] cm
(25 [26: 27: 27½: 28½] in)

56 [61: 66.5: 73.5: 80] cm
(22 [24: 26: 29: 31½] in)

Cast off knitwise (on **WS**).
Join both shoulder seams using back stitch, or mattress stitch if preferred, joining ends of neck edging at centre back neck. (**Note**: There is no back neck edge as front shoulder edges meet at centre back neck.)

See information page for finishing instructions, setting in sleeves using the shallow set-in method.

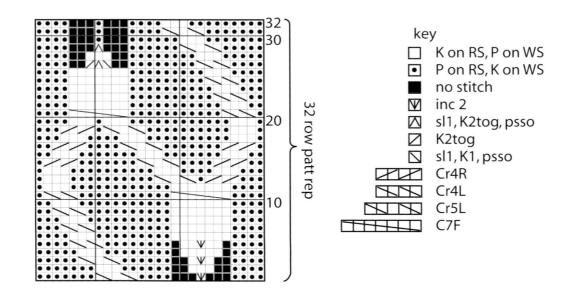

key
- ☐ K on RS, P on WS
- ⊡ P on RS, K on WS
- ■ no stitch
- inc 2
- sl1, K2tog, psso
- K2tog
- sl1, K1, psso
- Cr4R
- Cr4L
- Cr5L
- C7F

32 row patt rep

JOYCE
LISA RICHARDSON

Main image page 62 & 63

TENSION

30 sts and 40 rows to 10 cm measured over patt using 4mm (US 6) needles.

Pattern note: When working patt, work all slip sts with yarn at front of work - this is RS on RS rows, and WS on WS rows.

BACK

Using 4mm (US 6) needles cast on 135 [143: 151: 159: 167: 175: 183: 191] sts.
Now work in patt (see pattern note) as folls:
Row 1 (RS): K3, *sl 1, K3, rep from * to end.
Row 2: K1, *sl 1, K3, rep from * to last 2 sts, sl 1, K1.

YARN

8	10	12	14	16	18	20	22	

To fit bust

81	86	91	97	102	107	112	117	cm
32	34	36	38	40	42	44	46	in

Rowan Cashsoft DK

13	13	14	16	16	17	18	19	x 50 g

(photographed in Ballad Blue 508)

NEEDLES

1 pair 4mm (no 8) (US 6) needles

BUTTONS – 4 x RW5030 (20mm) Aged Silver 672 from Bedecked. Please see information page for contact details.

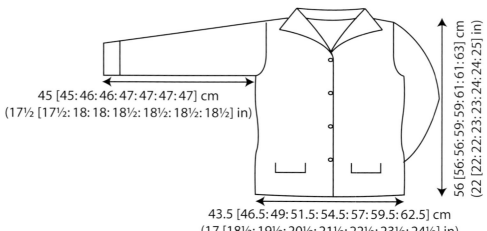

45 [45: 46: 46: 47: 47: 47: 47] cm
(17½ [17½: 18: 18: 18½: 18½: 18½: 18½] in)

56 [56: 56: 59: 59: 61: 61: 63] cm
(22 [22: 22: 23: 23: 24: 24: 25] in)

43.5 [46.5: 49: 51.5: 54.5: 57: 59.5: 62.5] cm
(17 [18½: 19½: 20½: 21½: 22½: 23½: 24½] in)

These 2 rows form patt.

Cont in patt, dec 1 st at each end of 13th and 7 foll 6th rows.

119 [127: 135: 143: 151: 159: 167: 175] sts.

Work 13 rows, ending with RS facing for next row.

Inc 1 st at each end of next and 5 foll 10th rows, taking inc sts into patt.

131 [139: 147: 155: 163: 171: 179: 187] sts.

Cont straight until back meas 34 [34: 33: 36: 35: 37: 36: 38] cm, ending with RS facing for next row.

Shape armholes

Keeping patt correct, cast off 5 [6: 6: 7: 7: 8: 8: 9] sts at beg of next 2 rows.

121 [127: 135: 141: 149: 155: 163: 169] sts.

Dec 1 st at each end of next 5 [5: 7: 7: 9: 9: 11: 11] rows, then on foll 4 [5: 6: 7: 6: 7: 7: 8] alt rows, then on 2 foll 4th rows.

99 [103: 105: 109: 115: 119: 123: 127] sts.

Cont straight until armhole meas 20 [20: 21: 21: 22: 22: 23: 23] cm, ending with RS facing for next row.

Shape shoulder

Cast off 6 [6: 7: 7: 8: 8: 9: 9] sts at beg of next 6 [2: 8: 4: 8: 4: 8: 4] rows, then 7 [7: –: 8: –: 9: –: 10] sts at beg of foll 2 [6: –: 4: –: 4: –: 4] rows.

Cast off rem 49 [49: 49: 49: 51: 51: 51: 51] sts.

POCKET FLAPS (make 2)

With 4mm (US 6) needles cast on 27 [27: 27: 31: 31: 31: 35: 35] sts.

Now work in patt (see pattern note) as folls:

Row 1 (RS): K1, ★sl 1, K3, rep from ★ to last 2 sts, sl 1, K1.

Row 2: K3, ★sl 1, K3, rep from ★ to end.

These 2 rows form patt.

Work in patt for a further 14 rows, ending with RS facing for next row.

Break yarn and leave sts on a holder.

LEFT FRONT

Using 4mm (US 6) needles cast on 73 [77: 81: 85: 89: 93: 97: 101] sts.

Now work in patt (see pattern note) as folls:

Row 1 (RS): ★K3, sl 1, rep from ★ to last st, K1.

Row 2: As row 1.

These 2 rows form patt.

Cont in patt, dec 1 st at beg of 13th and 5 foll 6th rows. 67 [71: 75: 79: 83: 87: 91: 95] sts.

Work 3 rows, ending with RS facing for next row.

Place pocket flap

Row 49 (RS): Patt 12 [16: 16: 16: 16: 20: 20: 20] sts, holding WS of pocket flap against RS of left front, patt tog first st of pocket flap with next st of front, (patt tog next st of flap with next st of front) 26 [26: 26: 30: 30: 30:

34: 34] times, patt 28 [28: 32: 32: 36: 36: 36: 40] sts.

Dec 1 st at beg of 2nd and foll 6th row.

65 [69: 73: 77: 81: 85: 89: 93] sts.

Work 13 rows, ending with RS facing for next row.

Inc 1 st at beg of next and 5 foll 10th rows, taking inc sts into patt.

71 [75: 79: 83: 87: 91: 95: 99] sts.

Cont straight until left front matches back to beg of armhole shaping, ending with RS facing for next row.

Shape armhole

Keeping patt correct, cast off 5 [6: 6: 7: 7: 8: 8: 9] sts at beg of next row.

66 [69: 73: 76: 80: 83: 87: 90] sts.

Work 1 row.

Dec 1 st at armhole edge of next 5 [5: 7: 7: 9: 9: 11: 11] rows, then on foll 4 [5: 6: 7: 6: 7: 7: 8] alt rows, then on 2 foll 4th rows.

55 [57: 58: 60: 63: 65: 67: 69] sts.

Cont straight until left front matches back to beg of shoulder shaping, ending with RS facing for next row.

Shape shoulder

Cast off 6 [6: 7: 7: 8: 8: 9: 9] sts at beg of next and foll 2 [0: 3: 1: 3: 1: 3: 1] alt rows, then 7 [7: –: 8: –: 9: –: 10] sts at beg of foll 1 [3: –: 2: –: 2: –: 2] alt rows.

Work 1 row, ending with RS facing for next row.

Break yarn and leave rem 30 [30: 30: 30: 31: 31: 31: 31] sts on a holder.

Mark positions for 4 buttons along left front opening edge - first to come in row 49, last to come 16 cm down from beg of shoulder shaping and rem 2 buttons evenly spaced between.

RIGHT FRONT

Using 4mm (US 6) needles cast on 73 [77: 81: 85: 89: 93: 97: 101] sts.

Now work in patt (see pattern note) as folls:

Row 1 (RS): K1, ★sl 1, K3, rep from ★ to end.

Row 2: As row 1.

These 2 rows form patt.

Cont in patt, dec 1 st at end of 13th and 5 foll 6th rows. 67 [71: 75: 79: 83: 87: 91: 95] sts.

Work 3 rows, ending with RS facing for next row.

Place pocket flap

Row 49 (RS): Patt 4 sts, work 2 tog tbl, yrn (to make first buttonhole), patt 22 [22: 26: 26: 30: 30: 30: 34] sts, holding WS of pocket flap against RS of right front, patt tog first st of pocket flap with next st of front, (patt tog next st of flap with next st of front) 26 [26: 26: 30: 30: 30: 34: 34] times, patt 12 [16: 16: 16: 16: 20:

20: 20] sts.

Making a further 3 buttonholes to correspond with positions marked for buttons on left front and as set by last row, complete to match left front, reversing shapings.

When right front is complete, ending with RS facing for next row, do NOT break yarn but set this ball of yarn to one side to be used for collar.

SLEEVES

Using 4mm (US 6) needles cast on 67 [67: 71: 71: 75: 75: 79: 79] sts.

Beg with row 1, work in patt as given for back, dec 1 st at each end of 3rd and 3 foll 6th rows.

59 [59: 63: 63: 67: 67: 71: 71] sts.

Cont in patt, shaping sides by inc 1 st at each end of 8th and every foll 8th row to 79 [89: 79: 89: 79: 89: 83: 93] sts, then on every foll 10th row until there are 95 [97: 99: 101: 103: 105: 107: 109] sts, taking inc sts into patt.

Cont straight until sleeve meas 50 [50: 51: 51: 52: 52: 52: 52] cm, ending with RS facing for next row.

Shape top

Keeping patt correct, cast off 5 [6: 6: 7: 7: 8: 8: 9] sts at beg of next 2 rows. 85 [85: 87: 87: 89: 89: 91: 91] sts.

Dec 1 st at each end of next 5 rows, then on foll 5 alt rows, then on 5 foll 4th rows. 55 [55: 57: 57: 59: 59: 61: 61] sts.

Work 1 row, ending with RS facing for next row.

Dec 1 st at each end of next and every foll alt row to 45 sts, then on foll 9 rows, ending with RS facing for next row. 27 sts.

Cast off 4 sts at beg of next 2 rows.

Cast off rem 19 sts.

MAKING UP

Press as described on the information page.

Join both shoulder seams using back stitch, or mattress stitch if preferred.

Collar

With RS facing, using 4mm (US 6) needles and ball of yarn set to one side with right front, patt 30 [30: 30: 30: 31: 31: 31: 31] sts from right front holder, pick up and knit 47 [47: 47: 47: 49: 49: 49: 49] sts from back, then patt 30 [30: 30: 30: 31: 31: 31: 31] sts from left front holder.

107 [107: 107: 107: 111: 111: 111: 111] sts.

Work in patt as set by sts from holders for 9 rows, ending with RS facing for next row.

Cast off in patt.

See information page for finishing instructions, setting in sleeves using the set-in method and reversing sleeve seam for first 6 cm for turn-back cuff. Fold 5 cm cuff to RS.

MAPLE
MARIE WALLIN

Main image page 12, 13, 14 & 15

● ● ●

YARN

	S	M	L	XL	XXL	

To fit bust
81–86 91–97 102–107 112–117 122–127 cm
32–34 36–38 40–42 44–46 48–50 in

Rowan Felted Tweed

A Bilberry 151
| 2 | 2 | 2 | 2 | 2 | x 50 g |

B Paisley 171
| 1 | 1 | 1 | 2 | 2 | x 50 g |

C Watery 152
| 1 | 1 | 1 | 2 | 2 | x 50 g |

D Maritime 167
| 1 | 2 | 2 | 2 | 2 | x 50 g |

E Seasalter 178
| 1 | 1 | 1 | 1 | 1 | x 50 g |

F Camel 157
| 1 | 1 | 2 | 2 | 2 | x 50 g |

G Ginger 154
| 1 | 1 | 1 | 2 | 2 | x 50 g |

H Pine 158
| 1 | 1 | 1 | 1 | 1 | x 50 g |

I Avocado 161
| 1 | 1 | 1 | 1 | 1 | x 50 g |

J Cinnamon 175
| 1 | 1 | 1 | 1 | 1 | x 50 g |

NEEDLES

1 pair 2¾mm (no 12) (US 2) needles
1 pair 3¼mm (no 10) (US 3) needles

BUTTONS – 9 x RW5013 (**WS facing**)
from Bedecked. Please see information page
for contact details.

TENSION

24 sts and 32 rows to 10 cm measured over st
st, 29 sts and 30 rows to 10 cm measured over
patterned st st, both using 3¼mm (US 3)
needles.

BACK

Using 2¾mm (US 2) needles and yarn A cast
on 105 [119: 131: 147: 163] sts.
***Row 1 (RS):** K1, *P1, K1, rep from
* to end.
Row 2: P1, *K1, P1, rep from * to end.
These 2 rows form rib.
**Joining in and breaking off colours as
required, cont in rib in stripes as folls:
Rows 3 and 4: Using yarn B.
Rows 5 and 6: Using yarn D.
Rows 7 and 8: Using yarn E.

Rows 9 and 10: Using yarn C.
Rows 11 and 12: Using yarn G.
Rows 13 and 14: Using yarn H.
Rows 15 and 16: Using yarn A.
Rows 3 to 16 form stripe sequence.***
Cont in rib in stripe sequence until work meas
10 cm, ending with **WS** facing for next row.**
Next row (WS): Using same colour yarn as
for previous row, rib 3 [5: 2: 6: 5], (rib 2, M1,
rib 5, M1, rib 2) 11 [12: 14: 15: 17] times, rib
3 [6: 3: 6: 5]. 127 [143: 159: 177: 197] sts.
Change to 3¼mm (US 3) needles.
Beg and ending rows as indicated, using a
combination of the **fairisle** and **intarsia**
techniques as described on the information
page and repeating the 80 row patt repeat
throughout, now work in patt from chart,
which is worked entirely in st st beg with a
K row, as folls:
Work 60 [64: 66: 70: 72] rows, ending with RS
facing for next row. (Back should meas 30 [31:
32: 33: 34] cm.)

Shape armholes
Keeping patt correct, cast off 6 [7: 8: 9: 10] sts
at beg of next 2 rows.
115 [129: 143: 159: 177] sts.
Dec 1 st at each end of next 7 [9: 11: 13: 17]
rows, then on foll 4 [6: 7: 8: 8] alt rows.
93 [99: 107: 117: 127] sts.
Cont straight until armhole meas 18 [19: 20:
21: 22] cm, ending with RS facing for next
row.

Shape shoulders and back neck
Next row (RS): Cast off 7 [8: 9: 10: 12] sts,
patt until there are 19 [21: 23: 27: 29] sts on
right needle and turn, leaving rem sts on a
holder.
Work each side of neck separately.
Cast off 3 sts at beg of next row, 7 [8: 9: 10: 12]
sts at beg of foll row, then 3 sts at beg of
next row.
Cast off rem 6 [7: 8: 11: 11] sts.
With RS facing, rejoin appropriate yarns to
rem sts, cast off centre 41 [41: 43: 43: 45] sts,
patt to end.
Complete to match first side, reversing
shapings.

LEFT FRONT
Using 2¾mm (US 2) needles and yarn A cast
on 52 [58: 64: 72: 80] sts.
Row 1 (RS): K1, *P1, K1, rep from * to last
st, K1.
Row 2: *K1, P1, rep from * to end.
These 2 rows form rib.
Work as given for back from ** to **.
Next row (WS): Using same colour yarn as
for previous row, rib 3 [2: 1: 3: 2], (rib 2, M1,
rib 5, M1, rib 2) 5 [6: 7: 7: 8] times, (rib 2, M1)
0 [0: 0: 1: 1] times, rib 4 [2: 0: 4: 4].
62 [70: 78: 87: 97] sts.
Change to 3¼mm (US 3) needles.
Beg and ending rows as indicated, now work in
patt from chart as folls:
Cont straight until left front matches back to
beg of armhole shaping, ending with RS facing
for next row.

Shape armhole
Keeping patt correct, cast off 6 [7: 8: 9: 10] sts
at beg of next row. 56 [63: 70: 78: 87] sts.
Work 1 row.
Dec 1 st at armhole edge of next 7 [9: 11: 13:
17] rows, then on foll 4 [6: 7: 8: 8] alt rows.
45 [48: 52: 57: 62] sts.
Cont straight until 25 [25: 27: 27: 29] rows less
have been worked than on back to beg of
shoulder shaping, ending with **WS** facing for
next row.

Shape neck
Keeping patt correct, cast off 12 sts at beg of
next row. 33 [36: 40: 45: 50] sts.
Dec 1 st at neck edge of next 7 rows, then on
foll 5 [5: 6: 6: 7] alt rows, then on foll 4th row.
20 [23: 26: 31: 35] sts.
Work 3 rows, ending with RS facing for
next row.

Shape shoulder
Cast off 7 [8: 9: 10: 12] sts at beg of next and
foll alt row.
Work 1 row.
Cast off rem 6 [7: 8: 11: 11] sts.

RIGHT FRONT
Using 2¾mm (US 2) needles and yarn A cast
on 52 [58: 64: 72: 80] sts.

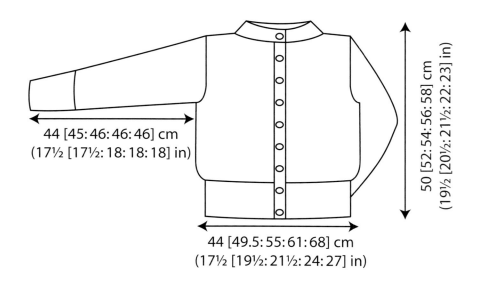

44 [45: 46: 46: 46] cm
(17½ [17½: 18: 18: 18] in)

44 [49.5: 55: 61: 68] cm
(17½ [19½: 21½: 24: 27] in)

50 [52: 54: 56: 58] cm
(19½ [20½: 21½: 22: 23] in)

Row 1 (RS): K2, *P1, K1, rep from * to end.
Row 2: *P1, K1, rep from * to end.
These 2 rows form rib.
Complete to match left front, reversing shapings.

SLEEVE STRIPE SEQUENCE
Rows 1 to 4: Using yarn G.
Rows 5 to 8: Using yarn J.
Rows 9 to 12: Using yarn I.
Rows 13 to 16: Using yarn F.
Rows 17 to 20: Using yarn D.
Rows 21 to 24: Using yarn B.
Rows 25 to 28: Using yarn A.
Rows 29 to 32: Using yarn C.
These 32 rows form sleeve stripe sequence and
are repeated.

SLEEVES
Using 2¾mm (US 2) needles and yarn A cast
on 45 [47: 49: 51: 53] sts.
Work as given for back from ★★★ to ★★★.
Cont in rib in stripe sequence until work meas
12 cm, ending with **WS** facing for next row.
Next row (WS): Using same colour yarn as
for previous row, rib 2 [3: 4: 5: 6], (M1, rib 6)
7 times, M1, rib 1 [2: 3: 4: 5].
53 [55: 57: 59: 61] sts.
Change to 3¼mm (US 3) needles.
Beg with sleeve stripe row 1 and a K row, now
work in st st in sleeve stripe sequence (see
above) as folls:
Inc 1 st at each end of 3rd [3rd: 3rd: next: next]
and every foll 4th [4th: 4th: alt: alt] row to
93 [97: 103: 63: 69] sts, then on every foll 6th
[6th: –: 4th: 4th] row until there are 95 [99: –:
107: 111] sts.
Cont straight until sleeve meas 44 [45: 46:
46: 46] cm, ending with RS facing for
next row.
Shape top
Keeping stripes correct, cast off 6 [7: 8: 9: 10] sts
at beg of next 2 rows. 83 [85: 87: 89: 91] sts.
Dec 1 st at each end of next 9 rows, then on
every foll alt row to 53 sts, then on foll 11
rows, ending with RS facing for next row.
31 sts.
Cast off 3 sts at beg of next 2 rows, then 4 sts
at beg of foll 2 rows.
Cast off rem 17 sts.

MAKING UP
Press as described on the information page.
Join both shoulder seams using back stitch, or
mattress stitch if preferred.
Neckband
With RS facing, using 2¾mm (US 2) needles
and yarn E, beg and ending at front opening
edges, pick up and knit 37 [37: 39: 39: 41] sts
up right side of neck, 53 [53: 55: 55: 57] sts
from back, then 37 [37: 39: 39: 41] sts down
left side of neck. 127 [127: 133: 133: 139] sts.
****Row 1 (WS): K1, *P1, K1, rep from * to
end.
Break off yarn E and join in yarn D.
Row 2: K2, *P1, K1, rep from * to last st, K1.
These 2 rows form rib.
Joining in and breaking off colours as required,
cont in rib in stripes as folls:
Row 3: Using yarn D.
Rows 4 and 5: Using yarn B.

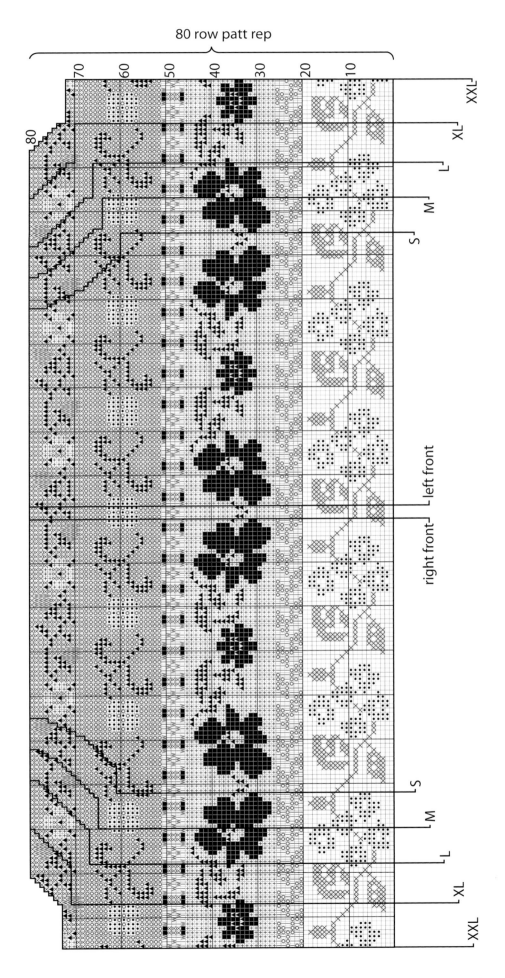

80 row patt rep

left front
right front

Row 6: Using yarn A.
Using yarn A, cast off in rib (on **WS**).
Button band
With RS facing, using 2¾mm (US 2) needles and yarn E, pick up and knit 119 [125: 131: 131: 137] sts evenly along left front opening edge,

between top of neckband and cast-on edge. Complete as given for neckband from ★★★★.
Buttonhole band
Work to match button band, picking up sts up right front opening edge and with the addition of 9 buttonholes worked in row 4 as folls:

Row 4 (RS): Rib 2, (work 2 tog, yrn, rib 9) twice, ★work 2 tog, yrn, rib 13 [14: 15: 15: 16], rep from ★ 5 times more, work 2 tog, yrn (to make 9th buttonhole), rib 3.
See information page for finishing instructions, setting in sleeves using the set-in method.

KIND
MARIE WALLIN
Main image page 104 & 105

●●

YARN

	S	M	L	XL	XXL	

To fit bust
81-86 91-97 102-107 112-117 122-127 cm
32-34 36-38 40-42 44-46 48-50 in
Rowan Lima

| 14 | 15 | 17 | 18 | 20 | x 50 g |

(photographed in Lima 888)

NEEDLES
1 pair 5mm (no 6) (US 8) needles
1 pair 5½mm (no 5) (US 9) needles
5mm (no 6) (US 8) circular needle,
100 cm long

BUTTONS – 5 x BN1367 (23mm) from Bedecked. Please see information page for contact details.

TENSION
20 sts and 26 rows to 10 cm measured over st st using 5½mm (US 9) needles.

BACK
Using 5mm (US 8) needles cast on 118 [130: 142: 154: 170] sts.
Row 1 (RS): K2, ★P2, K2, rep from ★ to end.
Row 2: P2, ★K2, P2, rep from ★ to end.
These 2 rows form rib.
Cont in rib, dec 1 st at each end of 21st and foll 18th row. 114 [126: 138: 150: 166] sts.
Work a further 7 rows, ending with RS facing for next row.

Change to 5½mm (US 9) needles.
Next row (RS): K4 [2: 3: 4: 4], K2tog, (K11 [10: 11: 12: 11], K2tog) 8 [10: 10: 10: 12] times, K4 [2: 3: 4: 4]. 105 [115: 127: 139: 153] sts.
Beg with a P row, work in st st for 3 rows, ending with RS facing for next row.
Beg and ending rows as indicated, working chart rows 1 to 102 **once only** and then repeating chart rows 103 and 104 **throughout**, now work in patt from chart for body as folls:
Dec 1 st at each end of 7th and 3 foll 18th rows. 97 [107: 119: 131: 145] sts.
Cont straight until back meas 50 [51: 52: 53: 54] cm, ending with RS facing for next row.
Shape armholes
Keeping patt correct, cast off 4 [5: 6: 7: 8] sts at beg of next 2 rows. 89 [97: 107: 117: 129] sts.
(**Note:** Armhole shaping is **NOT** shown on chart.)
Dec 1 st at each end of next 3 [5: 7: 9: 11] rows, then on foll 5 [5: 6: 6: 7] alt rows.

73 [77: 81: 87: 93] sts.
Cont straight until armhole meas 20 [21: 22: 23: 24] cm, ending with RS facing for next row.
Shape shoulders and back neck
Next row (RS): Cast off 6 [7: 7: 8: 9] sts, patt until there are 19 [20: 21: 23: 24] sts on right needle and turn, leaving rem sts on a holder.
Work each side of neck separately.
Cast off 3 sts at beg of next row, 6 [7: 7: 8: 9] sts at beg of foll row, then 3 sts at beg of next row.
Cast off rem 7 [7: 8: 9: 9] sts.
With RS facing, rejoin yarn to rem sts, cast off centre 23 [23: 25: 25: 27] sts, patt to end.
Complete to match first side, reversing shapings.

POCKET LININGS (make 2)
With 5½mm (US 9) needles cast on 24 [24: 26: 26: 28] sts.
Beg with a K row, work in st st for 12 cm, ending with RS facing for next row.
Break yarn and leave sts on a holder.

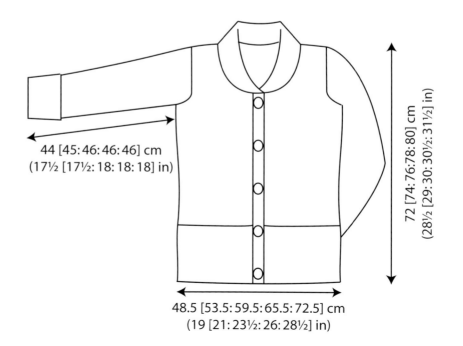

44 [45: 46: 46: 46] cm
(17½ [17½: 18: 18: 18] in)

72 [74: 76: 78: 80] cm
(28½ [29: 30: 30½: 31½] in)

48.5 [53.5: 59.5: 65.5: 72.5] cm
(19 [21: 23½: 26: 28½] in)

LEFT FRONT

Using 5mm (US 8) needles cast on 59 [63: 71: 75: 83] sts.

Row 1 (RS): K2, *P2, K2, rep from * to last st, K1.

Row 2: K1, P2, *K2, P2, rep from * to end. These 2 rows form rib.

Cont in rib, dec 1 st at beg of 21st and foll

18th row. 57 [61: 69: 73: 81] sts.

Work a further 6 rows, ending with **WS** facing for next row.

Place pocket

Next row (WS): Rib 20 [24: 26: 30: 33], cast off next 26 [26: 28: 28: 31] sts in rib, rib to end. Change to 5½mm (US 9) needles.

Next row (RS): K4 [5: 3: 5: 4], K2tog, K3 [4:

8: 8: 11], (K2tog) 1 [0: 1: 0: 0] times, with RS facing K across 24 [24: 26: 26: 28] sts of first pocket lining, K4 [4: 0: 7: 12], (K2tog, K8) 0 [0: 1: 0: 0] times, K2tog, K7 [10: 8: 13: 12], K2tog, K5 [6: 4: 6: 5]. 51 [56: 62: 68: 75] sts.

Beg with a P row, work in st st for 3 rows, ending with RS facing for next row.

Beg and ending rows as indicated, working

2 row patt rep

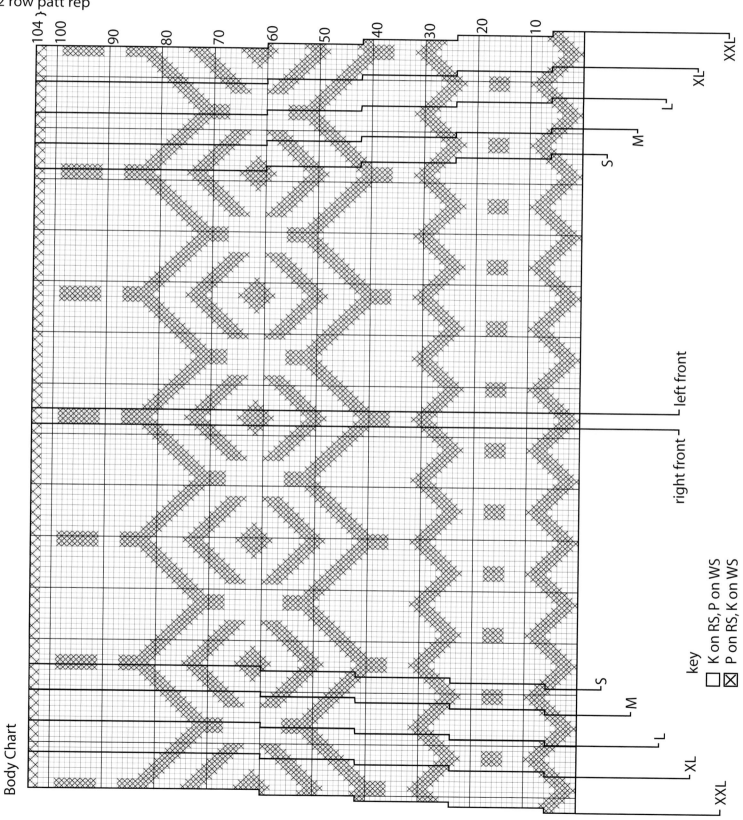

Body Chart

key
☐ K on RS, P on WS
☒ P on RS, K on WS

left front

right front

Sleeve Chart

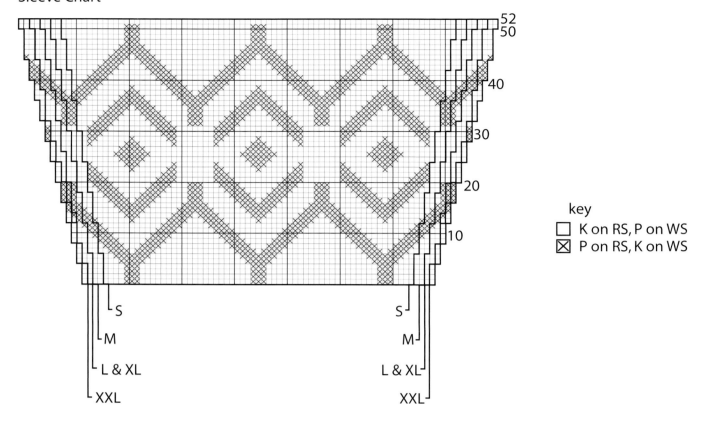

key
☐ K on RS, P on WS
☒ P on RS, K on WS

chart rows 1 to 102 **once only** and then repeating chart rows 103 and 104 **throughout**, now work in patt from chart for body as folls:
Dec 1 st at beg of 7th and 3 foll 18th rows. 47 [52: 58: 64: 71] sts.
Cont straight until left front matches back to beg of armhole shaping, ending with RS facing for next row.
Shape armhole
Keeping patt correct, cast off 4 [5: 6: 7: 8] sts at beg of next row. 43 [47: 52: 57: 63] sts.
Work 1 row.
Dec 1 st at armhole edge of next 3 [4: 4: 4: 4] rows. 40 [43: 48: 53: 59] sts.
Work 1 [0: 0: 0: 0] row, ending with RS facing for next row.
Shape front slope
Keeping patt correct, dec 1 st at end (front slope edge) of next and foll 4 [5: 7: 8: 10] alt rows **and at same time** dec 1 st at armhole edge of next 1 [1: 3: 5: 7] rows, then on foll 4 [5: 6: 6: 7] alt rows. 30 [31: 31: 33: 34] sts.
Dec 1 st at front slope edge **only** of 2nd and foll 7 [5: 3: 1: 0] alt rows, then on 3 [4: 5: 6: 6] foll 4th rows. 19 [21: 22: 25: 27] sts.
Cont straight until left front matches back to beg of shoulder shaping, ending with RS facing for next row.
Shape shoulder
Cast off 6 [7: 7: 8: 9] sts at beg of next and foll alt row.
Work 1 row.
Cast off rem 7 [7: 8: 9: 9] sts.

RIGHT FRONT
Using 5mm (US 8) needles cast on 59 [63: 71: 75: 83] sts.

Row 1 (RS): K3, *P2, K2, rep from * to end.
Row 2: P2, *K2, P2, rep from * to last st, K1.
These 2 rows form rib.
Cont in rib, dec 1 st at end of 21st and foll 18th row. 57 [61: 69: 73: 81] sts.
Work a further 6 rows, ending with **WS** facing for next row.
Place pocket
Next row (WS): Rib 11 [11: 15: 15: 17], cast off next 26 [26: 28: 28: 31] sts in rib, rib to end.
Change to 5½mm (US 9) needles.
Next row (RS): K5 [6: 4: 6: 5], K2tog, K7 [10: 8: 13: 12], K2tog, (K8, K2tog) 0 [0: 1: 0: 0] times, K4 [4: 0: 7: 12], with RS facing K across 24 [24: 26: 26: 28] sts of second pocket lining, (K2tog) 1 [0: 1: 0: 0] times, K3 [4: 8: 8: 11], K2tog, K4 [5: 3: 5: 4]. 51 [56: 62: 68: 75] sts.
Beg with a P row, work in st st for 3 rows, ending with RS facing for next row.
Beg and ending rows as indicated, working chart rows 1 to 102 **once only** and then repeating chart rows 103 and 104 **throughout**, now work in patt from chart for body as folls:
Dec 1 st at end of 7th and 3 foll 18th rows. 47 [52: 58: 64: 71] sts.
Complete to match left front, reversing shapings.

SLEEVES
Using 5½mm (US 9) needles cast on 50 [50: 54: 54: 54] sts.
Work in rib as given for back for 12 cm.
Change to 5mm (US 8) needles.
Cont in rib until work meas 20 cm, dec [inc: dec: dec: inc] 1 st at end of last row and ending with RS facing for next row.
49 [51: 53: 53: 55] sts.
Change to 5½mm (US 9) needles.

Beg with a K row, work in st st, shaping sides by inc 1 st at each end of 3rd and 3 [4: 4: 4: 4] foll 4th rows. 57 [61: 63: 63: 65] sts.
Work 5 [3: 3: 3: 3] rows, ending with RS facing for next row.
Beg and ending rows as indicated, now work in patt from chart for sleeve as folls:
Inc 1 st at each end of next and 0 [0: 2: 8: 11] foll 4th rows, then on 8 [8: 7: 3: 1] foll 6th rows, taking inc sts into patt.
75 [79: 83: 87: 91] sts.
Work 3 [3: 1: 1: 1] rows, ending after chart row 52 and with RS facing for next row.
Beg with a K row, complete sleeve in st st as folls:
Inc 1 st at each end of 3rd [3rd: 5th: 5th: 5th] row. 77 [81: 85: 89: 93] sts.
Cont straight until sleeve meas 54 [55: 56: 56: 56] cm, ending with RS facing for next row.
Shape top
Cast off 4 [5: 6: 7: 8] sts at beg of next 2 rows. 69 [71: 73: 75: 77] sts.
Dec 1 st at each end of next 5 rows, then on every foll alt row to 45 sts, then on foll 9 rows, ending with RS facing for next row. 27 sts.
Cast off 4 sts at beg of next 2 rows.
Cast off rem 19 sts.

MAKING UP
Press as described on the information page.
Join both shoulder seams using back stitch, or mattress stitch if preferred.
Front bands and collar
With RS facing and using 5mm (US 8) circular needle, beg and ending at cast-on edges, pick up and knit 115 [117: 119: 121: 123] sts up right front opening edge to beg of front slope

shaping, 46 [48: 53: 55: 56] sts up right front slope, 38 [38: 40: 40: 42] sts from back, 46 [48: 53: 55: 56] sts down left front slope to beg of front slope shaping, then 115 [117: 119: 121: 123] sts down left front opening edge.
360 [368: 384: 392: 400] sts.
Row 1 (WS): K1, P2, *K2, P2, rep from * to last st, K1.
Row 2: K3, *P2, K2, rep from * to last st, K1.
These 2 rows form rib.
Now shape collar as folls:
Row 3 (WS of body, RS of collar): Rib 199 [203: 212: 216: 221], wrap next st (by slipping next st from left needle to right needle, taking yarn to opposite side of work between needles, then slipping same st back onto left needle – when working back across wrapped sts, work the wrapped st and the wrapping loop tog as 1 st) and turn.
Row 4: Rib 38 [38: 40: 40: 42], wrap next st and turn.
Row 5: Rib 41 [41: 43: 43: 45], wrap next st and turn.
Row 6: Rib 44 [44: 46: 46: 48], wrap next st and turn.
Row 7: Rib 47 [47: 49: 49: 51], wrap next st and turn.
Row 8: Rib 50 [50: 52: 52: 54], wrap next st and turn.
Cont in this way, working 3 more sts on every row before wrapping next st and turning, until the foll row has been worked:
Next row (WS of collar): Rib 128 [128: 142: 148: 150], wrap next st and turn.
Next row: Rib to end.
Now working across all sts, cont as folls:
Next row (RS of body): Rib 4 [5: 4: 5: 4], *yrn (to make a buttonhole), work 2 tog, rib 25 [25: 26: 26: 27], rep from * 3 times more, yrn (to make 5th buttonhole), work 2 tog, rib to end.
Work a further 4 rows, ending with **WS** of body (RS of collar) facing for next row.
Cast off **very loosely** in rib.
See information page for finishing instructions, setting in sleeves using the set-in method and reversing sleeve seam for first 12 cm for turn-back cuff. Fold 10 cm cuff to RS.

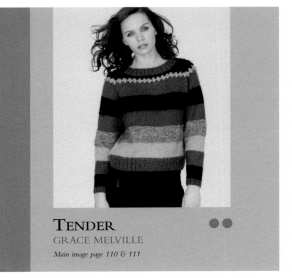

TENDER
GRACE MELVILLE
Main image page 110 & 111

YARN

	S	M	L	XL	XXL	

To fit bust
81–86 91–97 102–107 112–117 122–127 cm
32–34 36–38 40–42 44–46 48–50 in

Rowan Kid Classic and Kidsilk Haze

	S	M	L	XL	XXL	
A KCl Bear 817						
	2	2	2	2	2	x 50 g
B KCl Straw 851						
	3	3	3	3	4	x 50 g
C KSH Blood 627						
	2	2	2	2	3	x 25 g
D KCl Earth 872						
	2	2	3	3	3	x 50 g
E KCl Peat 832						
	1	1	1	1	1	x 50 g

NEEDLES
1 pair 4½mm (no 7) (US 7) needles
1 pair 5mm (no 6) (US 8) needles

TENSION
19 sts and 25 rows to 10 cm measured over st st using 5mm (US 8) needles.

SPECIAL ABBREVIATION
MB = (K1, P1, K1, P1) all into next st, turn and P4, turn and K4, lift 2nd, 3rd and 4th sts on right needle over first st and off right needle.

BACK
Using 4½mm (US 7) needles and yarn A cast on 102 [110: 122: 134: 146] sts.
Row 1 (RS): K2, *P2, K2, rep from * to end.
Row 2: P2, *K2, P2, rep from * to end.
These 2 rows form rib.
Work in rib for a further 16 rows, dec [inc: dec: dec: inc] 1 st at end of last row and ending with RS facing for next row.
101 [111: 121: 133: 147] sts.
Change to 5mm (US 8) needles.

Beg with a K row, cont in st st throughout as folls:
Using yarn A, work 0 [0: 2: 2: 2] rows.
Break off yarn A and join in yarn B.
Using yarn B, work 18 [18: 20: 20: 20] rows. Join in yarn C.
Using yarns B and C held together, work 18 [18: 20: 20: 20] rows.
Break off yarns B and C and join in yarn D.
Using yarn D, work 18 [18: 20: 20: 20] rows, ending with RS facing for next row.
Break off yarn D and join in yarn E.
Using yarn E, work 2 [4: 0: 2: 6] rows, ending with RS facing for next row. (Back should meas 29 [30: 32: 33: 34] cm.)
Shape raglan armholes
Cast off 3 sts at beg of next 2 rows.

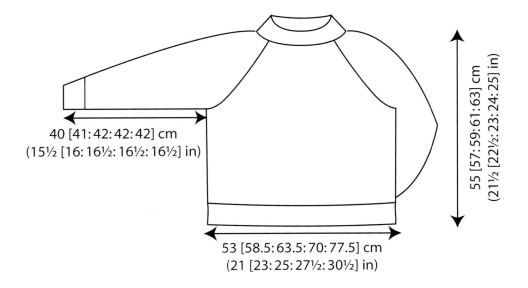

40 [41: 42: 42: 42] cm
(15½ [16: 16½: 16½: 16½] in)

53 [58.5: 63.5: 70: 77.5] cm
(21 [23: 25: 27½: 30½] in)

55 [57: 59: 61: 63] cm
(21½ [22½: 23: 24: 25] in)

95 [105: 115: 127: 141] sts.

Dec 1 st at each end of next 1 [5: 11: 16: 12] rows, then on 2 [0: 0: 0: 0] foll 4th rows, then on foll 2 [3: 3: 0: 0] alt rows.
85 [89: 87: 95: 117] sts.

Work 1 [1: 1: 0: 0] row, ending with RS facing for next row.

Break off yarn E and join in yarn A.

Using yarn A, dec 1 st at each end of next 1 [1: 1: 5: 19] rows, then on foll 8 [8: 9: 7: 0] alt rows. 67 [71: 67: 71: 79] sts.

Work 1 row, ending with RS facing for next row.

Break off yarn A and join in yarn B.

Next row (RS): Using yarn B, K2tog, K1, MB, ★K3, MB, rep from ★ to last 3 sts, K1, K2tog. 65 [69: 65: 69: 77] sts.

Using yarn B and beg with a P row, work in st st for 3 rows, dec 1 st at each end of 2nd of these rows and ending with RS facing for next row. 63 [67: 63: 67: 75] sts.

Break off yarn B, join in yarn E and complete work using yarn E **only.★★**

Now work in bobble patt as folls:

Row 1 (RS): K2tog, K1, MB, ★K3, MB, rep from ★ to last 3 sts, K1, K2tog. 61 [65: 61: 65: 73] sts.

Row 2: Purl.

Row 3: K2tog, K to last 2 sts, K2tog. 59 [63: 59: 63: 71] sts.

Row 4: Purl.

These 4 rows form bobble patt and cont raglan shaping.

Cont in bobble patt, dec 1 st at each end of next and foll 7 [9: 6: 8: 11] alt rows. 43 [43: 45: 45: 47] sts.

Work 1 row, ending with RS facing for next row.

Cast off.

FRONT

Work as given for back to ★★.

Now working in bobble patt as given for back, cont as folls:

Work 2 [6: 0: 2: 8] rows, dec 1 st at each end of next [next: –: next: next] and foll 0 [2: –: 0: 3] alt rows and ending with RS facing for next row. 61 [61: 63: 65: 67] sts.

Shape front neck

Next row (RS): K2tog, patt 12 [12: 12: 14: 14] sts and turn, leaving rem sts on a holder.

Work each side of neck separately.

Keeping patt correct, dec 1 st at neck edge of next 6 rows, then on foll 1 [1: 1: 2: 2] alt rows **and at same time** dec 1 st at raglan armhole edge of 2nd and foll 3 [3: 3: 4: 4] alt rows. 2 sts.

Work 1 row.

Next row (RS): K2tog and fasten off.

With RS facing, rejoin yarn to rem sts, cast off centre 33 [33: 35: 33: 35] sts, patt to last 2 sts, K2tog. 13 [13: 13: 15: 15] sts.

Complete to match first side, reversing shapings.

SLEEVES

Using 4½mm (US 7) needles and yarn D [D: D: D: E] cast on 38 [42: 42: 42: 46] sts.

Working in rib as given for back, cont as folls:

Sizes S, M, L and XL only

Using yarn D, work 8 [8: 6: 4: –] rows.

Break off yarn D and join in yarn E.

All sizes

Using yarn E, work 10 [10: 12: 14: 18] rows, inc [dec: inc: inc: dec] 1 st at centre of last row and ending with RS facing for next row. 39 [41: 43: 43: 45] sts.

Change to 5mm (US 8) needles.

Beg with a K row, now work in st st as folls:

Using yarn E, work 8 [8: 8: 6: 2] rows, inc 1 [1: 1: 1: 0] st at each end of 3rd [3rd: 3rd: 3rd: 0] and 1 [1: 1: 0: 0] foll 4th row.
43 [45: 47: 45: 45] sts.

Break off yarn E and join in yarn A.

Using yarn A, work 18 [18: 20: 20: 20] rows, inc 1 st at each end of 3rd [3rd: 3rd: next: next] and 3 [3: 4: 4: 4] foll 4th rows.
51 [53: 57: 55: 55] sts.

Break off yarn A and join in yarn B.

Using yarn B, work 18 [18: 20: 20: 20] rows, inc 1 st at each end of next [next: 3rd: next: next] and 4 foll 4th rows.
61 [63: 67: 65: 65] sts.

Join in yarn C.

Using yarns B and C held together, work 18 [18: 20: 20: 20] rows, inc 1 st at each end of 3rd [3rd: 3rd: next: next] and 3 [3: 2: 4: 4] foll 4th rows, then on 0 [0: 1: 0: 0] foll 6th row.
69 [71: 75: 75: 75] sts.

Break off yarns B and C and join in yarn D.

Using yarn D, work 18 [18: 20: 20: 20] rows, inc 1 st at each end of next [next: 3rd: next: next] and 2 [1: 0: 1: 2] foll 4th rows, then on 1 [2: 2: 2: 1] foll 6th rows.
77 [79: 81: 83: 83] sts.

Break off yarn D and join in yarn E.

Using yarn E, work 2 [4: 0: 2: 6] rows, inc 0 [0: 0: 0: 1] st at each end of 0 [0: 0: 0: next] row and ending with RS facing for next row.
77 [79: 81: 83: 85] sts. (Sleeve should meas 40 [41: 42: 42: 42] cm.)

Shape raglan

Cast off 3 sts at beg of next 2 rows. 71 [73: 75: 77: 79] sts.

Dec 1 st at each end of next 7 rows, then on foll 3 [2: 5: 4: 2] alt rows. 51 [55: 51: 55: 61] sts.

Work 1 row, ending with RS facing for next row.

Break off yarn E and join in yarn A.

Using yarn A, dec 1 st at each end of next and foll 8 [8: 9: 9: 9] alt rows. 33 [37: 31: 35: 41] sts.

Work 1 row, ending with RS facing for next row.

Break off yarn A and join in yarn B.

Next row (RS): Using yarn B, K2tog, K2 [2: 1: 1: 2], MB, ★K3, MB, rep from ★ to last 4 [4: 3: 3: 4] sts, K2 [2: 1: 1: 2], K2tog.
31 [35: 29: 33: 39] sts.

Using yarn B and beg with a P row, work in st st for 3 rows, dec 1 st at each end of 2nd of these rows and ending with RS facing for next row. 29 [33: 27: 31: 37] sts.

Break off yarn B, join in yarn E and complete work using yarn E **only**.

Now work in bobble patt as folls:

Row 1 (RS): K2tog, K2 [2: 1: 1: 2], MB, ★K3, MB, rep from ★ to last 4 [4: 3: 3: 4] sts, K2 [2: 1: 1: 2], K2tog. 27 [31: 25: 29: 35] sts.

Row 2: Purl.

Row 3: K2tog, K to last 2 sts, K2tog. 25 [29: 23: 27: 33] sts.

Row 4: Purl.

These 4 rows form bobble patt and cont raglan shaping.

Cont in bobble patt, dec 1 st at each end of next and foll 3 [5: 2: 4: 7] alt rows. 17 sts.

Work 1 row, ending with RS facing for next row.

Left sleeve only

Dec 1 st at each end of next row, then cast off 3 sts at beg of foll row. 12 sts.

Dec 1 st at beg of next row, then cast off 3 sts at beg of foll row. 8 sts.

Dec 1 st at each end of next row, then at beg of foll row. 5 sts.

Right sleeve only

Cast off 3 sts at beg and dec 1 st at end of next row. 13 sts.

Work 1 row.

Cast off 3 sts at beg and dec 1 st at end of next row, then dec 1 st at end of foll row. 8 sts.

Dec 1 st at each end of next row, then at end of foll row. 5 sts.

Both sleeves

Rep last 2 rows once more.

Next row (RS): K2tog and fasten off.

MAKING UP

Press as described on the information page.

Join both front and right back raglan seams using back stitch, or mattress stitch if preferred.

Neckband

With RS facing, using 4½mm (US 7) needles and yarn A, pick up and knit 10 sts from top of left sleeve, 10 [10: 10: 12: 12] sts down left side of neck, 32 [32: 34: 33: 35] sts from front, 10 [10: 10: 12: 12] sts up right side of neck, 10 sts from top of right sleeve, then 42 [42: 44: 45: 47] sts from back.
114 [114: 118: 122: 126] sts.

Beg with row 2, work in rib as given for back for 10 rows, ending with **WS** facing for next row.

Cast off in rib (on **WS**).

See information page for finishing instructions.

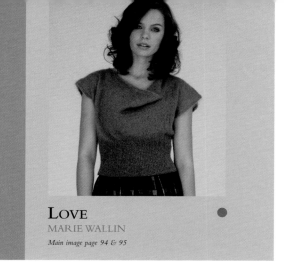

LOVE
MARIE WALLIN
Main image page 94 & 95

YARN

	S	M	L	XL	XXL
To fit bust					
	81-86	91-97	102-107	112-117	122-127 cm
	32-34	36-38	40-42	44-46	48-50 in

Rowan Baby Alpaca DK and Kidsilk Haze
A Alp Cheviot 207

2	3	3	3	3	x 50 g

B KSH Majestic 589

3	3	3	4	4	x 25 g

NEEDLES

1 pair 3¼mm (no 10) (US 3) needles

TENSION

25 sts and 34 rows to 10 cm measured over st st using 3¼mm (US 3) needles and Kidsilk Haze.

BACK

Using 3¼mm (US 3) needles and yarn A cast on 115 [127: 143: 157: 175] sts.
Row 1 (RS): K1, *P1, K1, rep from * to end.
Row 2: P1, *K1, P1, rep from * to end.
These 2 rows form rib.
Cont in rib until back meas 16 cm, ending with RS facing for next row.
Break off yarn A and join in yarn B.
Beg with a K row, cont in st st throughout as folls:**★★**
Work 20 [24: 28: 30: 34] rows, ending with RS facing for next row. (Back should meas 22 [23: 24: 25: 26] cm.)
Shape for cap sleeves
Place markers at both ends of last row to denote base of armhole openings.
Inc 1 st at each end of 7th and 3 [1: 7: 5: 3] foll 8th [8th: 10th: 10th: 10th] rows, then on 4 [6:

0: 2: 4] foll 10th [10th: 0: 12th: 12th] rows.
131 [143: 159: 173: 191] sts.
Work 11 rows, ending with RS facing for next row. (Work should meas 24 [25: 26: 27: 28] cm from markers.)
Shape shoulders and back neck
Cast off 13 [15: 17: 19: 22] sts at beg of next 2 rows. 105 [113: 125: 135: 147] sts.
Next row (RS): Cast off 13 [15: 17: 19: 22] sts, K until there are 16 [18: 21: 24: 26] sts on right needle and turn, leaving rem sts on a holder.
Work each side of neck separately.
Cast off 4 sts at beg of next row.
Cast off rem 12 [14: 17: 20: 22] sts.
With RS facing, rejoin yarn to rem sts, cast off centre 47 [47: 49: 49: 51] sts, K to end.
Complete to match first side, reversing shapings.

FRONT

Work as given for back to **★★**.
Inc 1 st at each end of 3rd and 5 [7: 8: 9: 6] foll 3rd rows, then on 0 [0: 0: 0: 3] foll 4th rows.
127 [143: 161: 177: 195] sts.
Work 2 [0: 1: 0: 1] rows, ending with RS facing for next row.
Shape for cap sleeves
Place markers at both ends of last row to denote base of armhole openings.
Inc 1 st at each end of next [3rd: 2nd: 3rd: 3rd] and 26 [18: 11: 4: 0] foll 3rd rows, then on 0 [6: 12: 18: 22] foll 4th rows.

181 [193: 209: 223: 241] sts.
Work 3 [5: 5: 5: 5] rows, ending with RS facing for next row.
Shape shoulders
Cast off 13 [15: 17: 19: 22] sts at beg of next 4 rows, then 12 [14: 17: 20: 22] sts at beg of foll 2 rows.
Leave rem 105 [105: 107: 107: 109] sts on a holder but do **NOT** break yarn.

MAKING UP

Press as described on the information page.
Join right shoulder seam using back stitch, or mattress stitch if preferred.
Neckband
With RS facing, using 3¼mm (US 3) needles and ball of yarn B left with front, K across 105 [105: 107: 107: 109] sts on front holder, then pick up and knit 55 [55: 57: 57: 59] sts from back. 160 [160: 164: 164: 168] sts.
Work in g st for 2 rows, ending with **WS** facing for next row.
Cast off **very loosely** knitwise (on **WS**).
Join left shoulder and neckband seam.
Armhole borders (both alike)
With RS facing, using 3¼mm (US 3) needles and yarn B, pick up and knit 120 [124: 130: 134: 140] sts evenly along row-end edges between markers.
Work in g st for 2 rows, ending with **WS** facing for next row.
Cast off knitwise (on **WS**).
See information page for finishing instructions.

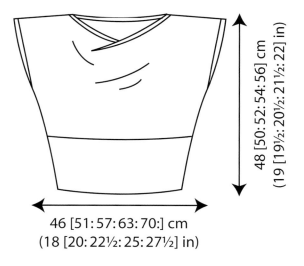

48 [50: 52: 54: 56] cm
(19 [19½: 20½: 21½: 22] in)

46 [51: 57: 63: 70:] cm
(18 [20: 22½: 25: 27½] in)

BIRCH
MARTIN STOREY

Main image page 20 & 21

YARN

	S	M	L	XL	XXL	

To fit bust
81-86 91-97 102-107 112-117 122-127 cm
32-34 36-38 40-42 44-46 48-50 in

Rowan Felted Tweed Aran

A Mahogany 734
13   13   14   15   16   x 50 g
B Cork 721
1   1   1   2   2   x 50 g
C Pebble 720
3   3   3   4   4   x 50 g

NEEDLES

1 pair 4½mm (no 7) (US 7) needles
1 pair 5mm (no 6) (US 8) needles
4½mm (no 7) (US 7) circular needle,
40 cm long

TENSION

16 sts and 23 rows to 10 cm measured over
patterned st st using 5mm (US 8) needles.

BACK

Using 4½mm (US 7) needles and yarn A cast
on 91 [99: 109: 119: 129] sts.
Row 1 (RS): K0 [0: 2: 1: 0], P2 [0: 3: 3: 3],
*K3, P3, rep from * to last 5 [3: 2: 1: 0] sts,
K3 [3: 2: 1: 0], P2 [0: 0: 0: 0].
Row 2: P0 [0: 2: 1: 0], K2 [0: 3: 3: 3], *P3,
K3, rep from * to last 5 [3: 2: 1: 0] sts, P3 [3: 2:
1: 0], K2 [0: 0: 0: 0].
These 2 rows form rib.
Work in rib for a further 16 rows, ending with
RS facing for next row.
Change to 5mm (US 8) needles.
Beg with a K row, work in st st for 2 rows,
ending with RS facing for next row.
Beg and ending rows as indicated and using the
intarsia technique as described on the
information page, now work in patt from chart
for body, which is worked entirely in st st beg
with a K row, until all 32 rows have been
completed, ending with RS facing for
next row.
Break off contrasts and cont using yarn A **only**.
Beg with a K row, cont straight in st st until
back meas 48 [49: 50: 51: 52] cm, ending with
RS facing for next row.
Shape armholes
Cast off 3 sts at beg of next 2 rows.
85 [93: 103: 113: 123] sts.

Next row (RS): K1, sl 1, K1, psso, K to last
3 sts, K2tog, K1.
Work 1 row.
Rep last 2 rows 3 times more.
77 [85: 95: 105: 115] sts.
Cont straight until armhole meas 23 [24: 25:
26: 27] cm, ending with RS facing for next
row.
Shape shoulders and back neck
Cast off 8 [9: 10: 12: 13] sts at beg of next
2 rows. 61 [67: 75: 81: 89] sts.
Next row (RS): Cast off 8 [9: 10: 12: 13] sts,
K until there are 11 [13: 15: 16: 18] sts on right
needle and turn, leaving rem sts on a holder.
Work each side of neck separately.
Cast off 4 sts at beg of next row.
Cast off rem 7 [9: 11: 12: 14] sts.
With RS facing, rejoin yarn to rem sts, cast off
centre 23 [23: 25: 25: 27] sts, K to end.
Complete to match first side, reversing
shapings.

FRONT

Work as given for back until 10 [10: 12: 12: 14]
rows less have been worked than on back to
beg of shoulder shaping, ending with RS facing
for next row.
Shape front neck
Next row (RS): K29 [33: 38: 43: 48] and
turn, leaving rem sts on a holder.
Work each side of neck separately.
Next row (WS): P1, P2tog, P to end.
Next row: K to last 3 sts, K2tog, K1.
Working all decreases as set by last 2 rows, dec
1 st at neck edge of next 2 rows, then on foll
2 [2: 3: 3: 4] alt rows. 23 [27: 31: 36: 40] sts.
Work 1 row, ending with RS facing for
next row.
Shape shoulder
Cast off 8 [9: 10: 12: 13] sts at beg of next and
foll alt row.
Work 1 row.
Cast off rem 7 [9: 11: 12: 14] sts.
With RS facing, rejoin yarn to rem sts, cast off

centre 19 sts, K to end.
Next row (WS): P to last 3 sts, P2tog tbl, P1.
Next row: K1, sl 1, K1, psso, K to end.
Complete to match first side, reversing
shapings.

SLEEVES

Using 4½mm (US 7) needles and yarn A cast
on 45 [47: 49: 49: 51] sts.
Row 1 (RS): K0 [1: 2: 2: 3], P3, *K3, P3, rep
from * to last 0 [1: 2: 2: 3] sts, K0 [1: 2: 2: 3].
Row 2: P0 [1: 2: 2: 3], K3, *P3, K3, rep from
* to last 0 [1: 2: 2: 3] sts, P0 [1: 2: 2: 3].
These 2 rows form rib.
Work in rib for a further 6 rows, ending with
RS facing for next row.
Change to 5mm (US 8) needles.
Beg with a K row, work in st st for 2 rows, inc
1 st at each end of first of these rows and
ending with RS facing for next row.
47 [49: 51: 51: 53] sts.
Beg and ending rows as indicated and using the
intarsia technique as described on the
information page, now work in patt from chart
for sleeve, which is worked entirely in st st beg
with a K row, as folls:
Inc 1 st at each end of 5th [5th: 5th: 3rd: 3rd]
and 0 [0: 0: 3: 6] foll 4th rows, then on 4 [4: 4:
2: 0] foll 6th rows, taking inc sts into patt.
57 [59: 61: 63: 67] sts.
Work 3 [3: 3: 5: 5] rows, ending after chart row
32 and with RS facing for next row.
Break off contrasts and cont using yarn A **only**.
Beg with a K row, work in st st, shaping sides
by inc 1 st at each end of 3rd [3rd: 3rd: next:
next] and every foll 6th row to 67 [75: 75:
83: 87] sts, then on every foll 8th [8th: 8th: -: -]
row until there are 73 [77: 79: -: -] sts.
Cont straight until sleeve meas 45 [46: 47:
47: 47] cm, ending with RS facing for
next row.
Shape top
Cast off 3 sts at beg of next 2 rows.
67 [71: 73: 77: 81] sts.

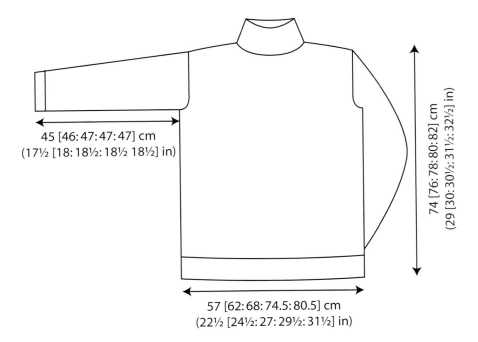

45 [46: 47: 47: 47] cm
(17½ [18: 18½: 18½: 18½] in)

57 [62: 68: 74.5: 80.5] cm
(22½ [24½: 27: 29½: 31½] in)

74 [76: 78: 80: 82] cm
(29 [30: 30½: 31½: 32½] in)

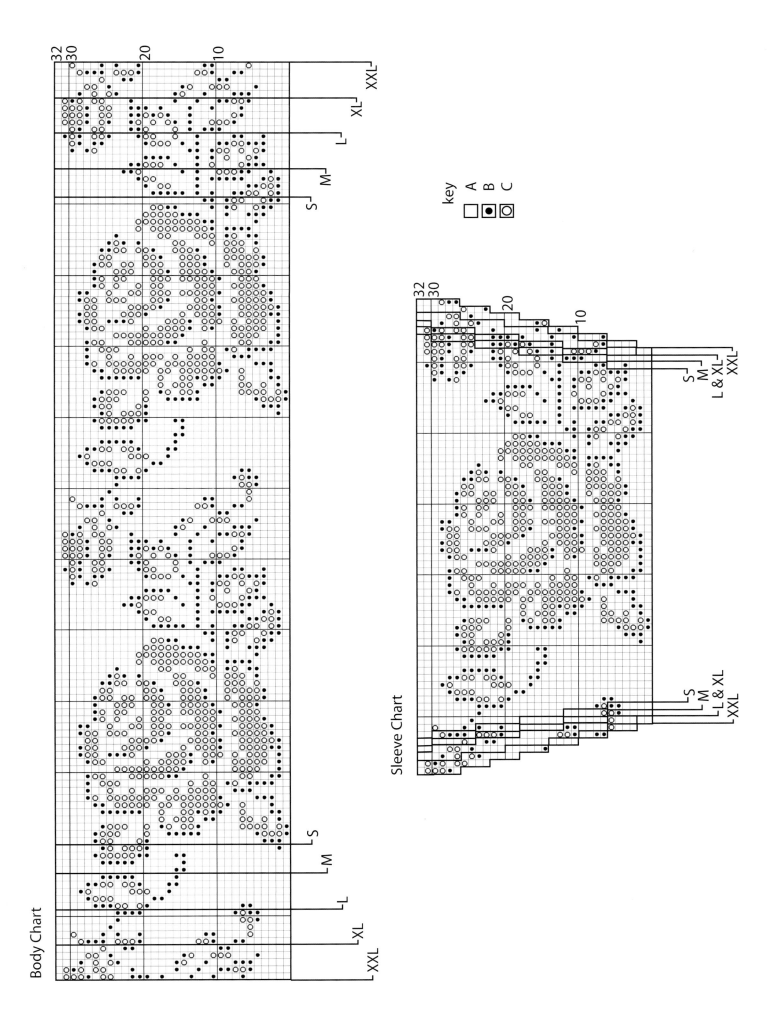

Body Chart

Sleeve Chart

key
A
B
C

Next row (RS): K1, sl 1, K1, psso, K to last 3 sts, K2tog, K1.
Work 1 row.
Rep last 2 rows twice more, then first of these 2 rows again, ending with **WS** facing for next row. 59 [63: 65: 69: 73] sts.
Next row (WS): P1, P2tog, P to last 3 sts, P2tog tbl, P1.
Cast off rem 57 [61: 63: 67: 71] sts.

MAKING UP
Press as described on the information page.
Join both shoulder seams using back stitch, or mattress stitch if preferred.
Neckband
With RS facing, using 4½mm (US 7) circular needle and yarn A, pick up and knit 14 [14: 16: 16: 18] sts down left side of neck, 19 sts from front, 14 [14: 16: 16: 18] sts up right side of neck, then 31 [31: 33: 33: 35] sts from back. 78 [78: 84: 84: 90] sts.
Round 1 (RS): ★K3, P3, rep from ★ to end.
Rep this round 20 times more.
Cast off in rib.
See information page for finishing instructions, setting in sleeves using the shallow set-in method.

HORNBEAM
MARTIN STOREY
Main image page 16 & 17

YARN

	S	M	L	XL	XXL	
To fit bust
81-86 91-97 102-107 112-117 122-127 cm
32-34 36-38 40-42 44-46 48-50 in
Rowan Felted Tweed Aran
A Cassis 723

| 9 | 10 | 11 | 11 | 12 | x 50 g |

B Plum 731

| 4 | 4 | 5 | 5 | 5 | x 50 g |

NEEDLES
1 pair 4½mm (no 7) (US 7) needles
1 pair 5mm (no 6) (US 8) needles
4½mm (no 7) (US 7) circular needle, 60 cm long

TENSION
16 sts and 23 rows to 10 cm measured over patterned st st using 5mm (US 8) needles.

BACK
Using 4½mm (US 7) needles and yarn A cast on 85 [93: 103: 113: 123] sts.
Row 1 (RS): K2 [0: 0: 0: 0], P3 [3: 2: 1: 0], ★K3, P3, rep from ★ to last 2 [0: 5: 4: 3] sts, K2 [0: 3: 3: 3], P0 [0: 2: 1: 0].
Row 2: P2 [0: 0: 0: 0], K3 [3: 2: 1: 0], ★P3, K3, rep from ★ to last 2 [0: 5: 4: 3] sts, P2 [0: 3: 3: 3], K0 [0: 2: 1: 0].
These 2 rows form rib.
Work in rib for a further 16 rows, ending with RS facing for next row.

Change to 5mm (US 8) needles.
Beg and ending rows as indicated, using a combination of the **fairisle** and **intarsia** techniques as described on the information page, working chart rows 1 to 34 **once only** and then repeating chart rows 35 to 114 **throughout**, now work in patt from chart, which is worked entirely in st st beg with a K row, as folls:
Work 91 [93: 95: 97: 99] rows, ending with **WS** facing for next row.★★ (Back should meas 47 [48: 49: 50: 51] cm.)
Shape for cap sleeves
Keeping patt correct, inc 1 st at each end of next 3 rows. 91 [99: 109: 119: 129] sts.
Place markers at both ends of last row to denote base of armhole openings.
Cont straight until armhole opening meas 23 [24: 25: 26: 27] cm from markers, ending with RS facing for next row.
Shape shoulders and back neck
Cast off 10 [12: 13: 15: 16] sts at beg of next 2 rows. 71 [75: 83: 89: 97] sts.
Next row (RS): Cast off 10 [12: 13: 15: 16] sts, patt until there are 15 [15: 17: 18: 20] sts on

right needle and turn, leaving rem sts on a holder.
Work each side of neck separately.
Cast off 4 sts at beg of next row.
Cast off rem 11 [11: 13: 14: 16] sts.
With RS facing, rejoin yarns to rem sts, cast off centre 21 [21: 23: 23: 25] sts, patt to end.
Complete to match first side, reversing shapings.

FRONT
Work as given for back to ★★.
Shape for cap sleeves
Keeping patt correct, inc 1 st at each end of next row, ending with RS facing for next row. 87 [95: 105: 115: 125] sts.
Divide for neck
Next row (RS): Inc in first st, patt 42 [46: 51: 56: 61] sts and turn, leaving rem sts on a holder.
Work each side of neck separately.
(**Note:** Front neck shaping is **NOT** shown on chart.)
Inc 1 st at end of next row.
45 [49: 54: 59: 64] sts.
Place marker at end of last row to denote base

74 [76: 78: 80: 82] cm
(29 [30: 30½: 31½: 32½] in)

53 [58: 64.5: 70.5: 77] cm
(21 [23: 25½: 28: 30½] in)

of armhole opening.
Keeping patt correct, dec 1 st at neck edge
of next and foll 4 [3: 4: 3: 3] alt rows, then on
9 [10: 10: 11: 12] foll 4th rows.
31 [35: 39: 44: 48] sts.
Cont straight until front matches back to beg
of shoulder shaping, ending with RS facing for
next row.

Shape shoulder
Cast off 10 [12: 13: 15: 16] sts at beg of next
and foll alt row.
Work 1 row.
Cast off rem 11 [11: 13: 14: 16] sts.
With RS facing, slip centre st onto a holder,
rejoin yarns to rem sts, patt to last st, inc in
last st.
Complete to match first side, reversing
shapings.

MAKING UP
Press as described on the information page.
Join both shoulder seams using back stitch, or
mattress stitch if preferred.

Neckband
With RS facing, using 4½mm (US 7) circular
needle and yarn A, pick up and knit 60 [60: 64:
64: 68] sts down left side of neck, K st on
holder at base of V and mark this st with a
coloured thread, pick up and knit 60 [60: 64:
64: 68] sts up right side of neck, then 34 [34:
34: 34: 38] sts from back.
155 [155: 163: 163: 175] sts.
Round 1 (RS): *K2, P2, rep from * to within
4 sts of marked st, K2, K2tog tbl, K marked st,
K2tog, **K2, P2, rep from ** to end.
This round sets position of rib.
Keeping rib correct, cont as folls:

Round 2: Rib to within 2 sts of marked st,
K2tog tbl, K marked st, K2tog, rib to end.
Rep last round 5 times more.
141 [141: 149: 149: 161] sts.
Cast off in rib, still dec either side of marked
st as before.

Armhole borders (both alike)
With RS facing, using 4½mm (US 7) needles
and yarn A, pick up and knit 102 [106: 106:
110: 110] sts evenly along armhole opening
edge between markers.
Row 1 (WS): P2, *K2, P2, rep from * to end.
Row 2: K2, *P2, K2, rep from * to end.
These 2 rows form rib.
Work in rib for a further 5 rows, ending with
RS facing for next row.
Cast off in rib.
See information page for finishing instructions.

key
□ A
▣ B

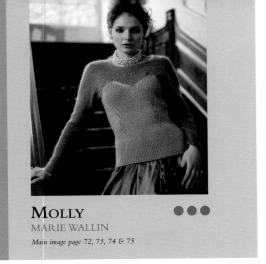

MOLLY
MARIE WALLIN

Main image page 72, 73, 74 & 75

● ● ●

YARN

	S	M	L	XL	XXL	

To fit bust
81-86 91-97 102-107 112-117 122-127 cm
32-34 36-38 40-42 44-46 48-50 in

Rowan Cashsoft DK and Kidsilk Haze
A DK Dusty 542
    5   5   6   6   7 x 50 g
B KSH Majestic 589
    4   4   5   5   5 x 25 g

NEEDLES

1 pair 2¼mm (no 13) (US 1) needles
1 pair 3¼mm (no 10) (US 3) needles
1 pair 3¾mm (no 9) (US 5) needles

TENSION

32 sts and 34 rows to 10 cm measured over rib using 3¾mm (US 5) needles and yarn A. 38 sts and 46 rows to 10 cm measured over st st using 2¼mm (US 1) needles and yarn B.

LOWER BACK

Using 3¼mm (US 3) needles and yarn A cast on 135 [151: 169: 189: 211] sts.
Row 1 (RS): K1 [1: 0: 0: 1], *P1, K1, rep from * to last 0 [0: 1: 1: 0] st, P0 [0: 1: 1: 0].
Row 2: P1 [1: 0: 0: 1], *K1, P1, rep from * to last 0 [0: 1: 1: 0] st, K0 [0: 1: 1: 0].
These 2 rows form rib.
Work in rib for a further 18 rows, dec 1 st at each end of 17th of these rows and ending with RS facing for next row.
133 [149: 167: 187: 209] sts.
Change to 3¾mm (US 5) needles.
Cont in rib, shaping side seams by dec 1 st at each end of 5th and 4 foll 6th rows.
123 [139: 157: 177: 199] sts.★★
Work 15 rows, ending with RS facing for next row.
Inc 1 st at each end of next and 5 foll 8th rows, taking inc sts into rib.
135 [151: 169: 189: 211] sts.
Cont straight until lower back meas 34 [35: 36: 37: 38] cm, ending with RS facing for next row.
Cast off in rib.

UPPER BACK

Using 2¼mm (US 1) needles and yarn B cast on 160 [180: 200: 224: 250] sts **loosely**.
Beg with a K row, work in st st as folls:
Work 8 rows, ending with RS facing for next row.

Shape armholes

Cast off 6 [8: 10: 12: 14] sts at beg of next 2 rows. 148 [164: 180: 200: 222] sts.
Dec 1 st at each end of next 7 [9: 11: 13: 15] rows, then on foll 6 [8: 9: 11: 13] alt rows.
122 [130: 140: 152: 166] sts.
Cont straight until armhole meas 18 [19: 20: 21: 22] cm, ending with RS facing for next row.

Shape shoulders and back neck

Next row (RS): Cast off 7 [8: 9: 10: 12] sts, K until there are 31 [34: 36: 41: 44] sts on right needle and turn, leaving rem sts on a holder. Work each side of neck separately.
Cast off 3 sts at beg of next row, 7 [8: 9: 10: 12] sts at beg of foll row, 3 sts at beg of next row, 7 [8: 9: 11: 12] sts at beg of foll row, then 3 sts at beg of next row.
Cast off rem 8 [9: 9: 11: 11] sts.
With RS facing, rejoin yarn to rem sts, cast off centre 46 [46: 50: 50: 54] sts, K to end.
Complete to match first side, reversing shapings.
Sew cast-on edge of upper back to cast-off edge of lower back.

MOTIFS (11 sts)

Row 1 (RS): K1, P1, K1, K2tog, M1P, P1, M1P, sl 1, K1, psso, K1, P1, K1.
Row 2: P1, K1, P2, K3, P2, K1, P1.
Row 3: K1, P1, K2tog, M1P, K1, P1, K1, M1P, sl 1, K1, psso, P1, K1.
Row 4: P1, (K1, P1) 5 times.
Row 5: K1, K2tog, M1P, (P1, K1) twice, P1, M1P, sl 1, K1, psso, K1.
Row 6: P2, K2, P1, K1, P1, K2, P2.
Row 7: K2tog, M1P, (K1, P1) 3 times, K1, M1P, sl 1, K1, psso.
Row 8: As row 4.
Row 9: K1, (P1, K1) 5 times.
Row 10: P1, (K1, P1) 5 times.
Rows 11 and 12: As rows 9 and 10.
Rows 13 to 36: As rows 1 to 12, twice.
Rows 37 to 44: As rows 1 to 8.
These 44 rows complete motif.

LOWER FRONT

Work as given for lower back to ★★.
Work 1 row, ending with RS facing for next row.

Place motifs

Next row (RS): Rib 30 [36: 43: 51: 60], work next 11 sts as row 1 of motif, rib 41 [45: 49: 53: 57], work next 11 sts as row 1 of motif, rib to end.
Next row: Rib 30 [36: 43: 51: 60], work next 11 sts as row 2 of motif, rib 41 [45: 49: 53: 57], work next 11 sts as row 2 of motif, rib to end.
These 2 rows set position of motifs.
Working appropriate rows of motifs until all 44 rows have been completed and then working all sts in rib, cont as folls:
Work 12 rows, ending with RS facing for next row.
Inc 1 st at each end of next and 5 foll 8th rows, taking inc sts into rib.
135 [151: 169: 189: 211] sts.
Cont straight until 1 row less has been worked than on lower back to cast-off edge, ending with WS facing for next row.
Next row (WS): Rib 67 [75: 84: 94: 105], inc in next st, rib 67 [75: 84: 94: 105].
136 [152: 170: 190: 212] sts.

Shape upper edge

Next row (RS): Cast off 15 [19: 24: 30: 37] sts in rib, rib 53 [57: 61: 65: 69] and slip these sts onto a holder, rib 53 [57: 61: 65: 69], cast off rem 15 [19: 24: 30: 37] sts in rib.
Break yarn.
With WS facing, rejoin yarn to last set of 53 [57: 61: 65: 69] sts and shape first point as folls:
★★★**Row 1 (WS):** K1, (P1, K1) twice, P2tog, rib to last 7 sts, P2tog tbl, (K1, P1) twice, K1.
Row 2: K2, P1, K1, P1, sl 1, K1, psso, rib to last 7 sts, K2tog, P1, K1, P1, K2.
49 [53: 57: 61: 65] sts.
Rep last 2 rows 9 [10: 11: 12: 13] times more, ending with WS facing for next row. 13 sts.

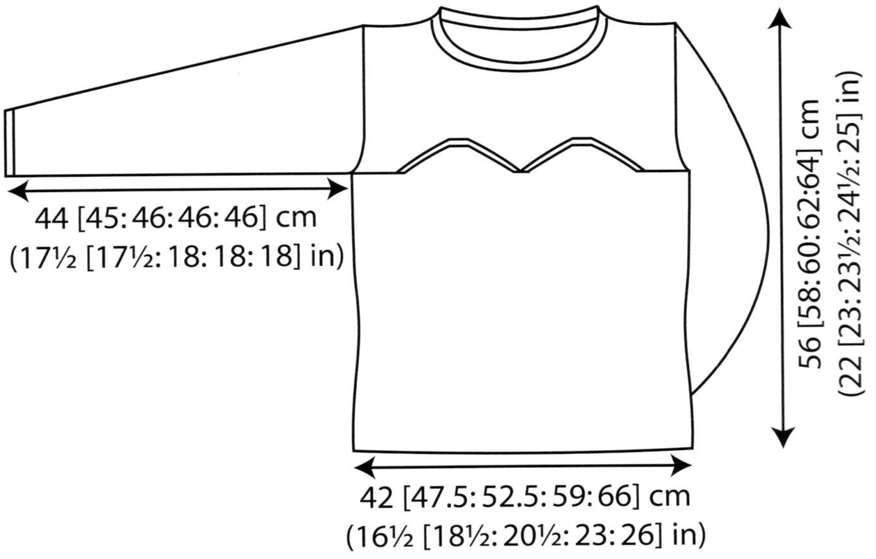

44 [45: 46: 46: 46] cm
(17½ [17½: 18: 18: 18] in)

56 [58: 60: 62: 64] cm
(22 [23: 23½: 24½: 25] in)

42 [47.5: 52.5: 59: 66] cm
(16½ [18½: 20½: 23: 26] in)

Next row (WS): K1, (P1, K1) twice, sl 1 purlwise, P2tog, psso, (K1, P1) twice, K1. Cast off rem 11 sts in rib.
With **WS** facing, rejoin yarn to rem set of 53 [57: 61: 65: 69] sts and work as given for first point from ★★★.

UPPER FRONT

Right side section
Using 2¼mm (US 1) needles and yarn B cast on 17 [23: 27: 35: 44] sts.
Beg with a K row, work in st st as folls:
Work 1 row, ending with **WS** facing for next row.
Inc 1 st at end of next row and at same edge on foll 3 rows. 21 [27: 31: 39: 48] sts.
Work 1 row.
Inc 1 st at shaped edge of next 3 rows, ending with **WS** facing for next row.
24 [30: 34: 42: 51] sts.

Shape armhole
Cast off 6 [8: 10: 12: 14] sts at beg and inc 1 st at end of next row. 19 [23: 25: 31: 38] sts.
★★★★Dec 1 st at armhole edge and inc 1 st at inner shaped edge of next row.
19 [23: 25: 31: 38] sts.
Dec 1 st at armhole edge of next row.
18 [22: 24: 30: 37] sts.
Inc 1 st at inner shaped edge of next 5 rows **and at same time** dec 1 st at armhole edge of next 5 rows. 18 [22: 24: 30: 37] sts.
Dec 0 [1: 1: 1: 1] st at armhole edge of next row. 18 [21: 23: 29: 36] sts.
Inc 1 st at inner shaped edge of next 5 rows **and at same time** dec 1 st at armhole edge of next 1 [1: 3: 5: 5] rows, then on foll 2 [2: 1: 0: 0] alt rows. 20 [23: 24: 29: 36] sts.
Dec 0 [0: 0: 0: 1] st at armhole edge of next row. 20 [23: 24: 29: 35] sts.

Sizes L, XL and XXL only
Inc 1 st at inner shaped edge of next 5 rows **and at same time** dec 1 st at armhole edge of next and foll 2 alt rows. - [-: 26: 31: 37] sts.
Work 1 row.

All sizes
Inc 1 st at inner shaped edge of next 6 [8: 6: 8: 10] rows, ending with RS facing for next row, **and at same time** dec 1 st at armhole edge of next and foll 2 [3: 2: 3: 4] alt rows.
23 [27: 29: 35: 42] sts.★★★★
Break yarn and leave sts on a holder.

Centre section
Using 2¼mm (US 1) needles and yarn B cast on 2 sts.

Beg with a K row, work in st st as folls:
Work 1 row, ending with **WS** facing for next row.
Inc 1 st at each end of next 4 rows. 10 sts.
Work 1 row.
Inc 1 st at each end of next 5 rows. 20 sts.
Rep last 6 rows 2 [2: 3: 3: 3] times more.
40 [40: 50: 50: 50] sts.
Work 1 row.
Inc 1 st at each end of next 6 [8: 6: 8: 10] rows, ending with RS facing for next row.
52 [56: 62: 66: 70] sts.
Break yarn and leave sts on a 2nd holder.

Left side section
Using 2¼mm (US 1) needles and yarn B cast on 17 [23: 27: 35: 44] sts.
Beg with a K row, work in st st as folls:
Work 1 row, ending with **WS** facing for next row.
Inc 1 st at beg of next row and at same edge on foll 3 rows. 21 [27: 31: 39: 48] sts.
Work 1 row.
Inc 1 st at shaped edge of next 2 rows, ending with RS facing for next row.
23 [29: 33: 41: 50] sts.

Shape armhole
Cast off 6 [8: 10: 12: 14] sts at beg and inc 1 st at end of next row. 18 [22: 24: 30: 37] sts.
Inc 1 st at beg of next row.
19 [23: 25: 31: 38] sts.
Now work as given for right side section from ★★★★ to ★★★★.

Join sections
Next row (RS): Work across sts of left side section as folls: (K2tog) 0 [1: 1: 1: 1] times, K to end, turn and cast on 12 sts, turn and K 52 [56: 62: 66: 70] sts of centre section, turn and cast on 12 sts, turn and work across sts of right side section as folls: K to last 0 [2: 2: 2: 2] sts, (K2tog) 0 [1: 1: 1: 1] times.
122 [132: 142: 158: 176] sts.
Dec 0 [1: 1: 1: 1] st at each end of 2nd and foll 0 [0: 0: 2: 4] alt rows.
122 [130: 140: 152: 166] sts.
Cont straight until 30 [30: 34: 34: 38] rows less have been worked than on upper back to beg of shoulder shaping, ending with RS facing for next row.

Shape front neck
Next row (RS): K46 [50: 54: 60: 66] and turn, leaving rem sts on a holder.
Work each side of neck separately.
Dec 1 st at neck edge of next 10 rows, then on foll 5 alt rows, then on 2 [2: 3: 3: 4] foll 4th

rows. 29 [33: 36: 42: 47] sts.
Work 1 row, ending with RS facing for next row.

Shape shoulder
Cast off 7 [8: 9: 10: 12] sts at beg of next and foll alt row, then 7 [8: 9: 11: 12] sts at beg of foll alt row.
Work 1 row.
Cast off rem 8 [9: 9: 11: 11] sts.
With RS facing, rejoin yarn to rem sts, cast off centre 30 [30: 32: 32: 34] sts, K to end.
Complete to match first side, reversing shapings.
Sew shaped lower edge of upper front to shaped upper edge of lower front.

SLEEVES
Using 2¼mm (US 1) needles and yarn B cast on 65 [69: 73: 73: 77] sts.
Work in g st for 6 rows, ending with RS facing for next row.
Beg with a K row, work in st st, shaping sides by inc 1 st at each end of 5th [5th: 5th: 5th: 3rd] and every foll 6th row to 91 [97: 105: 129: 139] sts, then on every foll 8th [8th: 8th: 8th: -] row until there are 115 [121: 127: 133: -] sts.
Cont straight until sleeve meas 44 [45: 46: 46: 46] cm, ending with RS facing for next row.

Shape top
Cast off 6 [8: 10: 12: 14] sts at beg of next 2 rows. 103 [105: 107: 109: 111] sts.
Dec 1 st at each end of next 7 rows, then on every foll alt row to 51 sts, then on foll 11 rows, ending with RS facing for next row.
29 sts.
Cast off 4 sts at beg of next 2 rows.
Cast off rem 21 sts.

MAKING UP
Press as described on the information page.
Join right shoulder seam using back stitch, or mattress stitch if preferred.
Neckband
With RS facing, using 2¼mm (US 1) needles and yarn B, pick up and knit 30 [30: 34: 34: 38] down left side of neck, 30 [30: 32: 32: 34] sts from front, 30 [30: 34: 34: 38] sts up right side of neck, then 64 [64: 68: 68: 72] sts from back.
154 [154: 168: 168: 182] sts.
Work in g st for 4 rows, ending with **WS** facing for next row.
Cast off knitwise (on **WS**).
See information page for finishing instructions, setting in sleeves using the set-in method.

BONNIE

MARTIN STOREY

Main image page 58 & 59

YARN

8	10	12	14	16	18	20	22

To fit bust

81	86	91	97	102	107	112	117	cm
32	34	36	38	40	42	44	46	in

Rowan Cashsoft DK

13	14	14	15	15	16	17	17	x 50 g

(photographed in Lime 509)

NEEDLES

1 pair 3¼mm (no 10) (US 3) needles
1 pair 4mm (no 8) (US 6) needles
Cable needle

TENSION

36 sts and 30 rows to 10 cm measured over patt using 4mm (US 6) needles.

SPECIAL ABBREVIATION

C7F = slip next 3 sts onto cable needle and leave at front of work, (K1 tbl, P1) twice, then K1 tbl, P1, K1 tbl from cable needle.

BACK

Using 3¼mm (US 3) needles cast on 145 [153: 161: 171: 181: 193: 203: 215] sts.
Row 1 (RS): (K1 tbl) 0 [1: 1: 1: 0: 1: 1: 1] times, (P1, K1 tbl) 7 [4: 6: 4: 7: 5: 3: 6] times, ★(P1, K1 tbl) 4 times, P1, rep from ★ 12 [14: 14: 16: 16: 18: 20: 20] times more, (K1 tbl, P1) 7 [4: 6: 4: 7: 5: 3: 6] times, (K1 tbl) 0 [1: 1: 1: 0: 1: 1: 1] times.
Row 2: (P1 tbl) 0 [1: 1: 1: 0: 1: 1: 1] times, (K1, P1 tbl) 7 [4: 6: 4: 7: 5: 3: 6] times, ★(K1, P1 tbl) 4 times, K1, rep from ★ 12 [14: 14: 16: 16: 18: 20: 20] times more, (P1 tbl, K1) 7 [4: 6: 4: 7: 5: 3: 6] times, (P1 tbl) 0 [1: 1: 1: 0: 1: 1: 1] times.
These 2 rows form rib.
Work in rib for a further 14 rows, ending with RS facing for next row.
Change to 4mm (US 6) needles.
Now work in patt as folls:
Row 1 (RS): P14 [9: 13: 9: 14: 11: 7: 13], ★(P1, K1 tbl) 4 times, P1, rep from ★ 12 [14: 14: 16: 16: 18: 20: 20] times more, P14 [9: 13: 9: 14: 11: 7: 13].
Row 2: K14 [9: 13: 9: 14: 11: 7: 13], ★(K1, P1 tbl) 4 times, K1, rep from ★ 12 [14: 14: 16: 16: 18: 20: 20] times more, K14 [9: 13: 9: 14: 11: 7: 13].
Row 3: P14 [9: 13: 9: 14: 11: 7: 13], (P1, C7F, P1) 13 [15: 15: 17: 17: 19: 21: 21] times, P14 [9:

13: 9: 14: 11: 7: 13].
Row 4: As row 2.
Rows 5 to 10: As rows 1 and 2, 3 times.
These 10 rows form patt.
Cont in patt, dec 1 st at each end of 3rd and foll 10th row, then on 2 foll 8th rows, then on 2 foll 6th rows.
133 [141: 149: 159: 169: 181: 191: 203] sts.
Work 9 rows, ending with RS facing for next row.
Inc 1 st at each end of next and 5 foll 8th rows, taking inc sts into rev st st.
145 [153: 161: 171: 181: 193: 203: 215] sts.
Cont straight until back meas 41 [41: 40: 43: 42: 44: 43: 45] cm, ending with RS facing for next row.

Shape armholes

Keeping patt correct, cast off 6 [7: 7: 8: 8: 9: 9: 10] sts at beg of next 2 rows.
133 [139: 147: 155: 165: 175: 185: 195] sts.
Dec 1 st at each end of next 5 [5: 7: 7: 9: 9: 11: 13] rows, then on foll 2 [3: 3: 5: 5: 7: 7: 8] alt rows, then on 2 foll 4th rows.
115 [119: 123: 127: 133: 139: 145: 149] sts.
Cont straight until armhole meas 20 [20: 21: 21: 22: 22: 23: 23] cm, ending with RS facing for next row.

Shape shoulders and back neck

Cast off 10 [10: 11: 12: 12: 13: 14: 15] sts at beg of next 2 rows.
95 [99: 101: 103: 109: 113: 117: 119] sts.
Next row (RS): Cast off 10 [10: 11: 12: 12: 13: 14: 15] sts, patt until there are 13 [15: 15: 15: 16: 17: 18: 18] sts on right needle and turn, leaving rem sts on a holder.
Work each side of neck separately.
Cast off 4 sts at beg of next row.
Cast off rem 9 [11: 11: 11: 12: 13: 14: 14] sts.
With RS facing, rejoin yarn to rem sts, cast off centre 49 [49: 49: 49: 53: 53: 53: 53] sts, patt to end.
Complete to match first side, reversing shapings.

FRONT

Work as given for back until 20 [20: 20: 22: 22: 22: 24: 24] rows less have been worked than on back to beg of shoulder shaping, ending with RS facing for next row.

Shape front neck

Next row (RS): Patt 39 [41: 43: 46: 47: 50: 54: 56] sts and turn, leaving rem sts on a holder. Work each side of neck separately.
Keeping patt correct, dec 1 st at neck edge of next 4 rows, then on foll 5 [5: 5: 6: 6: 6: 7: 7] alt rows, then on foll 4th row.
29 [31: 33: 35: 36: 39: 42: 44] sts.
Work 1 row, ending with RS facing for next row.

Shape shoulder

Cast off 10 [10: 11: 12: 12: 13: 14: 15] sts at beg of next and foll alt row.
Work 1 row.
Cast off rem 9 [11: 11: 11: 12: 13: 14: 14] sts.
With RS facing, rejoin yarn to rem sts, cast off centre 37 [37: 37: 35: 39: 39: 37: 37] sts, patt to end.
Complete to match first side, reversing shapings.

SLEEVES

Using 3¼mm (US 3) needles cast on 81 [81: 85: 85: 89: 89: 91: 91] sts.
Row 1 (RS): (K1 tbl) 0 [0: 0: 0: 0: 0: 1: 1] times, (P1, K1 tbl) 0 [0: 1: 1: 2: 2: 2: 2] times, ★(P1, K1 tbl) 4 times, P1, rep from ★ 8 times more, (K1 tbl, P1) 0 [0: 1: 1: 2: 2: 2: 2] times, (K1 tbl) 0 [0: 0: 0: 0: 0: 1: 1] times.
Row 2: (P1 tbl) 0 [0: 0: 0: 0: 0: 1: 1] times, (K1, P1 tbl) 0 [0: 1: 1: 2: 2: 2: 2] times, ★(K1, P1 tbl) 4 times, K1, rep from ★ 8 times more, (P1 tbl, K1) 0 [0: 1: 1: 2: 2: 2: 2] times, (P1 tbl) 0 [0: 0: 0: 0: 0: 1: 1] times.
These 2 rows form rib.
Work in rib for a further 22 rows, ending with RS facing for next row.
Change to 4mm (US 6) needles.
Now work in patt as folls:

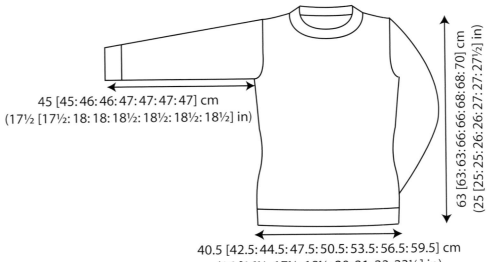

45 [45: 46: 46: 47: 47: 47: 47] cm
(17½ [17½: 18: 18: 18½: 18½: 18½: 18½] in)

63 [63: 63: 66: 66: 68: 68: 70] cm
(25 [25: 25: 26: 26: 27: 27: 27½] in)

40.5 [42.5: 44.5: 47.5: 50.5: 53.5: 56.5: 59.5] cm
(16 [16½: 17½: 18½: 20: 21: 22: 23½] in)

Row 1 (RS): P0 [0: 2: 2: 4: 4: 5: 5], ★(P1, K1 tbl) 4 times, P1, rep from ★ 8 times more, P0 [0: 2: 2: 4: 4: 5: 5].

Row 2: K0 [0: 2: 2: 4: 4: 5: 5], ★(K1, P1 tbl) 4 times, K1, rep from ★ 8 times more, K0 [0: 2: 2: 4: 4: 5: 5].

Row 3: P0 [0: 2: 2: 4: 4: 5: 5], (P1, C7F, P1) 9 times, P0 [0: 2: 2: 4: 4: 5: 5].

Row 4: As row 2.

These 4 rows set **position** of the 10 row patt rep as given for back.

Keeping patt correct as now set, inc 1 st at each end of 3rd [3rd: 3rd: next: next: next: next] and every foll 8th [8th: 8th: 6th: 8th: 6th: 6th: 6th] row to 95 [105: 105: 89: 115: 99: 109: 117] sts, then on every foll 10th [–: 10th: 8th: –: 8th: 8th: 8th] row until there are 103 [–: 109: 111: –: 117: 121: 123] sts, taking inc sts into rev st st.

Cont straight until sleeve meas 45 [45: 46: 46: 47: 47: 47: 47] cm, ending with RS facing for next row.

Shape top

Keeping patt correct, cast off 6 [7: 7: 8: 8: 9: 9: 10] sts at beg of next 2 rows. 91 [91: 95: 95: 99: 99: 103: 103] sts.

Dec 1 st at each end of next 5 rows, then on foll 3 alt rows, then on 4 foll 4th rows. 67 [67: 71: 71: 75: 75: 79: 79] sts.

Work 1 row.

Dec 1 st at each end of next and every foll alt row to 57 [57: 61: 61: 65: 65: 69: 69] sts, then on foll 5 [5: 7: 7: 9: 9: 11: 11] rows, ending with RS facing for next row. 47 sts.

Cast off 5 sts at beg of next 2 rows.

Cast off rem 37 sts.

MAKING UP

Press as described on the information page. Join right shoulder seam using back stitch, or mattress stitch if preferred.

Neckband

With RS facing and using 3¼mm (US 3) needles, pick up and knit 24 [24: 24: 26: 26: 26: 28: 28] sts down left side of neck, 37 [37: 37: 35: 39: 39: 37: 37] sts from front, 24 [24: 24: 26: 26: 26: 28: 28] sts up right side of neck, then 56 [56: 56: 56: 60: 60: 60: 60] sts from back. 141 [141: 141: 143: 151: 151: 153: 153] sts.

Row 1 (WS): K1, ★P1 tbl, K1, rep from ★ to end.

Row 2: P1, ★K1 tbl, P1, rep from ★ to end.

These 2 rows form rib.

Work in rib for a further 7 rows, ending with RS facing for next row.

Cast off in rib.

See information page for finishing instructions, setting in sleeves using the set-in method.

Belt

Using 3¼mm (US 3) needles cast on 9 sts.

Row 1 (RS): K2, (P1, K1) 3 times, K1.

Row 2: K1, (P1, K1) 4 times.

These 2 rows form rib.

Cont in rib until belt meas 145 [150: 155: 160: 165: 170: 175: 180] cm, ending with RS facing for next row.

Cast off in rib.

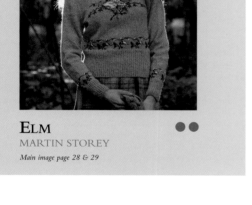

ELM

MARTIN STOREY ● ●

Main image page 28 & 29

YARN

8	10	12	14	16	18	20	22	

To fit bust

81	86	91	97	102	107	112	117	cm
32	34	36	38	40	42	44	46	in

Rowan Felted Tweed and Cashsoft 4 ply

A FTwd Scree 165
5	5	6	6	6	7	7	8	x 50 g

B 4ply Pretty 460
1	1	1	1	1	1	1	1	x 50 g

C 4ply Jewel 461
1	1	1	1	1	1	1	1	x 50 g

D 4ply Fennel 436
1	1	1	1	1	1	1	1	x 50 g

E 4ply Forest 442
1	1	1	1	1	1	1	1	x 50 g

F 4ply Quartz 446
1	1	1	1	1	1	1	1	x 50 g

G 4ply Loganberry 430
1	1	1	1	1	1	1	1	x 50 g

H 4ply Toxic 459
1	1	1	1	1	1	1	1	x 50 g

I 4ply Cream 433
1	1	1	1	1	1	1	1	x 50 g

NEEDLES

1 pair 2¾mm (no 12) (US 2) needles
1 pair 3¼mm (no 10) (US 3) needles

TENSION

23 sts and 32 rows to 10 cm measured over patterned st st using 3¼mm (US 3) needles.

BACK

Using 2¾mm (US 2) needles and yarn A cast on 89 [93: 97: 105: 111: 119: 125: 133] sts.

Row 1 (RS): K1, ★P1, K1, rep from ★ to end.

Row 2: P1, ★K1, P1, rep from ★ to end.

These 2 rows form rib.

Work in rib for a further 42 rows, inc 1 st at centre of last row and ending with RS facing for next row.

90 [94: 98: 106: 112: 120: 126: 134] sts.

Change to 3¼mm (US 3) needles.

Beg and ending rows as indicated and using the

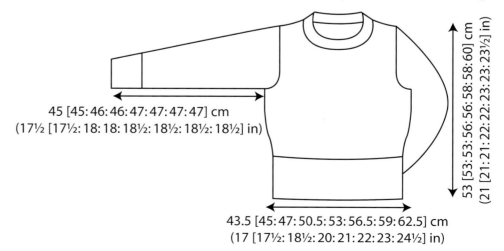

45 [45: 46: 46: 47: 47: 47: 47] cm
(17½ [17½: 18: 18: 18½: 18½: 18½: 18½] in)

43.5 [45: 47: 50.5: 53: 56.5: 59: 62.5] cm
(17 [17½: 18½: 20: 21: 22: 23: 24½] in)

53 [53: 53: 56: 56: 58: 58: 60] cm
(21 [21: 21: 22: 22: 23: 23: 23½] in)

Border Chart

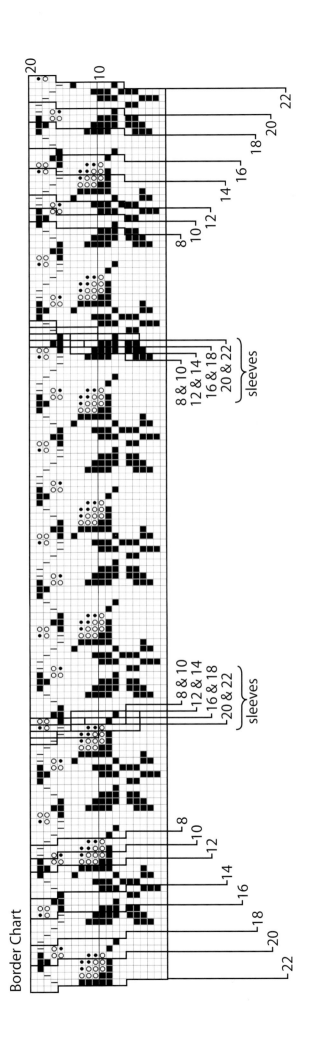

20
10

22
20
18
16
14
12
10
8

8 & 10
12 & 14
16 & 18
20 & 22
sleeves

8 & 10
12 & 14
16 & 18
20 & 22
sleeves

8
10
12
14
16
18
20
22

key
A □
B ◉
C ●
D ⊟
E ■
F ◪
G ◩
H ◨
I ⊠

Motif Chart

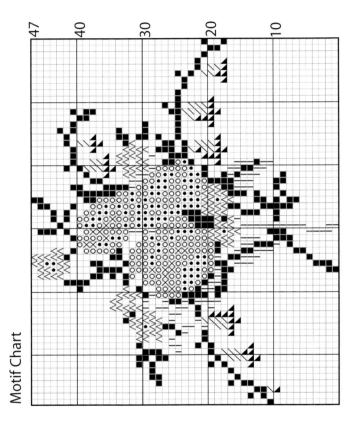

47
40
30
20
10

intarsia technique as described on the information page, now work in patt from chart for border, which is worked entirely in st st beg with a K row, as folls:

Inc 1 st at each end of 7th and foll 10th row, taking inc sts into patt. 94 [98: 102: 110: 116: 124: 130: 138] sts.

Work 3 rows, ending after chart row 20 and with RS facing for next row.

Break off contrasts and cont using yarn A **only**.

Beg with a K row, work in st st, inc 1 st at each end of 7th and 2 foll 10th rows. 100 [104: 108: 116: 122: 130: 136: 144] sts.**★★**

Cont straight until back meas 31 [31: 30: 33: 32: 34: 33: 35] cm, ending with RS facing for next row.

Shape armholes

Cast off 6 [7: 7: 8: 8: 9: 9: 10] sts at beg of next 2 rows. 88 [90: 94: 100: 106: 112: 118: 124] sts.

Dec 1 st at each end of next 3 [3: 5: 5: 7: 7: 9: 9] rows, then on foll 3 [3: 2: 3: 2: 4: 3: 4] alt rows, then on foll 4th row. 74 [76: 78: 82: 86: 88: 92: 96] sts.

Cont straight until armhole meas 20 [20: 21: 21: 22: 22: 23: 23] cm, ending with RS facing for next row.

Shape shoulders and back neck

Cast off 5 [6: 6: 7: 7: 7: 8: 9] sts at beg of next 2 rows. 64 [64: 66: 68: 72: 74: 76: 78] sts.

Next row (RS): Cast off 5 [6: 6: 7: 7: 7: 8: 9] sts, K until there are 10 [9: 10: 10: 11: 12: 12: 12] sts on right needle and turn, leaving rem sts on a holder.

Work each side of neck separately.

Cast off 4 sts at beg of next row.

Cast off rem 6 [5: 6: 6: 7: 8: 8: 8] sts.

With RS facing, rejoin yarn to rem sts, cast off centre 34 [34: 34: 34: 36: 36: 36: 36] sts, K to end.

Complete to match first side, reversing shapings.

FRONT

Work as given for back to ★★.

Place motif chart

Using the **intarsia** technique as described on the information page, now place chart for motif, which is worked entirely in st st beg with a **P** row, as folls:

Next row (WS): P21 [23: 25: 29: 32: 36: 39: 43], work next 58 sts as row 1 of chart for motif, P to end.

Next row: K21 [23: 25: 29: 32: 36: 39: 43], work next 58 sts as row 2 of chart for motif, K to end.

These 2 rows set the sts - centre 58 sts in patt from chart for motif with edge sts still in st st using yarn A.

Working rem 45 rows of chart for motif and then completing front in st st using yarn A **only**, cont as folls:

Cont straight until front matches back to beg of armhole shaping, ending with RS facing for next row.

Shape armholes

Keeping patt correct, cast off 6 [7: 7: 8: 8: 9: 9: 10] sts at beg of next 2 rows. 88 [90: 94: 100: 106: 112: 118: 124] sts.

Dec 1 st at each end of next 3 [3: 5: 5: 7: 7: 9: 9] rows, then on foll 3 [3: 2: 3: 2: 4: 3: 4] alt rows, then on foll 4th row. 74 [76: 78: 82: 86: 88: 92: 96] sts.

Cont straight until 22 [22: 22: 26: 26: 26: 30: 30] rows less have been worked than on back to beg of shoulder shaping, ending with RS facing for next row.

Shape front neck

Next row (RS): K26 [27: 28: 31: 32: 33: 36: 38] and turn, leaving rem sts on a holder.

Work each side of neck separately.

Dec 1 st at neck edge of next 4 rows, then on foll 4 alt rows, then on 2 [2: 2: 3: 3: 3: 4: 4] foll 4th rows. 16 [17: 18: 20: 21: 22: 24: 26] sts.

Work 1 row, ending with RS facing for next row.

Shape shoulder

Cast off 5 [6: 6: 7: 7: 7: 8: 9] sts at beg of next and foll alt row.

Work 1 row.

Cast off rem 6 [5: 6: 6: 7: 8: 8: 8] sts.

With RS facing, rejoin yarn to rem sts, cast off centre 22 [22: 22: 20: 22: 22: 20: 20] sts, K to end.

Complete to match first side, reversing shapings.

SLEEVES

Using 2¾mm (US 2) needles and yarn A cast on 51 [51: 53: 53: 55: 55: 57: 57] sts.

Work in rib as given for back for 30 rows, inc 1 st at centre of last row and ending with RS facing for next row. 52 [52: 54: 54: 56: 56: 58: 58] sts.

Change to 3¼mm (US 3) needles.

Beg and ending rows as indicated and using the **intarsia** technique as described on the information page, now work in patt from chart for border, which is worked entirely in st st beg with a K row, as folls:

Inc 1 st at each end of 7th [7th: 7th: 5th: 7th: 5th: 5th: 5th] and 1 [1: 1: 1: 1: 2: 2: 2] foll 8th [8th: 8th: 8th: 8th: 6th: 6th: 6th] rows, taking inc sts into patt.

56 [56: 58: 58: 60: 62: 64: 64] sts.

Work 5 [5: 5: 7: 5: 3: 3: 3] rows, ending after chart row 20 and with RS facing for next row.

Break off contrasts and cont using yarn A **only**.

Beg with a K row, work in st st, shaping sides by inc 1 st at each end of 3rd [3rd: 3rd: next: 3rd: 3rd: 3rd: 3rd] and every foll 8th [8th: 8th: 8th: 8th: 8th: 6th] row to 64 [74: 72: 80: 82: 84: 86: 74] sts, then on every foll 10th [10th: 10th: –: –: –: –: 8th] row until there are 74 [76: 78: –: –: –: –: 88] sts.

Cont straight until sleeve meas 45 [45: 46: 46: 47: 47: 47: 47] cm, ending with RS facing for next row.

Shape top

Cast off 6 [7: 7: 8: 8: 9: 9: 10] sts at beg of next 2 rows. 62 [62: 64: 64: 66: 66: 68: 68] sts.

Dec 1 st at each end of next 3 rows, then on foll 3 alt rows, then on 7 foll 4th rows. 36 [36: 38: 38: 40: 40: 42: 42] sts.

Work 1 row.

Dec 1 st at each end of next and every foll alt row to 30 sts, then on foll 3 rows, ending with RS facing for next row.

Cast off rem 24 sts.

MAKING UP

Press as described on the information page.

Join right shoulder seam using back stitch, or mattress stitch if preferred.

Neckband

With RS facing, using 2¾mm (US 2) needles and yarn A, pick up and knit 24 [24: 24: 28: 28: 28: 32: 32] sts down left side of neck, 22 [22: 22: 20: 22: 22: 20: 20] sts from front, 24 [24: 24: 28: 28: 28: 32: 32] sts up right side of neck, then 43 [43: 43: 43: 45: 45: 45: 45] sts from back.

113 [113: 113: 119: 123: 123: 129: 129] sts.

Beg with row 2, work in rib as given for back for 9 rows, ending with RS facing for next row.

Cast off in rib.

See information page for finishing instructions, setting in sleeves using the set-in method.

WILLOW
BRANDON MABLY
Main image page 26 & 27

YARN

	S	M	L	XL	XXL	
To fit bust						
	81-86	91-97	102-107	112-117	122-127	cm
	32-34	36-38	40-42	44-46	48-50	in

Rowan Kid Classic

A Earth 872						
	5	5	5	6	6	x 50 g
B Rosewood 870						
	2	2	2	2	3	x 50 g

NEEDLES

1 pair 3¾mm (no 9) (US 5) needles
1 pair 4mm (no 8) (US 6) needles
1 pair 5mm (no 6) (US 8) needles

BUTTONS – 2 x BN1368 (31mm) from
Bedecked. Please see information page for
contact details.

TENSION

19 sts and 25 rows to 10 cm measured over st st
using 5mm (US 8) needles.

BACK

Using 4mm (US 6) needles and yarn A cast on
94 [106: 114: 126: 142] sts.
Row 1 (RS): K2, *P2, K2, rep from * to end.
Row 2: P2, *K2, P2, rep from * to end.
These 2 rows form rib.
Work in rib for a further 8 rows, inc [dec: inc:
inc: dec] 1 st at end of last row and ending
with RS facing for next row.
95 [105: 115: 127: 141] sts.
Change to 5mm (US 8) needles.
Now work in striped st st as folls:
Row 1 (RS): Using yarn A, knit.
Row 2: Using yarn B, purl.
Row 3: Using yarn A, knit.
Row 4: Using yarn A, purl.
Row 5: Using yarn B, knit.
Row 6: Using yarn A, purl.
These 6 rows form striped st st.
Cont in striped st st until back meas 40 [42:
44: 46: 48] cm, ending with RS facing for
next row.
Shape shoulders and back neck
Keeping stripes correct, cast off 5 [6: 7: 8: 9] sts
at beg of next 2 rows, then 5 [6: 7: 8: 10] sts at
beg of foll 2 rows, ending with RS facing for
next row. 75 [81: 87: 95: 103] sts.
Next row (RS): Cast off 6 [7: 7: 9: 10] sts, patt
until there are 18 [20: 22: 24: 26] sts on right

needle and turn, leaving rem sts on a holder.
Work each side of neck separately.
Cast off 3 sts at beg of next row, 6 [7: 8: 9: 10] sts
at beg of foll row, then 3 sts at beg of next row.
Cast off rem 6 [7: 8: 9: 10] sts.
With RS facing, rejoin appropriate yarn to rem
sts, cast off centre 27 [27: 29: 29: 31] sts, patt
to end.
Complete to match first side, reversing shapings.

LEFT FRONT
Using 4mm (US 6) needles and yarn A cast on
51 [59: 63: 67: 75] sts.
Row 1 (RS): K2, *P2, K2, rep from * to
last st, K1.
Row 2: K1, P2, *K2, P2, rep from * to end.
These 2 rows form rib.
Work in rib for a further 8 rows, inc [dec: dec:
inc: -] 1 [2: 1: 1: -] sts evenly across last row and
ending with RS facing for next row.
52 [57: 62: 68: 75] sts.
Change to 5mm (US 8) needles.
Beg with stripe row 1, now work in striped st
st as given for back until 9 [9: 11: 11: 13] rows
less have been worked than on back to beg of
shoulder shaping, ending with **WS** facing for
next row.
Shape front neck
Keeping stripes correct, cast off 16 sts at beg of
next row. 36 [41: 46: 52: 59] sts.
Dec 1 st at neck edge of next 5 rows, then on
foll 1 [1: 2: 2: 3] alt rows. 30 [35: 39: 45: 51] sts.
Work 1 row, ending with RS facing for next row.
Shape shoulder
Keeping stripes correct, cast off 5 [6: 7: 8: 9] sts
at beg of next and foll 1 [1: 2: 1: 0] alt rows,
then 6 [7: 8: 9: 10] sts at beg of foll 2 [2: 1: 2: 3]
alt rows **and at same time** dec 1 st at neck
edge of next and foll alt row.
Work 1 row.
Cast off rem 6 [7: 8: 9: 10] sts.
Mark positions for 2 buttons along left front
opening edge – first to come 15 cm up from
lower edge, and 2nd to come 3 cm down from
beg of neck shaping.

RIGHT FRONT
Using 4mm (US 6) needles and yarn A cast on
51 [59: 63: 67: 75] sts.
Row 1 (RS): K3, *P2, K2, rep from * to end.
Row 2: P2, *K2, P2, rep from * to last st, K1.
These 2 rows form rib.
Work in rib for a further 8 rows, inc [dec: dec:
inc: -] 1 [2: 1: 1: -] sts evenly across last row and
ending with RS facing for next row.
52 [57: 62: 68: 75] sts.
Change to 5mm (US 8) needles.
Beg with stripe row 1, now work in striped st
st as given for back until right front meas
15 cm, ending with RS facing for next row.
Next row (buttonhole row) (RS): K3, cast
off 2 sts (to make a buttonhole - cast on 2 sts
over these cast-off sts on next row), K to end.
Complete to match left front, making a 2nd
buttonhole to correspond with position marked
for 2nd button on left front and reversing
shapings.

MAKING UP
Press as described on the information page.

Join both shoulder seams using back stitch, or
mattress stitch if preferred.
Left front facing
With RS facing, using 3¾mm (US 5) needles
and yarn A, pick up and knit 79 [83: 87: 91: 93]
sts evenly down left front opening edge, from
neck shaping to cast-on edge.
Row 1 (WS): Knit (to form fold line).
Row 2: K2, *P1, K1, rep from * to last st, K1.
Row 3: K1, *P1, K1, rep from * to end.
Last 2 rows form rib.
Work in rib for a further 8 rows, ending with
RS facing for next row.
Cast off in rib.
Right front facing
With RS facing, using 3¾mm (US 5) needles
and yarn A, pick up and knit 79 [83: 87: 91: 93]
sts evenly up right front opening edge, from
cast-on edge to neck shaping.
Row 1 (WS): Knit (to form fold line).
Place markers on last row level with positions
of buttonholes in right front, placing markers
between sts.
Beg with row 2, now work in rib as given for
left front facing as folls:
Work 4 rows, ending with RS facing for next row.
Row 6 (RS): Rib to first marker and turn,
leaving rem sts on a holder.
Work a further 2 rows in rib on this set of sts,
ending with **WS** facing for next row.
Break yarn and leave these sts on a 2nd holder.
Return to sts on first holder, rejoin yarn with
RS facing, rib to 2nd marker and turn, leaving
rem sts on first holder.
Work a further 2 rows in rib on this set of sts,
ending with **WS** facing for next row.
Break yarn and leave these sts on a 3rd holder.
Return to sts on first holder, rejoin yarn with
RS facing and rib to end.
Work a further 2 rows in rib on this set of sts,
ending with **WS** facing for next row.
Join sections
Next row (WS): Rib across sts on needle,
then rib across sts on 3rd holder, then rib across
sts on 2nd holder.
Buttonholes are now complete.
Work in rib for a further 2 rows, ending with
RS facing for next row.
Cast off in rib.
Collar
With RS facing, using 4mm (US 6) needles

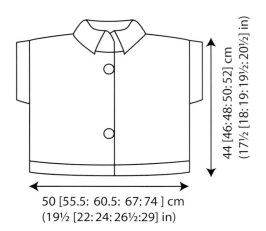

44 [46: 48: 50: 52] cm
(17½ [18: 19: 19½: 20½] in)

50 [55.5: 60.5: 67: 74] cm
(19½ [22: 24: 26½: 29] in)

and yarn A, beg and ending at front facing pick-up rows, pick up and knit 26 [26: 28: 28: 30] sts up right side of neck, 39 [39: 41: 41: 43] sts from back, then 26 [26: 28: 28: 30] sts down left side of neck. 91 [91: 97: 97: 103] sts.

Row 1 (RS of collar, WS of body): K3, *P1, K2, rep from * to last st, K1.
Row 2: K1, *P2, K1, rep from * to end.
Row 3: As row 1.
Row 4: K1, *P2, inc knitwise in next st, rep from * to last 3 sts, P2, K1.

120 [120: 128: 128: 136] sts.
Row 5: K3, *P2, K2, rep from * to last st, K1.
Row 6: K1, P2, *K2, P2, rep from * to last st, K1.

Rep last 2 rows until collar meas 16 cm from pick-up row, ending with RS of collar facing for next row.
Cast off **loosely** in rib.

Armhole borders (both alike)
Mark points along side seam edges 22 [23: 24: 25: 26] cm either side of shoulder seams.

With RS facing, using 4mm (US 6) needles and yarn A, pick up and knit 94 [98: 102: 106: 110] sts evenly along side edges between markers.
Beg with row 2, work in rib as given for back for 5 rows, ending with RS facing for next row.
Cast off in rib.
Fold front facings to inside along fold line rows and neatly sew in place. See information page for finishing instructions.

LARCH
MARIE WALLIN

● ● ●

Main image page 30 & 31

YARN

	S-M	L-XL	
To fit bust	81-97	102-117	cm
	32-38	40-46	in

Rowan Felted Tweed Aran

A Burnt 722			
	3	3	x 50 g
B Ivy 727			
	4	4	x 50 g
C Plum 731			
	6	7	x 50 g
D Cassis 723			
	3	3	x 50 g
E Cork 721			
	3	3	x 50 g

CROCHET HOOK
4.50mm (no 7) (US 7) crochet hook

TENSION
Basic motif meas 11 cm square using 4.50mm (US 7) crochet hook.

CROCHET ABBREVIATIONS
ch = chain; **dc** = double crochet; **dtr** = double treble; **dtr4tog** = *(yoh) twice and insert hook into next st, yoh and draw loop through, (yoh and draw through 2 loops) twice, rep from * 3 times more, yoh and draw through all 5 loops on hook; **dtr5tog** = *(yoh) twice and insert hook into next st, yoh and draw loop through, (yoh and draw through 2 loops) twice, rep from * 4 times more, yoh and draw through all 6

loops on hook; **qtr8tog** = *(yoh) 5 times and insert hook into next st, yoh and draw loop through, (yoh and draw through 2 loops) 5 times, rep from * 7 times more, yoh and draw through all 9 loops on hook; **qtr9tog** = *(yoh) 5 times and insert hook into next st, yoh and draw loop through, (yoh and draw through 2 loops) 5 times, rep from * 8 times more, yoh and draw through all 10 loops on hook; **sp(s)** = space(s); **ss** = slip stitch; **tr** = treble; **yoh** = yarn over hook.

BASIC MOTIF (make 32 in total)
Using 4.50mm (US 7) hook and first colour make 4 ch and join with a ss to form a ring. Joining in and breaking off colours as required, cont as folls:
Round 1 (RS): Using first colour, 5 ch (counts as 1 tr and 2 ch), (3 tr into ring, 2 ch) 3 times, 2 tr into ring, ss to 3rd of 5 ch at beg of round.
Round 2: Using 2nd colour, ss into first ch sp, 5 ch (counts as 1 tr and 2 ch), 3 tr into ch sp at base of 5 ch, *1 ch, miss 3 tr, (3 tr, 2 ch and 3 tr) into next ch sp, rep from * twice more, 1 ch, miss 3 tr, 2 tr into same ch sp as used at beg of round, ss to 3rd of 5 ch at beg of round.
Round 3: Using 3rd colour, ss into first ch sp, 5 ch (counts as 1 tr and 2 ch), 3 tr into ch sp at base of 5 ch, *1 ch, miss 3 tr, 3 tr into next ch sp, 1 ch, miss 3 tr**, (3 tr, 2 ch and 3 tr) into next ch sp, rep from * to end, ending last rep at **, 2 tr into same ch sp as used at beg of

round, ss to 3rd of 5 ch at beg of round.
Round 4: Using 4th colour, ss into first ch sp, 5 ch (counts as 1 tr and 2 ch), 3 tr into ch sp at base of 5 ch, *(1 ch, miss 3 tr, 3 tr into next ch sp) twice, 1 ch, miss 3 tr**, (3 tr, 2 ch and 3 tr) into next ch sp, rep from * to end, ending last rep at **, 2 tr into same ch sp as used at beg of round, ss to 3rd of 5 ch at beg of round.
Fasten off.

Completed basic motif is a square. In each corner there is a 2-ch sp and along each side, between the corner ch sps, there are 4 groups of 3 tr, each separated by a 1-ch sp. 17 sts (12 tr and 5 ch) along each side of motif.
Using colours as folls, make 32 basic motifs:

Motif A (make 8)
First colour: yarn A, 2nd colour: yarn B, 3rd colour: yarn C, 4th colour: yarn D.

Motif B (make 9)
First colour: yarn C, 2nd colour: yarn A, 3rd colour: yarn B, 4th colour: yarn E.

Motif C (make 8)
First colour: yarn E, 2nd colour: yarn C, 3rd colour: yarn D, 4th colour: yarn B.

Motif D (make 7)
First colour: yarn D, 2nd colour: yarn B, 3rd colour: yarn C, 4th colour: yarn A.

FRONT
Centre motif
Using 4.50mm (US 7) hook and yarn A, make 8 ch and join with a ss to form a ring.

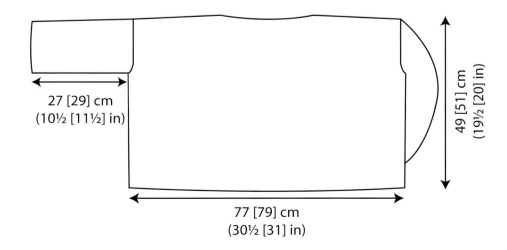

27 [29] cm
(10½ [11½] in)

77 [79] cm
(30½ [31] in)

49 [51] cm
(19½ [20] in)

Joining in and breaking off colours as required, cont as folls:

Round 1 (RS): Using yarn A, 9 ch (counts as 1 dtr and 5 ch), (1 dtr into ring, 5 ch) 7 times, ss to 4th of 9 ch at beg of round.

Round 2: Using yarn B, ss into first ch sp, 4 ch (counts as 1 dtr), 6 dtr into ch sp at base of 4 ch, 7 dtr into each of next 7 ch sps, ss to top of 4 ch at beg of round.

Round 3: Using yarn C, 4 ch (counts as 1 dtr), miss st at base of 4 ch, 1 dtr into each of next 6 dtr, ★5 ch★★, 1 dtr into each of next 7 dtr, rep from ★ to end, ending last rep at ★★, ss to top of 4 ch at beg of round.

Round 4: Using yarn D, ss into next dtr, 4 ch (does NOT count as st), miss dtr at base of 4 ch, dtr4tog over next 4 dtr, ★6 ch, miss 1 dtr, 1 dc into next ch sp★★, 6 ch, miss 1 dtr, dtr5tog over next 5 dtr, rep from ★ to end, ending last rep at ★★, 3 ch, 1 tr into top of dtr4tog at beg of round.

Round 5: Using yarn E, 1 ch (does NOT count as st), 1 dc into ch sp partly formed by tr at end of previous round, (8 ch, 1 dc into next ch sp) 15 times, 4 ch, 1 dtr into dc at beg of round.

Round 6: Using yarn B, 1 ch (does NOT count as st), 1 dc into ch sp partly formed by dtr at end of previous round, (9 ch, 1 dc into next ch sp) 15 times, 5 ch, 1 dtr into dc at beg of round.

Round 7: Using yarn E, 1 ch (does NOT count as st), 1 dc into ch sp partly formed by dtr at end of previous round, ★10 ch, 1 dc into next ch sp, rep from ★ to end, replacing dc at end of last rep with ss to first dc.

Round 8: Using yarn E, ss into first ch sp, 4 ch (counts as 1 dtr), 10 dtr into same ch sp, ★5 ch★★, 11 dtr into next ch sp, rep from ★ to end, ending last rep at ★★, ss to top of 4 ch at beg of round.

Round 9: Using yarn C, ss into next dtr, 7 ch (does NOT count as st), qtr8tog over next 8 dtr, ★8 ch, miss 1 dtr, 1 dc into next ch sp★★, 8 ch, miss 1 dtr, qtr9tog over next 9 dtr, rep from ★ to end, ending last rep at ★★, 4 ch, 1 dtr into top of qtr8tog at beg of round.

Round 10: Using yarn A, 1 ch (does NOT count as st), 1 dc into ch sp partly formed by dtr at end of previous round, ★12 ch, 1 dc into next ch sp, rep from ★ to end, replacing dc at end of last rep with ss to first dc. 32 ch sps.
Fasten off.

Number the ch sps around outer edge of this motif, from 1 to 32 counting clockwise around motif, so that correct ch sps are worked into when motif is attached to rest of front.

Right side panel
Join 6 basic motifs as shown in diagram A as folls:
With RS facing, 4.50mm (US 7) hook and yarn C, attach yarn to corner ch sp of motif A (this is motif number 1 on diagram), 3 ch (counts as 1 tr), holding RS of motif B (this is motif number 2 on diagram) against RS of motif A, work 1 ss into corresponding corner ch sp of motif B, ★(1 tr into next tr of motif A, 1 ss into correspond tr of motif B) 3 times, 1 tr into next ch sp of motif A, 1 ss into corresponding ch sp of motif B, rep from ★ until tr and ss have been worked into corner ch sps at other end of this edge of motifs.
Fasten off.
In same way, join motif number 3 to motif number 2, and motif number 4 to motif number 3.

Join motif number 5 to motif number 1 in same way but do **NOT** fasten off, now cont along edges of motifs number 2 and 3 as folls:
2 tr around stem of tr joining motifs number 1 and 2 placing marker on 2nd of these tr, 1 tr into corner ch sp of motif number 2, (1 tr into each of next 3 tr, 1 tr into next ch sp) 4 times, 2 tr around stem of tr joining motifs number 2 and 3, 1 tr into corner ch sp of motif number 3, (1 tr into each of next 3 tr, 1 tr into next ch sp) 4 times, 2 tr around stem of tr joining motifs number 3 and 4 placing marker on first of these tr, now join motif number 6 to motif number 4 as previous motifs were joined. 74 sts in total – 36 tr between marked tr, and 18 sts beyond marked tr at each end.
Fasten off.
Now work edging along motif number 5 as folls:
With RS facing, 4.50mm (US 7) hook and yarn C, attach yarn to corner ch sp of motif number 5 at point X on diagram, 3 ch (counts as 1 tr), miss ch sp at base of 3 ch, ★(1 tr into each of next 3 tr, 1 tr into next ch sp) 3 times, 1 tr into each of next 3 tr, 1 tr into corner ch sp, 1 ss into centre motif ch sp number 29 on diagram, 1 tr into same corner ch sp as last tr, (1 tr into each of next 3 tr, 1 tr into next ch sp) 4 times – last tr is worked in corner ch sp at point Y on diagram, 1 ss into top of marked tr joining motifs number 1 and 2.
Fasten off.
Now work edging along motif number 6 as folls:
With RS facing, 4.50mm (US 7) hook and yarn C, attach yarn with a ss into marked tr joining motifs number 3 and 4 at point X on diagram, 1 tr into corner ch sp of motif number 6, ★(1 tr into each of next 3 tr, 1 tr into next ch sp) 3 times, 1 tr into each of next 3 tr, 1 tr into corner ch sp, 1 ss into centre motif ch sp number 5 on diagram, 1 tr into same corner ch sp as last tr, (1 tr into each of next 3 tr, 1 tr into next ch sp) 4 times – last tr is worked in corner ch sp at point Y on diagram.
Fasten off.

Joining rows
With RS facing, 4.50mm (US 7) hook and yarn A, attach yarn with a ss to last-but-one tr along side of motif number 5, 2 ch, miss 2 tr after marked tr along edge of motif number 2, (3 tr into next tr, 1 ch, miss 3 tr) 8 times, 3 tr into next tr, miss last tr before other marked tr, 1 ss into 2nd tr along side of motif number 6, fasten off.
Fastening off yarn at end of each row and beg next row at beg of previous row (so that all rows are RS rows) and foll diagram A, cont as folls:
Row 2: Using yarn B, miss 1 tr along side of motif number 5, attach yarn to next tr with a ss, 3 tr into first ch sp of previous row, (1 ch, miss 3 tr, 3 tr into next ch sp) 9 times, miss 1 tr along side of motif number 6, 1 ss into next tr, fasten off.
Row 3: Using yarn E, miss 1 tr along side of motif number 5, attach yarn to next tr with a ss, 1 ch, miss first 3 tr of row 2, (3 tr into next ch sp, 1 ch, miss 3 tr) 4 times, 1 tr into next ch sp, (1 ss into centre motif ch sp number 1 on diagram, 1 tr into same place as last tr) twice, (1 ch, miss 3 tr, 3 tr into next ch sp) 4 times,

1 ch, miss last 3 tr of row 2 and next tr along side of motif number 6, 1 ss into next tr, fasten off.
Row 4: Using yarn D, miss 1 tr along side of motif number 5, attach yarn to next tr with a ss, 3 tr into first ch sp of row 3, (1 ch, miss 3 tr, 3 tr into next ch sp) twice, 1 ch, miss 3 tr, 1 tr into next ch sp, (1 ss into centre motif ch sp number 32, 1 tr into same ch sp as last tr) twice, 1 ss into centre motif ch sp number 32, fasten off.
Row 5: Using yarn B, miss 1 tr along side of motif number 5, attach yarn to next tr with a ss, 1 ch, miss 3 tr at beg of row 4, 3 tr into next ch sp, 1 ch, miss 3 tr, 1 tr into next ch sp, (1 ss into centre motif ch sp number 31, 1 tr into same ch sp as last tr) twice, 1 ss into centre motif ch sp number 31, fasten off.
Row 6: Using yarn E, miss 1 tr along side of motif number 5, attach yarn to next tr with a ss, 3 tr into first ch sp of row 5, 1 ch, miss 3 tr, 3 tr into next ch sp, 1 ss into centre motif ch sp number 31, fasten off.
Row 7: Using yarn A, miss 1 tr along side of motif number 5, attach yarn to next tr with a ss, 1 ch, miss 3 tr at beg of row 6, 1 tr into next ch sp, (1 ss into centre motif ch sp number 30, 1 tr into same ch sp as last tr) twice, 1 ss into centre motif ch sp number 30, fasten off.
Row 8: Using yarn D, attach yarn to first st along edge of motif number 5 at point X on diagram, 3 ch (counts as 1 tr), 2 tr into st at base of 3 ch, (1 ch, miss 3 tr, 3 tr into next tr) 4 times, 1 ss into centre motif ch sp number 29, fasten off.
Row 9: Using yarn E, attach yarn to top of 3 ch at beg of row 8, 4 ch (counts as 1 tr and 1 ch), miss first 3 sts of row 8, (3 tr into next ch sp, 1 ch, miss 3 tr) 3 times, 1 tr into next ch sp, (1 ss into centre motif ch sp number 28, 1 tr into same ch sp as last tr) twice, 1 ss into centre motif ch sp number 28, fasten off.
Row 10: Using yarn B, attach yarn to 3rd of 4 ch at beg of row 9, 3 ch (counts as 1 tr), 2 tr into next ch sp, (1 ch, miss 3 tr, 3 tr into next ch sp) 3 times, 1 ss into centre motif ch sp number 28, fasten off.
Row 11: Using yarn A, attach yarn to top of 3 ch at beg of row 10, 4 ch (counts as 1 tr and 1 ch), miss first 3 sts of row 10, (3 tr into next ch sp, 1 ch, miss 3 tr) twice, 1 tr into next ch sp, (1 ss into centre motif ch sp number 27, 1 tr into same ch sp as last tr) twice, 1 ss into centre motif ch sp number 27, fasten off.
Row 12: Using yarn E, attach yarn to 3rd of 4 ch at beg of row 11, 3 ch (counts as 1 tr), 2 tr into next ch sp, (1 ch, miss 3 tr, 3 tr into next ch sp) twice, 1 ss into centre motif ch sp number 27, fasten off.
Row 13: Using yarn B, attach yarn to top of 3 ch at beg of row 10, 4 ch (counts as 1 tr and 1 ch), miss first 3 sts of row 12, 3 tr into next ch sp, 1 ch, miss 3 tr, 1 tr into next ch sp, (1 ss into centre motif ch sp number 26, 1 tr into same ch sp as last tr) twice, 1 ss into centre motif ch sp number 26, fasten off.
Row 14: Using yarn D, attach yarn to 3rd of 4 ch at beg of row 13, 3 ch (counts as 1 tr), 2 tr into next ch sp, 1 ch, miss 3 tr, 3 tr into next ch sp, 1 ss into centre motif ch sp number 26, fasten off.

Row 15: Using yarn E, attach yarn to top of 3 ch at beg of row 10, 4 ch (counts as 1 tr and 1 ch), miss first 3 sts of row 14, 1 tr into next ch sp, (1 ss into centre motif ch sp number 25, 1 tr into same ch sp as last tr) twice, 1 ss into centre motif ch sp number 25, fasten off.

Row 16: Using yarn B, attach yarn to 3rd of 4 ch at beg of row 15, 3 ch (counts as 1 tr), 2 tr into next ch sp, 1 ss into centre motif ch sp number 25, fasten off.

These 16 rows join motifs number 1, 2 and 5 to centre motif. In same way, join motifs number 3, 4 and 6 to centre motif.

Left side panel

Work as given for right side panel, **but** using motifs as shown in main diagram and attaching joining row 3 to centre motif ch sp number 17. Join side panels by attaching yarn C to first st of row 16, work 3 ch, then work a ss into corresponding st of row 16 of other side panel, fasten off.

Lower edging

With RS facing, 4.50mm (US 7) hook and yarn C, attach yarn to lower (free) corner ch sp of motif number 1, 3 ch (counts as 1 tr), miss ch sp at base of 3 ch, (1 tr into each of next 3 tr, 1 tr into next ch sp) 4 times, 2 tr around stem of tr joining motifs number 1 and 5, 1 tr into corner ch sp of motif number 5, (1 tr into each of next 3 tr, 1 tr into next ch sp) 4 times, 2 tr around stem of tr at point X on diagram A, now work across row-end edges of joining rows, working 2 tr into each row-end and ch sp joining both rows 16, then work across lower edges of motifs of left front panel in same way as across motifs number 1 and 5**.

Size L–XL only

Turn and cont as folls:

Next row: 3 ch (counts as 1 tr), miss tr at base of 3 ch, 1 tr into each tr to end, working last tr into top of 3 ch at beg of previous row, turn. Rep last row once more.

Both sizes

Fasten off.

Upper edging

Work to match lower edging to **, working across top of front.

Fasten off.

BACK

Work as given for front, **but** using motifs as shown in main diagram.

Join left shoulder seam

With RS facing, 4.50mm (US 7) hook and yarn D, attach yarn to top of first tr of front upper edging, 3 ch (counts as 1 tr), holding RS of back against RS of front, work 1 ss into corresponding tr of back (this is last tr of edging), (1 tr into next tr of front, 1 ss into correspond tr of back) 37 times. Fasten off.

Join right shoulder seam in same way.

LEFT SLEEVE

Following main diagram and joining motifs as previously, join 4 basic motifs as folls:

Join motif B to motif A with one row of tr using yarn C.

Join motif C to motif D in same way.

Along both sides of both pairs of joined motifs,

work 1 row of tr using yarn C.

Using yarn D, join pairs of motifs in same way as shoulder seams are joined.

Using yarn B, work 1 row of tr along outer edges of joined motifs.

Work edging across lower edge of sleeves in same way as for front lower edging.

Work edging across upper edge of sleeves in same way as for front upper edging.

Join sleeve to front and back

Using yarn C, work edging along armhole edge of front and back in same way as upper edging, ensuring start and end points match width of sleeve and that same number of sts are worked as on upper sleeve edging.

Now join sleeve to body in same way as shoulder seams are joined.

RIGHT SLEEVE

Work as given for left sleeve, **but** using motifs as shown in main diagram.

MAKING UP

Press as described on the information page.

Join side seams

With RS facing, using 4.50mm (US 7) hook and yarn A, attach yarn at base of left front side seam, 3 ch (counts as 1 tr), then work in tr up left side seam, then down left sleeve seam.

Size L–XL only

Turn and cont as folls:

Next row: Using yarn B, 3 ch (counts as 1 tr), miss tr at base of 3 ch, 1 tr into each tr to end, working last tr into top of 3 ch at beg of previous row.

Both sizes

Fasten off.

In same way, work along left back and sleeve edges.

Now, using yarn B [C], join side seams in same way as shoulder seams.

Join right side and sleeve seam in same way.

See information page for finishing instructions.

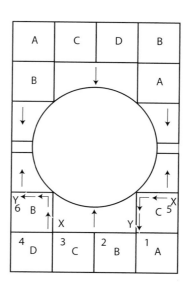

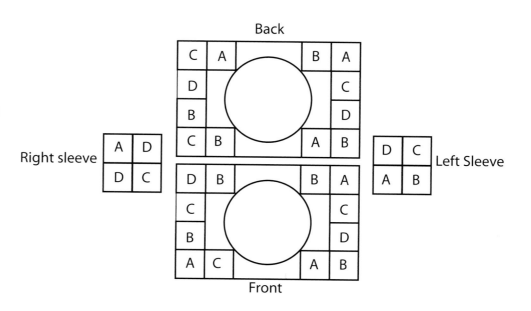

INFORMATION

TENSION

Obtaining the correct tension is perhaps the single factor which can make the difference between a successful garment and a disastrous one. It controls both the shape and size of an article, so any variation, however slight, can distort the finished garment. Different designers feature in our books and it is **their** tension, given at the **start** of each pattern, which you must match. We recommend that you knit a square in pattern and/or stocking stitch (depending on the pattern instructions) of perhaps 5 - 10 more stitches and 5 - 10 more rows than those given in the tension note. Mark out the central 10cm square with pins. If you have too many stitches to 10cm try again using thicker needles, if you have too few stitches to 10cm try again using finer needles. Once you have achieved the correct tension your garment will be knitted to the measurements indicated in the size diagram shown at the end of the pattern.

SIZING & SIZE DIAGRAM NOTE

The instructions are given for the smallest size. Where they vary, work the figures in brackets for the larger sizes. **One set of figures refers to all sizes.** Included with most patterns in this magazine is a **'size diagram'**, of the finished garment and its dimensions. The measurement shown at the bottom of each **'size diagram'** shows the garment width 2.5cm below the armhole shaping. To help you choose the size of garment to knit please refer to the sizing guide on page 98.

CHART NOTE

Many of the patterns in the book are worked from charts. Each square on a chart represents a stitch and each line of squares a row of knitting. Each colour used is given a different letter and these are shown in the **materials** section, or in the **key** alongside the chart of each pattern. When working from the charts, read odd rows (K) from right to left and even rows (P) from left to right, unless otherwise

stated. When working lace from a chart it is important to note that all but the largest size may have to alter the first and last few stitches in order not to lose or gain stitches over the row.

WORKING A LACE PATTERN

When working a lace pattern it is important to remember that if you are unable to work both the increase and corresponding decrease and vica versa, the stitches should be worked in stocking stitch.

KNITTING WITH COLOUR

There are two main methods of working colour into a knitted fabric: **Intarsia** and **Fairisle** techniques. The first method produces a single thickness of fabric and is usually used where a colour is only required in a particular area of a row and does not form a repeating pattern across the row, as in the fairisle technique. **Fairisle type knitting:** When two or three colours are worked repeatedly across a row, strand the yarn **not** in use loosely behind the stitches being worked. If you are working with more than two colours, treat the "floating" yarns as if they were one yarn and always spread the stitches to their correct width to keep them elastic. It is advisable not to carry the stranded or "floating" yarns over more than three stitches at a time, but to weave them under and over the colour you are working. The "floating" yarns are therefore caught at the back of the work.

FINISHING INSTRUCTIONS

After working for hours knitting a garment, it seems a great pity that many garments are spoiled because such little care is taken in the pressing and finishing process. Follow the text below for a truly professional-looking garment.

PRESSING

Block out each piece of knitting and following the instructions on the ball band press the garment pieces, omitting the ribs. Tip: Take special care to press the edges, as this will make sewing up both

easier and neater. If the ball band indicates that the fabric is not to be pressed, then covering the blocked out fabric with a damp white cotton cloth and leaving it to stand will have the desired effect. Darn in all ends neatly along the selvage edge or a colour join, as appropriate.

STITCHING

When stitching the pieces together, remember to match areas of colour and texture very carefully where they meet. Use a seam stitch such as back stitch or mattress stitch for all main knitting seams and join all ribs and neckband with mattress stitch, unless otherwise stated.

CONSTRUCTION

Having completed the pattern instructions, join left shoulder and neckband seams as detailed above. Sew the top of the sleeve to the body of the garment using the method detailed in the pattern, referring to the appropriate guide:
Straight cast-off sleeves: Place centre of cast-off edge of sleeve to shoulder seam. Sew top of sleeve to body, using markers as guidelines where applicable.
Square set-in sleeves: Place centre of cast-off edge of sleeve to shoulder seam. Set sleeve head into armhole, the straight sides at top of sleeve to form a neat right-angle to cast-off sts at armhole on back and front.
Shallow set-in sleeves: Place centre of cast off edge of sleeve to shoulder seam. Match decreases at beg of armhole shaping to decreases at top of sleeve. Sew sleeve head into armhole, easing in shapings.
Set- in sleeves: Place centre of cast-off edge of sleeve to shoulder seam. Set in sleeve, easing sleeve head into armhole.

Join side and sleeve seams.
Slip stitch pocket edgings and linings into place.
Sew on buttons to correspond with buttonholes.
Ribbed welts and neckbands and any areas of garter stitch should not be pressed.

ABBREVIATIONS

K	knit
P	purl
st(s)	stitch(es)
inc	increas(e)(ing)
dec	decreas(e)(ing)
st st	stocking stitch (1 row K , 1 row P)
g st	garter stitch (K every row)
beg	begin(ning)
foll	following
rem	remain(ing)
rev st st	reverse stocking stitch (1 row K , 1 row P)
rep	repeat
alt	alternate
cont	continue
patt	pattern
tog	together
mm	millimetres
cm	centimetres
in(s)	inch(es)
RS	right side
WS	wrong side
sl 1	slip one stitch
psso	pass slipped stitch over
p2sso	pass 2 slipped stitches over
tbl	through back of loop
M1	make one stitch by picking up horizontal loop before next stitch and knitting into back of it
M1P	make one stitch by picking up horizontal loop before next stitch and purling into back of it
yfwd	yarn forward
yrn	yarn round needle
meas	measures
0	no stitches, times or rows
-	no stitches, times or rows for that size
yon	yarn over needle
yfrn	yarn forward round needle
wyib	with yarn at back

CROCHET TERMS

UK crochet terms and abbreviations have been used throughout. The list below gives the US equivalent where they vary.

ABBREV.	UK	US
dc (sc)	double crochet	(single crochet)
htr (hdc)	half treble	(half double crochet)
tr (dc)	treble	(double crochet)
dtr (tr)	double treble	(treble)

EXPERIENCE RATING

● = Easy, straight forward knitting

● ● = Suitable for the average knitter

● ● ● = For the more experienced knitter

BUTTONS AND RIBBONS USED IN THIS MAGAZINE ARE SOURCED FROM:

Bedecked Limited, 1 Castle Wall, Back Fold, Hay-on-Wye, Via Hereford, HR3 5EQ

www.bedecked.co.uk

Shop tel: 01497 822769

Email: thegirls@bedecked.co.uk

ACCESSORY TRIMS USED IN THIS MAGAZINE ARE FROM:

MacCulloch & Wallis, 25-26 Dering Street, London, W1S 1AT

www.macculloch-wallis.co.uk

Shop tel: 020 7629 0311

Email: macculloch@psilink.co.uk

WASH CARE INFORMATION

You may have noticed over the last season that the wash care symbols on our ball bands and shade cards have changed. This is to bring the symbols we use up to date and hopefully help you to care for your knitting and crochet more easily. Below are the symbols you are likely to see and a brief explanation of each.

MACHINE WASH SYMBOLS

Machine Wash, Cold · Machine Wash, Cold, Gentle · Machine Wash, Warm · Machine Wash, Warm, Gentle

HAND WASH SYMBOLS

Do Not Wash · Hand Wash, Normal · Hand Wash, Cold · Hand Wash, Warm

DRY CLEAN SYMBOLS

Do Not Dry Clean · Dry Clean · Dry Clean, in Certain Solvents, Consult Cleaner · Dry Clean, Any Solvent

IRONING SYMBOLS

Do Not Iron · Iron Low Heat · Iron Medium Heat

DO NOT BLEACH SYMBOL

Do Not Bleach

DRYING SYMBOLS

Do Not Tumble Dry · Tumble Dry, Gentle, Low Heat · Dry Flat in Shade · Dry Flat · Do Not Wring

Rowan Overseas Stockists

For more information on overseas stockists and Mail Order details please contact the Rowan distributor / agent listed under each country. 'ROWAN AT ....' stockists carry a large range of Rowan Yarns.

AUSTRALIA

Melbourne	VIC	**Australian Country Spinners Pty Ltd (Dist)**	Level 7, 409 St. Kilda Road		3004	(03) 9380 3830
Albert Park	VIC	Wool Baa	124 Bridport Street	sales@woolbaa.com	3206	(03) 96906633
Avalon Beach	NSW	Avalon Fabrics & Crafts	Shop 4, 24 Avalon Parade	info@avalonfabrics.com	2107	(02) 9918 2978
Bowral	NSW	Wool Addiction	The Penders, 3/20 Station Street		2576	(02) 4862 4799
Claremont	WA	Remember Me	28 Freshwater Parade		6010	(08) 93853478
Geelong	VIC	Twisted Threads	106 Ryrie Street	mandy@twistedthreads.com.au	3220	(03) 52210099
Hornsby	NSW	Hornsby Wool & Craft Nook	Shop 3-3A, 25-31 Florence Street	hornsbywoolcraft@optusnet.com	2077	(02) 94824924
Innaloo	WA	The Wool Shack	5A Langley Place	emma@the woolshack.com	6918	(08) 94466344
Katoomba	NSW	Katoomba Knitting & Needle Craft	Shop 5, Town Centre Arcade, Katoomba St		2780	(02) 4782 6137
Kyneton	VIC	Pick Up Stitches Pty Ltd	46 Piper Street	pickupstitches@bigpond.com	3444	(03) 5422 6614
Loftus	NSW	Jules Craft Shoppe	Shop 3/69 National Avenue	judy@julescraftshoppe.com.au	2237	(02) 9542 3298
Melbourne	VIC	Clegs	60 Elizabeth St	clegsbrunswick@clegs.com.au	3000	(03) 96547677
Melbourne	VIC	Sunspun	185 Canterbury Road	shop@sunspun.com.au	3126	(03) 98301609
Mosman Park	WA	Calico and Ivy	1 Glyde Street	info@calicoandivy.com	6012	(08) 93833794
Mount Eliza	VIC	Windmills & Roses	36-38 Ranelagh Drive		3930	(03) 97874949
Oakleigh	VIC	Craftee Cottage	52-54 Atherton Road	info@crafteecottage.com.au	3166	(03) 9568 3606
Pennant Hills	NSW	Sue's Cherryhills	Shop 7, 354 Pennant Hills Road	pczerney@unwired.com.au	2120	(02) 94840212
Penrith	NSW	The Wool Inn	Sop 14, N & K Centre, 450 High Street	anitab@the_wool_inn.com.au	2750	(02) 4732-2201
Phillip	ACT	Stitch N Time	Unit 2, 55 Colby Court	robynmiranda@bigpond.com	2607	(02) 6282 8383
Phillip	NSW	Stitch N Time	Unit 2, 55 Colby Court	robynmiranda@bigpond.com	2607	(02) 6282 8383
Sassafras	VIC	Sassafras Wool Store	Shop 2, 372 Mt. Dandenong Tourist Road	sassafraswoolstore@bigpond.com	3787	(03) 9755 2510
Sherwood	QLD	Threads & More	Shop 7, 637 Sherwood Rd, cnr Oxley Road	accounts@threadsandmore.com.au	4075	(07) 3379 6699
Smeaton Grange	NSW	Tijuana Alpacas	Unit 1 / 8 Blackmore Road	sharon@tijuana-alpaca.com.au	2567	(02) 4647 1155
Surrey Hills	VIC	Wool Shop	486 Whitehorse Road		3127	(03) 98369614
Sydney	NSW	Tapestry Craft	50 York Street	email@tapestrycraft.com.au	2000	(02) 9298588
Wembley	WA	Woolly Latte's	46-48 Grantham Street	info@woollylattes.com	6014	(08) 92871492

AUSTRIA

Baden	Stick + Strick	Hauptplatz 8	susanne.hasieber@stickundstrick.at	2500	0043/2252/49570	www.stickundstrick.at
Feldkirch	**Zum Schwarzen Schaf (Rowan At)**	**Schlossergasse 1**	**wolle@zumschwarzenschaf.at**	**6800**	**0043/552281072**	**www.zumschwarzenschaf.at**
Hornstein	ROWAN AT Wollerei	Mühlgasse 5	shop@wollerei.at	7053	0043/2689/42528	www.wollerei.at
Innsbruck	Kogler Anton	Museumstr. 6		6020	0043/512584186	
Kitzbuehel	Kitzbuehel Handarbeiten	Im Gries Nr. 23		6370	0043/535672646	
Kolsass	Wolle + Staune (Sabine Kahn)	Auweg 2a	kahn@wolleundstaune.at	6114	0043/664/2629093	www.wolleundstaune.at
Salzburg	Graf Robert	Schrannengasse 2		5020	0043/662876038	
Wels	Zimmermann & Kroboth Gesmbh	Salzburgerstrasse 140		4600	0043/724241291	
Wien	Cadek Maria	Schultergasse 2		1010	0043/1/5354412	
Wien	**Zwei Glatt Zwei Verkehrt (Rowan At)**	**Josefstaeddter Str. 14**	**wolle@zweiglattzweiverkehrt.at**	**1080**	**0043/1/4035736**	**www.zweiglattzweiverkehrt.at**
Wien	Stick + Strick	Simmeringer Haupstrasse 86	susanne.hasieber@stickundstrick.at	1110	0043/1/7494268	www.stickundstrick.at
Wien	Wolle fuer Mode Fleischmann	Neubaugasse 59/3		1070	0043/1/5233394	
Wien	Wollstube Beck	Kalvarienbergasse 32		1170	0043/1/4037211	
Wien	Wollboutique Pinguin	Alserstrasse 21		1080	0043/1/4080010	

BELGIUM

Aalter	Angela's Wolboetiek	Stationstraat 40	angela.vercruysse@telenet.be	9880	09 / 374 27 28	
Antwerpen	**ROWAN AT Lana**	**Anselmostraat 92**	**info@lana-antwerpen.be**	**2018**	**03/ 238 70 17**	**www.lana-antwerpen.be**
Arlon	Brin De Soie	Rue des Faubourg 19		6700	063/ 445 680	
Brussel	Art et Fil	25, Rue du Baillie		1000	02/ 647 64 51	
Eeklo	Hobbyfarm	Pastoor Bontestraat, 37		9900	09/3786664	
Gent	Stoffenidee	Burgstraat 38 A	stoffenidee@skynet.be	9000		annemarie_dw@yahoo.co.uk
Geraardsbergen	Maxime's Hobby	Guilleminlaan 237	info@maximeshobby.be	9500	054/411145	
Hamme	Guy's Naaicentrum	Roodkruisstraat 98	info@guysnaaicentrum.be	9220	052/ 47 18 05	www.guysnaaicentrum.be
Ieper	ORIGAMI	Jules Capronstraat 10	nicole.origami@scarlet.be	8900	057.21.60.22	
Jemeppe	Boite a fils	Rue Joseph Wettinck, 40	laboiteafils@telenet.be	4101	04/2338710	
Kortrijk	Alle steken op een rij	Grote Kring 14		8500		
Kortrijk	Filati	Steenpoort 11		8500	056/210513	filatie-kortrijk@skynet.be
Leuven	t Wolwinkeltje	Parijsstraat 25		3000	016 22 75 48	deforcerosemie@hotmail.com
Lokeren	De Wolkamer	Gentsesteenweg 477		9160	09/355 20 55	
Mere	De Breinaald	Nieuwstraat 10		9420	0475/480234	
Merelbeke	t Wolhuisje	Oude Gaversesteenweg 45		9820	0497/80 61 71	
Sint Truiden	Govaerts	Van Mechelen, Markt 61			011/682288	
TORHOUT	LANA EXCLUSIF	Oostendestraat 88A		8820	050/21.36.32	www.lana-exclusif.be
TOURNAI	PAPRIKA COTTON	Rue Saint-Martin 62		7500	069.23.53.83	www.paprikacotton.be
Virton	La Compagnie des Laines	Grand Rue 56	lacompagniedeslaines@live.be	6760	063 67 78 00	
Wilsele	D.Yarns	P Van Langendoncklaan 17	d_van_nueten@hotmail.com	3012	(016) 20 13 81	

CANADA

South Carolina	***Greer***	***Westminster Fibers (Distributor)***	***8 Shelter Drive***		***29650***	***800 445-9276***	***www.westminsterfibers.com***
Alberta	**Calgary**	**Pudding Yarns (Rowan At)**	**1516-6th St, SW**		**T2R 0Z8**	**403 244 2996**	
Alberta	Edmonton	River City Yarns	3438 99th St	rivercityyarns@shaw.ca	T6E 5X5	780 477-9276	
British Columbia	Victoria	Beehive Wool Shop	1700 Douglas Street	beehivewoolshop@telus.net	V8W 2G7	250 385 2727	
British Columbia	Port Moody	Black Sheep Yarns	88 Grant St		V3H 0B6	778 355-9665	
British Columbia	Vancouver	Three Bags Full	4458 Main St		V5V 3R3	604 874 9665	
British Columbia	**N Vancouver**	**Urban Yarns (Rowan At)**	**3111 Highland Boulevard**	**knitting@urbanyarns.ca**	**V7R 2X5**	**604 984 2214**	**www.urbanyarns.ca**
British Columbia	**Vancouver**	**Urban Yarns (Rowan At)**	**4437 West 10th Ave**	**urbanyarns@telus.net**	**V6R 2H8**	**604 228 1122**	**www.urbanyarns.ca**
British Columbia	Richmond	Wool and Wicker	120-12051 2nd Ave		Y7E 3L6	604 275 1239	
Ontario	Perth	Janie H Knits	528 Glen Tay Rd	info@janiehknits.com	K7H 3C6	613 326-0626	www.janiehknits.com
Ontario	Barrie	Knit & Quilt.com	79 Anne Street South		L4N 2E2	705 737 4422	
Ontario	Milton	Main St.Yarns	15 Martin St, Unit AM8	info@mainstyarns.com	L9T 2R1	905 693-4299	www.mainstyarns.com
Ontario	**Toronto**	**Romni Wools Ltd (Rowan At)**	**658 Queen St West**		**M6J 1E5**	**416 703 0202**	
Ontario	**Ancaster**	**The Needle Emporium (Rowan At)**	**420 Wilson St. East**		**L9G 2C3**	**800 667-9167**	**www.needleemporium.com**
Ontario	**Ottawa**	**Wool NThings (Rowan At)**	**1439 Youville Drive, Unit 20**	**gisele@woolnthings.com**	**K1C 4M8**	**613 841 8689**	**www.woolnthings.com**
Quebec	**Montreal**	**Effiloche (Rowan At)**	**6252 Saint Hubert**	**ginette@effiloche.com**	**H2S 2M2**	**514 276-2547**	
Quebec	Montreal	Mouline Yarns	2657 Notre-Dame West	svetlana@moulineyarns.com	H3J 1N9	514 935-4401	www.moulineyarns.com

CHINA

Shanghai	***Coats Shanghai Ltd. (Distributor)***	***No. 9 Building, Baosheng Road, Songjiang Industrial Zone***	***victor.li@coats.com***		***86 21 5774 3733***
Beijing	Sanli Knitting Fashion Co., Ltd.	ROOM 204, Yunding Center, Block 2 Xiluoyuan, Fengtai.	zka@sina.com		+86-(0)10-88893570; 88865049
Shanghai	Shanghai Yujun Co. Ltd	Room 2404, World Trade Tower No.500 Guandong Road	jessechang@vip.163.com	200002	+86-(0)21-60529096; 60529097; 60529098

DENMARK

Copenhagen	***Distributor: Coats HP A/S***	***Tagensvej 85C, St.tv***			***45 35 86 90 49***	
Ålborg	**Rowan AT Design Vaerkstedet**	**Boulevarden 9**	**butik@design-vaerkstedet.dk**	**9000**	**45 98 12 07 13**	
Århus	**Rowan AT Inger's**	**Volden 19**	**design.club@mail.dk**	**8000**	**45 86 19 40 44**	**www.design-club.dk**
Århus C	**Rowan AT City Stoffer**	**Park Alle 9**	**mt@citystoffer.dk**	**8000**	**45 86 19 03 93**	**www.citystoffer.dk**
Blåvand	**Rowan AT Ho Strik**	**Hovej 21**	**info@hostrik.dk**	**6857**	**45 75 27 54 03**	**www.hostrik.dk**
Farum	Fingerbollet	Farum Hovedgade 85	fingerboellet@gmail.com	3520	45 44 95 70 01	
Fårup	Quiltefant	Spurvevej 1	camilla@quiltefant.dk	8990	45 96 68 00 28	www.quiltefant.dk
Fredriksberg	Wilfert's	Gammel Kongevej 102	britta@wilferts.dk	1850	45 33 22 54 90	www.wilferts.dk
Gilleleje	Gilleje Stof og Garn	Stationsvej 1		3250	45 48 30 31 10	
Grindsted	Cirkeline	Borgergade 14	anette.may@mail.tele.dk	7200	45 75 32 32 99	www.cirkelinegarn.dk
Helsinge	Uldgalleriet	Østergade 2	gitte@uldgalleriet.dk	3200	45 48 79 71 36	www.uldgalleriet.dk
Hornslet	Filt	Tingvej 7B	fischer-filt@mail.dk	8543	45 86 97 51 33	www.fischer-filt.dk
Horsens	**Rowan AT Strikkekunsten**	**Søndergade 41 B**	**kontakt@strikkekunsten.dk**	**8700**	**45 75 65 16 54**	**www.strikkekunsten.dk**
Hørsholm	Engle Stof	Usserød Kongevej 10 A	englestof@mail.dk	2970	45 45 86 33 78	
København	**Rowan AT Sommerfuglen**	**Vandkunsten 3, Kbh.K**	**mail@sommerfuglen.dk**	**1467**	**45 33 32 82 90**	**www.sommerfuglen.dk**
København	Uldstedet	Fiolstræde 13, Kbh.K	uldstedet@uldstedet.dk	1171	45 33 91 17 71	www.uldstedet.dk
Kolding	Martha	Sondergade 41 B	martha-garn@webspeed.dk	6600	45 75 52 48 08	
Lyngby	**Rowan AT Uldstedet**	**Gl. Jernbanevej 7**	**uldstedet@uldstedet.dk**	**2800**	**45 45 88 10 88**	**www.uldstedet.dk**
Nyborg	Ulrikka	Nørregade 13	ulrikkagarn@yahoo.dk	5800	45 65 30 22 80	www.ulrikkagarn.dk
Randers	Uldma	Rosengade 2	salg@uldma.dk	8900	45 86 46 64 66	www.uldma.dk
Ribe	Ribes Broderi & Garn	Dagmarsgade 4	symaskineland@symaskineland.dk	6760	45 75 42 16 75	www.symaskineland.dk
Roskilde	**Rowan AT Garnhøkeren**	**Karen Olsdatterstræde 9**		**4000**	**45 46 37 20 63**	
Silkeborg	Ønskegarn	Nygade 12	onskegarn@onskegarn.dk	8600	45 86 82 57 07	www.onskegarn.dk
Skanderborg	**Rowan AT Stof & Sy**	**Adelgade 123**	**info@stofogsy.dk**	**8660**	**45 86 52 02 45**	**www.stofogsy.dk**
Slangerup	**Rowan AT Paradisets Bamser,**	**Toj og Brugskonst, Kvinderupvej 17**	**pia.freck@mail.tele.dk**	**3550**	**45 47 33 58 66**	**www.butikparadiset.dk**
Svendborg	Ulrikka	Gerritsgade 2	ulrikkagarn@yahoo.dk	5700	45 62 22 21 17	www.ulrikkagarn.dk
Tarm	Uldgården	Fjerbaekvej 12, Vodstrup	uldgaarden@uldgaarden.dk	6880	45 97 37 42 71	www.uldgaarden.dk
Thisted	**Rowan AT Strikkefeen**	**Vestergade 18 C**	**strikkefeen@hotmail.com**	**7700**	**45 97 92 12 33**	**www.strikkefeenthisted.dk**
Varde	Cotton Wear	Smedegade 9	cccsejunge@hotmail.com	6800	45 75 22 33 00	www.cottonwear.dk
Vejle	**Rowan AT Garn & Design Arne S. Hansen**	**Vestergade 45**	**garn-design@mail.dk**	**7100**	**45 75 82 02 49**	**www.garn-design.dk**
Viborg	Mathilde	St. Sct. Mikkelsgade 37		8800	45 86 61 50 22	

FAERO ISLANDS

Klaksvik	Fa Búnin	N.P. Gøta 20, Postrum 282		F-700	00298 455210	
Torshavn	Igloo SP/F Spuni	Sverresgøta 19, Postbox 181		F-110	00298 315264	

FRANCE

Angers	Maison Marot	12 rue Champeronniere		49100	02 41 88 37 66	
Bordeaux	La Lainerie	22 rue des Ayres		33000	05 56 81 43 92	http://lalainerie.com
Colmar	Ambiance Laine	5 Rue Des Pretres	info@ambiance-laine.fr	68000	03 89 41 87 71	www.ambiance-laine.fr
Dijon	Planete Laines	20 rue du Chateau		21000	03 80 30 37 96	www.planete-laine.com
Joigny	Lady Laine	47 bis rue Gambetta	ladylaine.joigny@wanadoo.fr	89300	03 86 62 21 21	www.ladylaine.fr
Le Havre	Mercerie Zip	81 rue de Paris		76600	02 35 21 61 73	
Le Plessis Robinson	La Mercerie Carrée	8 place Francois Spoerry	contact@la-mercerie-carree.fr	92350	01 46 32 61 74	www.la-mercerie-carree.fr
Levallois-Perret	Laines en Vogue	36 rue Gabriel Peri		92300	01 47 57 58 64	
Lognes	Les Trouvailles d'Amandine	3 Grande Allée Le Notre	contact@lestrouvaillesdamandine.com	77185	09 50 37 93 95	www.lestrouvaillesdamandine.com/boutique
Montpellier	Anne Ouvrages	28 rue Paul Brousse		34000	04 67 92 50 92	
Moret sur Loing	La Patte de l'Ours	32 rue de l'Eglise	lapattedelours@orange.fr	77250	01 60 70 15 17	www.la-patte-de-lours.blogspot.co
Nancy	2 Aiguilles dans la Cafetière	5 rue Gustave Simon		54000	03 83 39 46 70	
Nantes	Laines, Fil et blablala	6 rue du Chapeau Rouge		44000	02 40 80 58 24	www.laine-fil-et-blablabla.com
Orléans	Au fil d'Emma	79 Boulevard A. Martin		45000	09 50 14 85 84	www.aufildemma.com
Osmoy	So ! Fil	6 chemin du moutier	tricothe.sofil@gmail.com	78910	01 34 87 29 15	http://tricothe.jimdo.com
Paris (16)	Le Grenier du Ranelagh - Elle Tricote,	7 rue Duban		75016	01 45 20 11 80	
Paris (7)	Le Bon Marche	115 rue du Bac		75007	01 44 39 80 00	
Paris (9)	Le Comptoir	26 rue Cadet		75009	01 42 46 20 72	http://lecomptoir.canalblog.com/
Poitiers	La Mercerie	4 rue Magenta		86000	05 49 52 59 22	http://lamercerie.commerces-poitiers.fr
Rennes	LTM	11 rue Poullain Duparc		35000	02 99 78 20 60	
Strasbourg	Elle Tricote	8 rue du coq	elletricote@agat.net	67000	03 88 23 03 13	www.elletricote.com
Thonon Les Bains	Au Vieux Rouet	7 rue Ferdinand Dubouloz		74200	04 50 71 07 33	
Toulouse	Fifi Jolipois	11 rue Cujas	fifijolipois@yahoo.fr	31000	05 62 30 80 09	www.perles-et-bijoux.com
Tours	La Boîte à Laine	"37, rue du Grand Marché"		37000	02 47 37 76 47	
Valence	Récré Action Imagine	1 rue Ferdinand Marie		26000	04 75 56 00 83	

GERMANY

Ahlen	Agnes Schubert	Gemmericher Str 39		59229	02382 - 72712	
Ammersbek	Angelika Lehmann	Schwarzerweg 21		22949	04532/4641	
Arnstein	Jutta Heurung	Marktstr. 8		97450	09363/6975	
Au a. Inn	Helga Holzner	Steinbach 1	bachmair-helga@t-online.de	83546	08073-916666	
Backnang	**Rowan AT Wollstube Wollin**	**Schillerstr. 19**	**info@wolle-wollin.com**	**71522**	**07191/902828**	**www.wolle-wollin.com**
Bad Brückenau	Inge Vogel	Ludwigstr. 42		97769	0974-14034	
Bad Laer	Gäbel	Mozartstr. 12		49196	05424-8939	
Bad Lippspringe	Marion Reinstädler	Arminiusstr. 10		33175	05252-971621	
Bad Neuenahr-Ahrweiler	**Rowan AT Dat Lädche**	**Niederhutstr. 17**	**dat-laedche_adams@t-online.de**	**53474**	**02641/4464**	
Bad Soden	**Rowan AT Beate Schilb**	**Hasselstr. 19**		**65812**	**06196/644113**	
Bamberg	**Rowan AT Friedericke Pfund**	**Promenadestr. 18**	**wollstudio@fritzi.pfund.de**	**96047**	**0951-202173**	**www.home.t-online.de/home/fritzi.pfund**
Bayreuth	**Rowan AT Strickart**	**Kirchplatz 7**	**strickwerk@gmx.de**	**95444**	**0921/5304870**	**www.strickart-cafe.de**
Berlin	Claudia Kottonau	Bahnhofstr. 3		12555	030 /6562697	
Berlin	Claudia Thees	Bahnhofstr. 3		12555	030 /6562697	
Berlin	Jolanta Schulze	Aßmannstr. 40		12587	030-65484239	
Berlin	Kerstin Hering	Helene-Weigl-Platz 13		12681	030 66 30 80 55	
Berlin	**Rowan AT Birgit Küttner**	**Teltower Damm 34**		**14169**	**030-8026500**	
Berlin	**Rowan AT Holz & Wolle**	**Warnemünder Str. 29**		**14199**	**030/83222762**	
Biberach	Regina Kreuzer-Krause	Gymnasiumstr. 14		88400	07351/1889980	
Bielefeld	Kercan	Friedrich-Ebert-Strasse 2		33602	0521/60296	
Bielefeld	WollZauber	Vilsendorferstr. 45		33739	05206/2992	
Bonn-Duisdorf	**Rowan AT Petra Klein**	**Rochusstr. 245**		**53123**	**0228-39047787**	**www.atelier-rosenbaum.de**
Braunschweig	**Rowan AT Susanne Wenke**	**Lange Str. 35**	**info@stil-bluete.net**	**38100**	**0177/3447082**	**www.stil-bluete.net**
Bremen	Wollstube A. Heyn	Brüggeweg 40-42		28309	0421/413869	
Bühl	Jasmin Radel	Hauptstr. I 70	mail@veilchenschoen-wollhandel.de	77815	07223/8010743	www.veilchenschoen-wollhandel.d
Coburg	Kristina Hackert	Steinweg 32	kristina.hackert@umgarnt.de	96450	09561-7958133	www.umgarnt.de
Dachau	Barbara Reischl	Konrad-Adenauer-Str. 20	info@cotton-club-dachau.com	85221	08131-736859	www.cotton-club-dachau.com
Dannenberg	Annette Gierow	Lange Str. 32		29451	05861/976050	
Darmstadt	G.u.B.Bachmann	Gute Gartenstr.36		64291	06151/372680	
Detmold	Handarbeitsgeschäft Müller	Krummestr. 19	info@handarbeitenmueller.de	32756	05231/28216	www.handarbeitenmueller.de
Dornhan	Regina Temelkoski	Roßgartenstr. 14		72175	07455/2785	
Dresden	**Rowan AT Strick und Faden**	**Rothenburger Str. 14**	**nachstrickundfaden@web.de**	**1099**	**0351/8104086**	
Duisburg	Zaudtke	Grabenstr. 90		47057	0203 - 355799	
Düsseldorf	Woll Duo	Scharnhorststr. 16		40477	0211/467776	
Düsseldorf	Zaudtke	Herderstr. 90		40237	0211 - 684935	
Erlangen	Joana Leyer		info@joana-leyer.de	91054	09131/6873290	www.joana-leyer.de
Erlangen	**Rowan AT Christa Peters-Keller**	**Hauptstr. 115**	**shop@wollkontor-erlangen.de**	**91054**	**09131/204327**	**www.wollkontor-erlangen.de**
Fallingbostel	Dagmar Ohlsen	Walsroder Str. 5		29683	05162/909320	
Felsberg	**Rowan AT Wollstube**	**Untergasse 30**		**34587**	**05662-3741**	
Finningen	Claudia Hager	Bergstr. 3	HagerClaudia@aol.com	89435	"09074-921008,"	www.handbags-and-more.de
Flensburg	Claus Greve	Dorotheenstrasse 24		24937	0177-1972315	
Frankfurt	Lana	Große Bockenheimer Str.35		60313	069/281758	
Frankfurt	**Rowan AT Wolle-Boutique**	**Eckenheimer Landstr. 34**		**60318**	**069/59792080**	
Frankfurt am Main	**Rowan AT Maschenwerke**	**Marburger Str. 4**	**info@maschenwerke.de**	**60487**	**069-71 58 89 80**	**www.maschenwerke.de**
Freiburg	**Rowan AT Welt der Handarbeit**	**Salzstr.37-39**		**79098**	**0761/2172135**	
Freudenberg	Gabriele Rosler	Mittelstrasse 2		57258	02734/436999	
Friedrichsdorf	Claudia Hahn	Hugenottenstr. 85a		61381	06172/72498	
Garmisch-Partenkirchen	Edith Vogel	Ludwigstr. 81		82467	0882/12200	
Gauting	**Rowan AT Dr. Melanie Graeb**	**Grubmühlerfeldstr. 25**	**mgraeb@aol.com**	**82131**	**089-89357858**	**www.bonifaktur.de**
Geretsried	Spinnrad-Handarbeiten	Drosselweg 1	spinnrad-handarbeiten@web.de	82538	08171/649100	
Günzburg	Nähzentrum Fuchs	Augsburger Str. 28	Naehzentrum-Fuchs@gmx.de	89312	"08221-1059,"	
Hamburg	Hand-Werk	Im Mühlenkamp 44		22303	040/2798254	
Hamburg	Pur-Pur-Wolle	"Heußweg 41b,"	info@purpurwolle.de	20255	040/4904579	www.purpurwolle.de
Hamburg	Wollboutique	Wandsbeker Chaussee 315	service@wollboutique.de	22089	040/2007620	
Hamburg	Wollvik	Ratsmühlendamm 26	wollvik@web.de	22335	040/41543767	
Hammelburg	Gabriele Schäfer	Kissingerstr. 10		97762	09732-2328	
Hanau	Anette Schnabl	Bangertstr. 7		63450	06181-5072732	
Hannover	**Rowan AT Zeier-Möller Sophie**	**Sallstr. 81**		**30171**	**0511/3009622**	
Heilbronn	Wollke	Am Kieselmarkt 2	wollke@t-online.de	74072	07131/629357	
Heppenheim	**Rowan AT Alpaka**	**Friedrichstr. 23**		**64646**	**06252/2889**	
Herborn	Sandra Vorländer	Hauptstr. 94		35745	02772-4499884	
Herzberg	Ursula Deppe-Krieger	Heidestr. 23		37412	0552-172861	
Hilden	Ellen Klaft	Worrington Platz 28		40721	02103-298249	
Hohenhameln-Soßnar	**Rowan AT Next Systems**	**Kleine Sackstr. 2**	**info@wollfactory.de**	**31249**	**05128/4091366**	**www.wollfactory.de**
Homburg	**Rowan AT Filatum**	**Saarbrücker Str.3**	**Ibeyersdorf@t-online.de**	**66424**	**06841/171300**	
Hoyerhagen	Waltraud Elsner	Hauptstr. 44	blumenstube-hoyerhagen@gmx.de	27318	0425 - 13478	
Hünfelden	Wolfgang Jäger	Mainzerlandstr. 6		65597	06438-928838	
Ibbenbüren	Pottmeier	Unterer Markt 4		49477	05451/936417	
Kamp-Lintfort	Elfi's Wollwelt	Mörser Strasse 270		47475	02842/10 226	
Kandel	Sybille Riehm	Waldstr. 10		76870	07275-729064	
Karlsruhe	Gabriele Bodesohn	Marienstr. 77/79		76137	0721/7597840	
Kassel	**Rowan AT Christina Geyer**	**Freidrich-Ebert-Str. 147**		**34117**	**0561/710029**	
Kelkheim	**Rowan AT Kelkheimer Masche**	**"Höchster Str. 8, "**		**65779**	**06195/975678**	
Kiel	Dörte Dietrich	Damaschkeweg 50a		24113	0431/2405493	www.wollwerkstatt-kiel.de
Kirchheim	Ulrike Beck-Kley	Schuhstr. 5		73230	0702/145275	
Kirchlengern	Corinna Schumacher	Lübbecker Str 5		32278	05223-9859721	
Koblenz	Birgit Reich	An der Liebfrauenkirche 11		56068	0261-9733224	
Köln	Maschenkunst	Christophstr. 9-11	info@maschenkunst.de	50670	0221/2783489	www.maschenkunst.de
Köln	Rapp	Goltsteinstr. 96		50568	0221-16906088	
Landsberg	Christel Sellwig	Herkom.Passage 111		86899	08191/21245	
Landshut	**Rowan AT Barbara Zeilhofer**	**Kirchgasse 247**		**84028**	**0871/2764217**	
Leutenbach	Astrid Bauchrowitz	Am Pfarrgarten 3		91359	09199-695460	
Leutkirch	Brigitta Schwarz-Frehner	Marktstr. 30	info@diezweigstelle.de	88299	07561-9834566	
Mainz	Andrea Seufert	Fuststr. 2		55116	06131-2407196	
Marburg	Saskia Krieger	Frauenbergstr. 13		35039	06421-34230	
Meckenheim	**Rowan AT Heidrun Bergau**	**Neuer Markt 17**		**53340**	**02225-887969**	
Melle	Freya Hoffknecht			49326	05428/927877	
Michelstadt	Haberkorn / Schütz GbR.	Neutorstr. 3		64720	06061-965891	
Moritzburg	Wollwunderland Schulze	Schlossallee 29	salonrokoko@web.de	01468	03520/799395	www.salon-rokoko.de
München	**Rowan AT Brigitte Kreische**	**Nordendstr. 17**	**info@strickeria-muenchen.net**	**80799**	**089/88904532**	**www.wool-concept.de**
Münster	Lacatus	Hörster Strasse 56	info@maschenrausch.com	48143	0049521/3846293	
Norderney	Patchwork-Stübchen	Jann-Berghaus-Str.13		26548	04932/927160	
Nürnberg	Anita Hammel	Weinmarkt 10	mail@tollewolle-online.de	90403	0911-209497	www.tollewolle-online.de
Oberasbach	Chic In Strick	Am Rathaus 14		90522	0911/697592	
Oberursel	Daniela Queißer	Rathausplatz 6		61440	06171/586555	
Oppenheim	Wolle in der Villa	Friedrich-Ebert Str.83	wolle-seufert@t-online.de	55276	06133/2131	
Osnabrück	Woll-Perle	Hakenstr. 3		49074	0541/258561	
Paderborn	**Rowan AT Nicole Kersek-Meilwes**		**Kürassierweg 8**		**33104**	**05254-10126**
Plauen	Heike Bromnitz	Stresemannstr. 6		08523	03741 221316	www.naehstuebl-bromnitz.de
Potsdam	**Rowan AT Rosmarie Adler**	**Friedrich-Ebert-Str. 27**		**14467**	**0331-2800609**	
Ratingen	Wollkörbchen (Frau Szczygielski)	Turmstr. 30		40878	02102-80844	www.wollkoerbchen-ratingen.de

GERMANY (cont)

City	Shop	Address	Email	Postal	Phone	Website
Regensburg	Rowan AT Birgit Birner	Fuchsengang 2	Strickeria@gmx.net	93047	0941-58612300	www.Strickeria.net
Reutlingen	Wolle und Mehr	Metzgerstr. 64		72764	07121/310488	
Rheinbach	Rowan AT Faszination Wolle	Vor dem Dreeser Tor 22	info@faszinationwolle.de	53359	02226 - 911 28 50	www.faszinationwolle.de
Salzhausen	Wollart Ute Rudat	Eyendorfer Str. 3		21376	04172-969123	
Schlüchtern	Dagmar Marburger	Obertorstr.8		36381	06661-1337	
Siegen	Rowan AT Stecknadel	Rathausstr. 2	creativ@stecknadel.info	57078	0271-89002667	
Sindelfingen	Hilde´s Stricklädle	Obere Vorstadt 26		71063	07031/688183	
Soest	Rowan AT Der Faden	Potsdamer Platz 1		59494	02921/3192277	
Solingen	Sabine Ziel	Grünewalderstr. 1		42657	0212-2437886	
Stadtlohn	Wolle und Design	Görkeskamp 6	info@wolleunddesign.de	48703	02563/98208	www.wolleunddesign.de
Stuttgart	Isabelle Roche	Sophienstr. 24		70178	0711-2265758	
Suhl	Steffi Hengelhaupt	Friedrich-König-Str. 5		98527	03681-723704	
Titisee-Neustadt	Ingeborg Steiert	Scheuerlenstr. 24		79822	07651/7218	
Troisdorf	Olga Wanner	Kölner Str. 83		53840	02241-72974	
Übach-Palenberg	Ute Ströbel	Von-Liebig-Str. 42	info@eunomia.de	52531	02451/909205	www.eunomia.de
Ulm	Rowan AT Wolle & Ideen	Pfauengasse 17	Heike@Redlinghaus.de	89073	0731/619491	
Undorf	Roswitha Baierl	Hofmarkstr. 38	rosis_wollstube@yahoo.de	93152	09404-6410341	
Vincenzbronn	Anita Krehn	Vincenzbronner Hauptstr. 26		90613	09105/9319	
Waghäusl-Wiesental	Petra Holzer	Mannheimer Str. 7		68753	07254-7799741	www.Bastelstubediesunddas.de
Weilburg	Christina Mundhenk	Am Eichenweg 1		35781	06471-629298	
Weimar	Steffi Hengelhaupt	Eisfeld 3		99423	03643/901748	
Weinheim	Rowan AT Heide Fabian	Giselherstr. 19		69469	06201/256910	
Wenden	Barbara Klur	Severinusstr. 2		57482	02762-490291	
Westerkappeln	Mode- und Wollpalette	Bahnhofstrasse 6		49492	05404/899939	
Wetter-Volmarstein	Christiane A. Struck	Osterfeldstrasse 11		58300	02335/8451940	
Wiesbaden	Rowan AT Fil a Fil Der Woll-Laden	Rathausstr. 61		65203	0611-66969	
Winsen/ Aller	Markus Schröter	Celler Str. 11		29308	0514-35336	
Wuppertal	Strick und Stick	Auer Schulstrasse 5	d.teege-schitthelm@hotmail.de	42103	0202/4292104	

HOLLAND

City	Shop	Address	Email	Postal	Phone	Website
Almere-Haven	Het Spoeltje	Meerstraat 52	handwerkzaak@hetspoeltje.nl	1353 AZ	036-5216817	www.hetspoeltje.nl
Amersfoort	H.W. Mur	Langestraat 13		3811 AA	033 461 7837	www.happytown.nl
AMSTELVEEN	AVERECHT	Groenhof 163	info@averecht.eu	1186 EZ	06-29010554	
Amsterdam	ROWAN AT de Afstap (Lonnie Bussink)	Oude Leliestraat 12	info@afstap.nl	1015 AW	020-6231445	www.afstap.nl
Bergen	ROWAN AT Finlandia(Rowan At)	Kleine Dorpsstraat 26	info@finlandiaimport.nl	1861 KN	0725 894642	
Dalen	ROWAN AT Breiweb	Hoofdstraat 44	info@breiweb.nl	7751 GD	052 4551597	www.breiweb.nl
De Rijp	Sylka Mode	Rechtestraat, 118	info@sylkamode.com	1483 BG	031/299674548	www.sylkamode.com
Eindhoven	ROWAN AT Breimode Brigitte	Ouverture 212	info@brigitte-handwerken.nl	5629 PX	040-2435576	www.brigitte-handwerken.nl
Etten-Leur	De Wolboetiek	Bisschopsmolenstraat 169		4876 AL	076-5022597	
Groningen	Sajet	Guldenstraat 6	sales@sajet.com	9712 CE	050/314 09 00	www.sajet.com
Heerlen	Ut Bolke	Benzenraderweg 92		6417 SV	045 /571 64 51	
Hoorn	FA Schouten	Grote Noord, 120		1621 KM	031/229215682	
Joure	Ajoure	Pastorielaan 2	www.ajoure.nl	8501 EZ	051/3413344	
Kampen	Pingouin wol & handwerken	Oudestraat 20	pingouinkampen@uwnet.nl	8261 CP	038-3322811	
KOEWACHT	WOLBOERDERIJ BLIJ BEZUIDEN	Het Zand 61	wolboerderij@planet.nl	4576CB	"114,361,402"	
Leeuwarden	Wereldwol	de Lauwers 2		8939 BW	058/2881301	
Leiden	ROWAN AT Ribbels	Pieterskerk-Choorsteeg 18	christa.kroon@ribbels.nl	2311 TR	071 5133126	www.ribbels.nl
Nieuwpoort	ROWAN AT De Schapekop	Hoogstraat 30	info@deschapekop.nl	2965 AL	0184-602678	www.deschapekop.nl
Oldenzaal	ROWAN AT Lohuis	Steenstraat 26	t.lohuis@planet.nl	7571 BK	05415-12626	www.lohuis-tijhuis.nl
Roden	Spinnewiel	Raadhuisstraat 2		9301 AB	050/5018893	
Rotterdam	Lydialaine	Goudsesingel 231 A		3031 EK	010/4136697	
Sittard	Wollstreet	Rijksweg Noord 61	info@wollstreet.nl	6131 CJ	0464-586330	
Someren	Het Weverke	Molenstraat 24		5711EW	0493-492092	
Utrecht	ROWAN AT Modilaine	Lijnmarkt 22	Johannes.aikema@orange.nl	3511 KH	030-2328911	
Voorburg	De Breikorf	Koningin Julianalaan 274	info@debreikorf.nl	2274 JR	070 3871286	www.breikorf.nl
Wapenveld	Klaziens Kreatie	Stationsweg 20		8191 AH	038/447 05 74	www.klazienskreatie.nl
Woudsend	Hannah Tricotage	Carmelieterstraat, 6		8551 RJ	031/514592343	
Zuidlaren	ROWAN AT Ryahuis (Rowan At)	Telefoonstraat 26	www.ryahuis.nl	9471 EN	050-4092618	
Zwolle	Rits-in	Assendorperstraat 105		8012 DH	0031/38421261	

HONG KONG

Shop	Address	Email	Phone
East Unity Company Ltd.	Unit B2, 7/F, Block B, Kailey Industrial Centre, 12 Fung Yip Street, Chai Wan, Hong Kong	eastunityco@yahoo.com.hk	(852)2869 7110

ICELAND

City	Shop	Address	Email	Postal	Phone	Website
Reykjavik	*Rowan At Storkurinn (Dist)*	*Laugavegur 59*	*storkurinn@simnet.is*	*101*	*551 8258*	*www.storkurinn.is*

ITALY

City	Shop	Address	Province	Postal	Phone
MILANO	*coats cucirini srl (Distributor)*	*viale sarca n° 223*	*MI*	*20126*	*02636151*
ARESE	MAPA SNC	PZZA 5 GIORNATE 6/D	MI	20020	029383921
ASTI	LA BOTTEGA DI EVELINA	VIA GIOBERTI 62	AT	14100	0141595579
AVENZA	MARIA VITTORIA	VIA CAMPO D'APPIO 12	MS	54033	058552943
BOLOGNA	CASA DELLA LANA	VIA AUGUSTO RIGHI 19	BO	40126	051227731
BUSNAGO	IL FILO DI ARIANNA	VIA ITALIA 157	MI	20040	
CAMPOSAMPIERO	BOTON E BUSETA S.A.S.	VIA G.PASCOLI 2/B	PD	35012	0495790302
CARATE BRIANZA	UNFILODI	VIA ARIOSTO 2	MI	20048	0362 991063
CASORATE PRIMO	IL GOMITOLO D'ORO	VIA SALICI 6	PV	27022	
CASTEL SAN PIETRO	MOLINARI	VIA MATTEOTTI 116	BO	40024	051 6958688
CESENA	L'AGO E IL DITALE	VIA ALBERTINI 35	FC	47023	0547610552
CLUSONE	BARETTI SNC	PIAZZA UCCELLI 2O	BG	24023	034621404
COMO	LA MERCERIA IMAC	VIA P.CARCANO 15	CO	22100	031260163
CORTINA D'AMPEZZO	LA COOPERATIVA DI CORTINA S.C.	CORSO ITALIA 40	BL	32043	0436861245
DOMODOSSOLA	IL GOMITOLO	VIA GALLETTI 28	VB	28845	
ESTE	FANIN LUCIA "NONSOLOMERCERIA"	VIA G. MARCONI 15	PD	35042	0429602513
GENOVA	FONTE DELLA LANA	GALATA 27 R.	GE	16121	010562594
IMOLA	2 COLONNE	VIA EMILIA 61	BO	40026	054225854
JESOLO PAESE	AGO & FILO	VIA PIAVE VECCHIO 1/B	VE	30016	0421952282
LA SPEZIA	CERRETTI E C. SNC	CORSO CAVOUR 178	SP	19122	0187735108
LEDRO - MEZZOLAGO	IL GOMITOLO	VIA PTICE 17	TN	38060	
LUCCA	L'ARCOLAIO	PIAZZA CITTADELLA 11	LU	55100	0583580248
MENFI	TURTURICI ROSALBA	VIA SANTI BIVONA 16	AG	92013	
MERANO	WOLLE ANITA	VIA GALILEI STR 10	BZ	39012	0473237025
MEZZOLOMBARDO	PUNTO MAGLIA & CUCITO	C.SO MAZZINI 36/A	TN	38017	0461 603263
MILANO	PLANA MERCERIA SNC	VIA PLANA 43	MI	20155	0233002241
MILANO	TRICOTS	PIAZZA SIENA 8	MI	20146	024075777
MODENA	DIRITTO E ROVESCIO	LARGO S. FRANCESCO 144	MO	41121	0594555316
MODENA	ILGOMITOLO	VIA CANALINO 74	MO	41121	059237468
MONSELICE	RANGON CHIARA	VIA ZANELLATO 14	PD	35043	042974417
MOZZATE	FILOFOLLIA	VIA ROSSELLI 24	CO	22076	0331831488
PADERNO DUGNANO	BIGATTI LANA	VIA ROMA 30/A	MI	20037	
PADOVA	AKI SAS	PIAZZA DEI SIGNORI 19	PD	35139	049663818
PARMA	ZUCCHERI SNC	VIA MAZZINI 10/A	PR	43121	0521281262
PISA	BRICO CHIC	VIA DELLE BELLE TORRI 50	PI	56127	
POGGIBONSI	SUL FILO DI LANA	LARGO GRAMSCI 14	SI	53036	0577 982110
PORTOGRUARO	LANE E FILATI GRAZIELLA	VIA MAZZINI 9	VE	30026	042174808
PROVAGLIO D'ISEO	L' AGORAIO	VIA FIUME 8	BS	25050	0306154578
RACALMUTO	AGNELLO MARIA GRAZIA	VIA REGINA MARGHERITA 7	AG	92020	
REGOLEDO DI COSIO VALTELLINO	EMPORIO DI LAZZARI FEDERICO	VIA STATALE 8	SO	23013	0342638150
ROMA	CAPUANI MARIANTONIETTA	PIAZZA DELLA TORRETTA 22	RM	*00186	06 6871215
SCANDIANO	IL FILO DI ARIANNA	VIA GARIBALDI 9/C	RE	42019	0522984736
TORINO	LA COMPAGNIA DEL COTONE	VIA MAZZINI 44	TO	10123	0118178381
TRIESTE	FONDA SILVA SAS	VIA DELLE TORRI 2	TS	34122	040771717
UDINE	ELISA CESSELLI	VIA SAVORGNANA 18	UD	33100	0432 295633
VEDELAGO	BARRICHELLO SAS	VIA MONTEGRAPPA 28	TV	31050	0423 700167
VERONA	DRITTO E ROVESCIO SNC	VIA ROSA MORANDO 32 A	VR	37131	

JAPAN

City	Prefecture	Shop	Address	Email	Postal	Phone	Website
Chiba	Chiba	Mitsukoshi Department Store	6F Mitsukoshi Bild, 2-6-1 Fujimi Cyuouku		260-8631	81-043-221-0515	
Hiroshima	Hiroshima	Puppy Hiroshima	8-16 kamihacchoubori, nakaku		730-0012	81-082-222-0537	
Kitakyusyu	Hukuoka	Izutsuya Department Store	2-4 igashiko, Kokurakitaku		803-0802	81-093-522-2729	
Kobe	Hyogo	Union Wool	1-30-22 Kitanagasadori, Chuouku		650-0012	81-078-331-8854	
KOBE	HYOGO	Union Wool Co., Ltd	1-30-22, Kitanagasadori Chuou-ku	union@smile.ocn.ne.jp	650-0012	078-331-8854	
Oosaka	Oosaka	Hankyu Department Store	8-7 kakudacho, Kitaku		530-8350	81-06-6313-8938	
Oosaka	Oosaka	Masuzakiya	4-5-4 Kawaramachi, Chuouku		541-0048	81-06-6222-1110	
Osaka	Japan	room amie	3-11-8-109 Yamate-cho, Suita-city	info@roomamie.jp	564-0073	06-6821-3717	http://roomamie.jp
Tokyo	Tokyo	Mitsubaya	1-1-1 Minamiaoyama, Minatoku		107-0062	81-03-3404-1677	
Tokyo	Tokyo	Mitsukoshi Department Store	Hobby & Craft Salon 8F Mitsukoshi New Bild, 1-4-1 Nihonbashi Chuouku		103-8001	81-03-3273-6500	
Tokyo	Tokyo	Puppy Shimokitazawa	2-26-4 Kitazawa, Setagayaku		155-0031	81-03-3468-0581	

KOREA

City	District	Store	Address	Email	Postal	Phone	Website
Seoul	Seocho-Gu	Coats Korea Co. Lt (Distributor)	5F Eyeon B/D, 935-40 Banghae-Dong	rozenpark@coats.com	137-060	82-2-521-6262	www.coatskorea.co.kr
Seoul	Jongno-Gu	Danju	1F, 35-3 Sogyeok-Dong	jade@danju.co.kr	110-200	82-2-720-1127	www.danju.co.kr
Seoul	Jongno-Gu	My Knit Studio	3F, 144 Kwanhoon-Dong	myknit@mykint.com	110-300	82-2-722-0006	www.myknit.com

LEBANON

Beirut	y.knot	Saifi Village, Mkhalissiya Street 162	y.knot@cyberia.net.lb	(961) 1 992211

LUXEMBOURG

City	Store	Address	Postal	Phone
ESCH s/ALZETTE	Ouvrages Elisabeth	Rue S. Bolivar 29	4037	00352.40.05.06
Luxembourg	Bastel Kiste	Rue Du Fort Elisabeth 17-19, Luxembourg	1463	00352/40 05 06

MALTA

City	District	Store	Address	Email	Postal	Phone
MALTA	Msida	John Gregory Ltd	8 Ta'Xbiex Sea Front	raygreg@onvol.net	MSD 1512	+356 2133 0202

NEW ZEALAND

City	Store	Address	Email	Phone	Website
Belfast	ACS New Zealand (Distributor)	1 March Place, Christchurch		64-3-323-6665	
Cuba Mall	Knit World	Shop 210b, Left Bank, Wellington		04 385 1918	wellington@knitworld.co.nz
Devonport	Wild & Woolly	38 Victoria Road, Auckland		09 445 3255	wildandwoollyyarns@gmail.com
Kaiwaka	The Apple Basket	1914 State Highway 1, Northland		09 4312 443	applebasketquilts@xtra.co.nz
Warkworth	Twinset and Pearls	Elizabeth Street, Northland		09 425 7246	twinsetandpearls@clear.net.nz
	Alterknitives	PO Box 47961, Auckland		(64 9) 376 0337	knitit@ihug.co.nz
	Creations Unlimited	118 Hardy Street, Nelson		03 548 4297	creations@jasnelson.co.na
	Fabryx	Unit 5a, 29 Totara Street, Taupo		07 376 7494	fabryx@clear.net.nz
	Knit World	189 Peterborough St, Christchurch		03 379 2300	christchurch@knitworld.co.nz
	Knit World Mail Order	PO Box 30 645	"info@knitting.co.nz,"	04 586 4530	www.knitworldstudio.co.nz
	Tauranga Knitting Centre	8/152, 11th Avenue, Tauranga		07 571 8892	tgaknitcentre@hotmail.com

NORWAY

City	District	Store	Address	Email	Postal	Phone	Website
Bergen	Ulset	Coats Knappehuset AS	Pb 100		5873	55 53 93 00	
Arendal		Blad Trad	Harebakksenteret	blatrad@online.no	4846	37 03 64 33	
Asker		Garnstua Asker	Knud Askersvei		1383	66 78 19 86	www.garnstua.no
Bryne		Idestova a/s Bryne	Arne Garborgs veg 15	anny@idestova.no	4370	99 29 30 03	www.idestova.no
Dombås		Tusenogen Tråd	Dombås Senter		2660	61 24 16 50	
Drammen		Ulla Garn & Broderi	Sankt Olavsgate 2	butikk@ullgarn.no	3018	32 89 00 58	www.ullagarn.no
Grimstad		Broderihjørnet Huslidstua	Storgata 32	Huslidstua@live.no	4876	37 04 89 14	
Horten		Flittig Lise Horten	Apotekergaten 16	flittiglise@c2i.net	3187	33 04 60 55	
Jessheim		Ull og Saker	Jessheim Storsenter		2050	63 97 34 74	post@ullogsaker.nu
Kongsberg		Strikkestua Kongsberg	Kirkegaten 12	tkolseth@online.no	3616	32 73 23 12	
Kragero		Strikk Inom	Sannidalsv. 196		3770	35 98 03 40	www.strikkinom.no
Kristiansand		Langfeldt Garn	H.Wergwlandsgt. 21-23		4612	38 02 20 29	
Laksevåg		Pinnsvin Design	Lyngboveien 160	kontakt@pinnsvinsdesign.no	5164	99 37 09 12	www.pinnsvinsdesign.no
Oslo		Ariadne Garn	Lilleakervn 16		283	22 73 06 20	
Oslo		Bentes Boutique	Chr. Michelsengt 1	garnbente@gmail.com	0568	22 37 44 86	
Oslo		Bentes Boutique	Gjovikgt. 1		0470	22 18 26 39	
Oslo		Linderud Garn og Hobby	Linderud Senter		0594	22 64 49 94	
Oslo		Nøstet Mitt	Tveita Senter		0671	22 75 50 65	
Oslo		Nøstet Mitt	Lambertseter Senter		1150	23 38 22 20	
Oslo		Strikkeriet	Stilla Senter	iren@strikkeriet.no	0491	22 95 78 13	www.strikkeriet.no
Oslo		Tjorven Garn og Gaver	Valkyriegt. 17	tina@tjorven.no	0366	22 69 33 60	www.tjorven.no
Sandnes		Kreaaktiv	Kvadrat Kjøpesenter	kreaktiv-kvadrat@quiltebutikken.com	4301	33 06 33 31	
Sarpsborg		Sarpsborg Garn og Broderi	Jernbanegaten 16	post@sarpsborggarnogbroderi.com	1706	69 15 27 60	
Ski		Trine Sv og Strikk	Idretsveien 6	post@trinestrikk.no	3018	64 87 25 68	
Skien		Strikkepinnen Skien	Ulefossveien 26	opgons@online.no	3730	35 52 72 21	

PORTUGAL

City	Store	Address	Postal	Phone
co, 22, Cx. Postal 155	9002	291201990		
Ponta Delgada	Eduardo J. Moura (Coats & Clark agent in Azores)	R. Arcanjo Lar, 11 Cave, Apartado 182	9500	296284341
Porto	Ovelha Negra	Rua da Conceição, 100	4050-214	+351 220935847

SINGAPORE

City	Store	Address	Email	Postal	Phone
Singapore	Golden Dragon Store (Distributor)	101 Upper Cross St. #02-51, People's Park Centre	gdscraft@hotmail.com	058357	(65) 65358454 /65358234

SOUTH AFRICA

City	Store	Address	Email	Postal	Phone	Website
Johannesburg	Arthur Bales Ltd (Distributor)	62 Fourth Avenue, Linden	arthurb@new.co.za	2195	(27) 118 882 401	www.arthurbales.co.za

SPAIN

City	Store	Address	Email	Postal	Phone	Website
Barcelona	Coats Fabra, SA (Distributor)	Sant Adrià, 20	atencion.clientes@coats.com	8030	(34) 93 290 84 00	www.coatscrafts.es
Álava	Vitoria-Gasteiz LOG CABIN	C/ Manuel Iradier, Pza. Iglesia del Carmen		1005	(+34) 945142430	
Barcelona	Badalona	Montserrat Mata, Maria Cristina 11		8912	(34) 93 3832657	
Barcelona	VILASSAR DE MAR	Iulia Komarova, ENRIC GRANADOS 153				www.lanadeioulia.com
Barcelona	Club de la Aguja	Ganduxer 72		08021	(34) 93 4143815	
Barcelona	El Corte Inglés Barcelona	Plaza Catalunya 14		8002		
Barcelona	Lanas Rodriguez	Providencia 130		8024	(34) 93 2196970	
Barcelona	Mercería Santana	Avda. Portal de l'Angel, 26		8002	(34) 933020948	
Bilbao	Oyambre	Pau Claris 145		08009	(34) 93 4872672	
Eibar	El Corte Inglés Bilbao	Gran Via 9		48001		
La Coruña	Guipuzcoa	Artile, Bidebarrieta 18		20600	(34) 94 3207227	www.artilepunto.com, www.artile.net
La Rioja	El Corte Inglés Coruña	Ramón y Cajal SN		15006		
Madrid	Logroño M.J. Patchwork	Duques de Najera, 2		26002	941585222	www.mjpatchwork.com
Madrid	Alcobendas ISABEL PRIETO	Pº Alcobendas, 10 (C.C. Bulevar)		28109		
Madrid	El club de labores	Infanta Ma Teresa 11		28016	(+34) 913441068	www.clubdelabores.com
Madrid	El Corte Inglés Madrid Castellana	Raimundo Fernandez Villaverde 79		28003	(34) 91 418 88 00	
Madrid	El Corte Inglés Madrid Preciados	Calle Preciados nº3		28013	(34) 91 3798000	
Palma de Mallorca	INKE LABORES S.L.	Don Ramón de la Cruz, 47		28001	915762847	
Pamplona	El Corte Inglés Palma Mallorca - Rosselló	Alexandre Rosselló 12 (suc.23)		7002	(34) 971770177	
Zaragoza	La Chica de las lanas	San Miguel, 5		31001	(34) 948221684	
	El Corte Inglés Zaragoza	Pº Sagasta 3		50008		
	Tira del ovillo				(34) 686361083	www.tiradelovillo.com

SWEDEN

City	Store	Address	Email	Postal	Phone	Website
Goteborg	Coats Expotex AB (Distributor)	JA Wettergrensgata 7, Göteborg, Västra Frölunda		421 30	(46) 33 720 79 00	
Åhus	PP CO	Gamla Skeppsbron 10	kristina@ppco.se	296 31	(044) 240521	
Älvsjö	ZigZag	Långsjövägen 25	bergqvist.katarina@telia.com	125 30	(0705) 13 33 09	
Bollebygd	Nedergården	Stationsvagen 12	nedergardensgarn@telia.com	517 35	(033) 28 94 28	www.nedergardens.com
Boras	Stickat och Klart	Hallbergsgatan 2	kristina.karlson@hotmail.com	503 30	(033) 10 32 38	
Degerberga	Hemslojdsboden	Tingsvagen 23	lina@hemslojdsboden.com	297 31	(044) 350262	www.hemslojdsboden.com
Gårdsjö	Garntorpet	Håhult 1	ingrid@garntorpet.se	548 74	(0706) 196 200	www.garntorpet.se
Goteborg	2 Knit	Bondegatan 7	info@2knit.se	416 65	(031) 199080	www.2knit.se
Goteborg	Strikk	Vallgatan 23	info@strikkdesign.com	411 16	(031) 711 37 99	www.strikkdesign.com
Haljarp	Hedenskougs Garnhorna	Olofstorpsvagen 25		261 72	(0418) 430485	
Helsingborg	Tant Thea AB	Möllegränden 15	info@tantthea.se	252 23	(042) 13 51 53	www.tantthea.se
Hörby	Garnverandan	Gamla Torg 5	info@garnverandan.se	242 31	(0415) 31 13 00	www.garnverandan.se
Kristianstad	Helylle Hantverk	Vastra Storgatan 510	eva.martinsson@helylle.se	291 31	(044) 353250	www.helylle.se
Linkoping	Garnverket	Storgatan 54	maya@garnverket.se	582 28	(013)13 59 09	www.garnverket.com
Lund	Slandan	Lilla Fiskaregatan 1	slandan@telia.se	222 22	046 128077	www.slandaninlund.se
Malmo	Irmas Hus	Kalendegatan 13	annkarin@irmashus.se	211 35	(040) 611 08 00	www.irmashus.se
Orebro	Trend Tyg & Garn	Oscar C Kopmangatan 9	trend-tyg-garn@hotmail.com	702 10	019 103055	
Stockholm	Garnverket	Hantverkargatan 14	lena@garnverket.se	112 21	(08) 651 78 08	www.garnverket.com
Stockholm	NK Tyg & Sy	Hamngatan 18-20	sidencarlson@swipnet.se	111 77	(08) 762 88 50	
Stockholm	**Rowan At Wincent**	**Norrtullsgatan 27**	**butik.wincent@gmail.com**	**113 27**	**(08) 33 70 60**	www.wincentgarner.se or wincentyarn.com
Falkenberg	Sticka Latt	Brogatan 2		311 31	(0346) 17166	www.stickalatt.se
Stockholm	Sticka by Marie Viktoria	Osterlanggatan 20	marievictoria@gmail.com	111 31	(08)21 18 31	www.knitting.se
Stockholm	**Wincent (Rowan At)**	**Norrtullsgatan 27**	**butik.wincent@gmail.com**	**113 27**	**(08) 33 70 60**	**www.wincentgarner.se or wincentyarn.com**
Sundsvall	Garnkorgen	Klackvagen 17	info@garnkorgen.se	856 53	(060) 124 501	www.garnkorgen.se
Taby	Trasselgarn & Broderi	Stationsvagen 25	info@trassel.se	187 30	(08) 638 00 59	www.trassel.se
Torslanda	Karma Garn	Gösta Andrés Gata 2	info@karmagarn.se	423 36	(031)92 00 98	www.karmagarn.se
Umea	Hemflit	Kungsgatan 51	eva@hemflit.com	903 26	(090) 77 03 84	www.hemflit.se
Uppsala	Yll & Tyll	Bredgatan 7c	info@yllotyll.com	753 20	(018) 10 51 90	www.yllotyll.com
Vasteras	Upplings Garn	Kungsgatan 2	info@upplings.se	722 11	(021) 13 00 94	
Västerhaninge	Mia´s Garn & Färgstudio	Bokstigen 3	mia@miasgarnstudio.se	137 34	(08) 400 11 891	
Vaxsjo	Umbra	Batmanstorget 2	info@umbra.nu	352 80	4647077901	

Omaha	Nebraska	String of Purls	8721 Shamrock Rd	68114	(402)393-5648	
RENO	**NEVADA**	**JIMMY BEANS WOOL (ROWAN AT)**	**5000 Smithridge Dr, #A11**	**89502**	**(775) 827-9276**	**www.jimmybeanswool.com**
Basking Ridge	New Jersey	Angelfire Studio	403 King George Road	07920	(908) 604-4294	
Basking Ridge	New Jersey	Down Cellar	25 South Finley Ave	07920	(908) 766-2300	
Haddonfield	New Jersey	Woolplay	22 N. Haddon Ave	08033	856 428 0110	
Hoboken	New Jersey	Patricia's Yarns	107 4th St	07030	(201) 217-9276	
Madison	New Jersey	The Blue Purl	92 Green Ave	07940	(973)377-5648	
Martinsville	New Jersey	A Yarn for All Seasons	1944 Washington Valley Rd	08836	(732) 560-1111	
Westfield	New Jersey	Knit A Bit	66 Elm St, suite 2	07090	(908) 301-0053	www.knit-a-bit.com
Santa Fe	New Mexico	Tutto, Santa Fe	218 Galisteo St	87501	(877) 603-6725	www.tuttosantafe.com
East Rochester	New York	The Village Yarn & Fiber	350 West Commercial St	14445	(585)586-5470	
Ithaca	New York	Knitting Etc	2255 North Triphammer Rd	14850	(607) 277-1164	
Katonah	New York	Katonah Yarn Co	120 Bedford Rd	10536	(914) 977-3145	
New York City	New York	Annie & Co	1325 Madison Ave	10128	(212) 289-2944	
New York City	New York	Knitty City	208 W 79th Street	10024	(212) 787-5896	
New York City	New York	Purl	137 Sullivan St	10012	(212) 420-8796	www.purlsoho.com
SAYVILLE	**NEW YORK**	**RUMPELSTILTSKIN (ROWAN AT)**	**22 Main Street**	**11782**	**(631)750-1790**	
SCARSDALE	**NEW YORK**	**STICKS & STRINGS (ROWAN AT)**	**45 Spencer Pl.,**	**10583**	**(914) 723-5478**	
CHAPEL HILL	**NORTH CAROLINA**	**YARNS ETC (ROWAN AT)**	**99 S Elliott Rd, Ste 2**	**27514**	**(919) 928-8810**	
RALEIGH	**NORTH CAROLINA**	**GREAT YARNS (ROWAN AT)**	**1208 Ridge Rd**	**27607**	**(919)832-3599**	
Wilmington	North Carolina	The Quarter at Oleander	5725 Oleander Drive, #B2	28403	(910)392-0020	
Fargo	North Dakota	Prairie Yarns	2615 South University	58103	(701) 280-1478	
Cincinnati	Ohio	Fiberge	9901 Montgomery Road	45242	513-831-9276	
Cleveland	Ohio	Fine Points	12620 Larchmere Blvd	44120	(216) 229-6644	www.shopfinepoints.com
COLUMBUS	**OHIO**	**KNITTER'S MERCANTILE (ROWAN AT)**	**214 Graceland Blvd**	**43214**	**(614) 888-8551**	**www.knittersmercantile.com**
Dublin	Ohio	Temptations	35 South High Street	43017	(614) 734-0618	
Granville	Ohio	Wisp, LLC	447 West College Street	43023	740-975-1946	
Lakewood	Ohio	River Colors Studio	1387 Sloane Ave	44107	(216)228-9276	
PICKERINGTON	**OHIO**	**YARN MARKET (ROWAN AT)**	**12936 Stonecreek Dr, unit D**	**43147**	**(888) 996-9276**	**www.yarnmarket.com**
Uniontown	Ohio	My Sister's Yarn Shop	3477 Massillon Road	44685	(330)896-7040	
Tulsa	Oklahoma	Loops	2042 Utica Sq	74114	(918) 742-9276	www.loopsknitting.com
ASHLAND	**OREGON**	**THE WEB-STERS (ROWAN AT)**	**11 North Main St**	**97520**	**(800) 482-9801**	**www.yarnatwebsters.com**
BEAVERTON	**OREGON**	**FOR YARN SAKE (ROWAN AT)**	**11679 SW Beaverton**	**97005**	**(503)469-9500**	
McMinnville	Oregon	Boersma's Knitting Center	203 NE 3rd Street	97128	503-472-4611	
Portland	Oregon	Close Knit	2140 NE Alberta St	97211	(503)288-4568	
PORTLAND	**OREGON**	**KNIT PURL (ROWAN AT)**	**1101 SW Alder**	**97205**	**(503) 227-2999**	**www.knit-purl.com**
Portland	Oregon	Knitting Bee	18305 NW West Union Rd	97229	(503)439-3316	
Sisters	Oregon	Stitchin' Post	311 West Cascade St	97759	(541) 549-6061	www.stitchinpost.com
Chambersburg	Pennsylvania	Yarn Basket	150 Falling Spring Rd	17202	(717) 263-3236	
Doylestown	Pennsylvania	Forever Yarn	15 W Oakland Ave	18901	215) 348-5648	
Mcmurray	Pennsylvania	Bloomin Yarns	3323 Washington Rd, Ste 102	15317	(724) 942-1025	
New Hope	Pennsylvania	Twist Knitting & Spinning	6220 Lower York Road	18938	(215) 862-8075	
Newtown Square	Pennsylvania	Slip Knot	3719 W Chester Pike	19073	(610) 359-9070	
Philadelphia	Pennsylvania	Rosie's Yarn Cellar	2017 Locust Street	19103	(215) 977-9276	
Pittsburgh	Pennsylvania	Knit One	2721 Murray Ave	15217	412-421-6666	
SEWICKLEY	**PENNSYLVANIA**	**YARNS UNLIMITED (ROWAN AT)**	**435 Beaver St**	**15143**	**(412) 741-8894**	**www.yarnsunlimitedpa.com**
East Greenwich	Rhode Island	Unwind RI Inc	458 1st Ave	02818	401-398-7780	
TIVERTON	**RHODE ISLAND**	**SAKONNET PURLS (ROWAN AT)**	**3988 Main Rd**	**02878**	**(888) 624-9902**	**www.letsknit.com**
Hilton Head Island	South Carolina	The Courtyard	32 Palmetto Bay Rd, Ste 10A	29928	(843) 842 5614	
Sioux Falls	South Dakota	Athena Fibers	3915 South Hawthorne Ave	57105	(605) 271 0741	
Brentwood	Tennessee	Threaded Bliss Yarn	127 Franklin Rd #170	37027	(615) 370 8717	
AUSTIN	**TEXAS**	**HILL COUNTRY WEAVERS (ROWAN AT)**	**1701 South Congress**	**78704**	**(512) 707 7396**	**www.hillcountryweavers.com**
Austin	Texas	Yarnbow	1607 Ranch Rd, 620 North,Ste 800	78734	(512) 535 2332	www.yarnbow.com
Beaumont	Texas	Strings and Things	885 Evergreen Lane	77706	(409)225-5185	
Dallas	Texas	Holley's Yarn Shoppe	5211 Forest Lane	75244	972-345-8033	
HOUSTON	**TEXAS**	**YARNS 2 EWE INC (ROWAN AT)**	**518 Shepherd Dr**	**77007**	**(713) 880 5648**	**www.yarns2ewe.com**
Norwich	Vermont	Northern Nights Yarn Shop	289 Main Street	05055	(802) 649 2000	
RICHMOND	**VIRGINIA**	**LETTUCE KNIT (ROWAN AT)**	**3030 Stony Point Rd**	**23235**	**(804) 323 5777**	
Richmond	Virginia	The Yarn Lounge	3003 West Cary St	23221	(804) 340 2880	
Vienna	Virginia	Uniquities	421-D Church St NE	22180	(703) 242 0520	
Williamsburg	Virginia	Knitting Sisters	1915 Pocahontas Trail, ste B1	23185	(757) 258 5005	
BAINBRIDGE IS	**WASHINGTON**	**CHURCHMOUSE YARN AND TEAS (ROWAN AT)**	**118 Madrone Lane**	**98110**	**(206) 780 2686**	
Mount Vernon	Washington	Wildfibers	706 South First St	98273	(360)336-5202	
Preston	Washington	Yarn Country	30540 SE 84th St, Unit 4	98050	(425) 818 8096	www.yarncountry.com
Seattle	Washington	Little Knits	3221 California Ave SW	98116	(206)935-4072	
SEATTLE	**WASHINGTON**	**THE WEAVING WORKS (ROWAN AT)**	**4717 Brooklyn Ave, N.E.**	**98105**	**(888) 524 1221**	**www.weavingworks.com**
Seattle	Washington	Tricoter	3121 East Madison St	98112	(206) 328 6505	www.tricoter.com
APPLETON	**WISCONSIN**	**IRIS FINE YARNS (ROWAN AT)**	**132 E. Wisconsin Ave**	**54911**	**(920) 954 9001**	
Delafield	Wisconsin	Knitch	608 Milwaukee Street	53018	262-646-9392	
Madison	Wisconsin	The Knitting Tree	2614 Monroe St	53711	(608)238-0121	
MILWAUKEE	**WISCONSIN**	**RUHAMA'S (ROWAN AT)**	**420 E Silver Spring Dr**	**53217**	**(888) 669 4726**	**www.ruhamas.com**
Sturgeon Bay	Wisconsin	Spin LLC	108 South Madison Ave	54235	(920) 746 7746	

UNITED KINGDOM

'ROWAN AT ....' stockists carry a large range of Rowan Yarns.

Avon	**Brislington**	**Get Knitted (Rowan At)**	**39 @ Brislington, Brislington Hill**	**sales@getknitted.com**	**BS4 5BE**	**0117 3005211**	**www.getknitted.com**
Avon	**Bristol**	**John Lewis (Rowan At)**	**Cribbs Causeway**		**BS12 5TP**	**0117 959 1100**	
Bedfordshire	Leighton Buzzard	Nutmeg Needlecrafts	1-4 Peacock Mews		LU7 1JH	01525 376456	
Berkshire	**Reading**	**John Lewis (Rowan At)**	**Broad Street**		**RG7 4AH**	**01189 575955**	
Booterstown	Winnie's Craft Café	Inspirations	19 Victoria Street, Newton Stewart	rose.lawther@btconnect.com	Co Dublin	+353 1 2603734	
Buckinghamshire	Buckingham	The Nimble Thimble	9 Bridge Street	sales@nimble-thimble.co.uk	MK18 1EL	01280 822236	www.nimble-thimble.co.uk
Buckinghamshire	Great Missenden	Rainbow Silks	85 High Street	caroline@rainbowsilks.co.uk	HP16 0AL	01494 862111	www.rainbowsilks.co.uk
Buckinghamshire	**Milton Keynes**	**John Lewis (Rowan At)**	**Central Milton Keynes**		**MK1 1NN**	**01908 679171**	
Cambridgeshire	**Cambridge**	**John Lewis (Rowan At)**	**10 Downing Street**		**CB2 3DS**	**01223 361292**	
Cambridgeshire	**Peterborough**	**John Lewis (Rowan At)**	**Queensgate Centre**		**PE1 1NL**	**01733 344644**	
Cheshire	**Cheadle**	**John Lewis (Rowan At)**	**Wilmslow Road**		**SK9 3RN**	**0161 491 4914**	
Cheshire	**Chester**	**Stash (Rowan At)**	**Unit 48, Evan's Business Park, Minerva Ave**	**stash@celticove.com**	**CH1 4QL**	**01244 389310**	**www.celticove.com**
Cheshire	**Knutsford**	**Fibre and Clay (Rowan At)**	**11-13 Minshull Street**	**info@fibreandclay.co.uk**	**WA16 6HG**	**01565 652035**	**www.fibreandclay.co.uk**
Cheshire	Nantwich	Homemade	3 Mill Street	lizzydrippingsales@btopenworld.com	CW5 5ST	01270 625318	
Cheshire	Northwich	Thimble Town	Blakemere Craft Centre	thimbletown@hotmail.co.uk	CW8 2EB	01606 883133	
Chipping Norton	The Knitting Shed					01608 811902	
Co Durham	Barnard Castle	Button and Bowes	3 The Bank		DL12 8PH	01833 631133	
Co. Fermanagh	Enniskillen	Boston Quay Craft Shop	Down Street		BT74 7DU	028 6632 3837	
Cornwall	Launceston	The Cornwall Yarn Shop	1 Madford Lane	info@thecornwallyarnshop.co.uk	PL15 9EB	01566 779930	www.thecornwallyarnshop.co.uk
Cornwall	Penzance	Iriss	66 Chapel Street	rowan@iriss.co.uk	TR18 4AD	01736 366568	www.rowan-at-iriss.co.uk
Cornwall	**Truro**	**Truro Fabrics (Rowan At)**	**Lemon Quay**	**info@trurofabrics.co.uk**	**TR1 2LW**	**01872 222130**	**www.trurofabrics.com**
Cornwall	Wadebridge	ArtyCrafts	41 Molesworth Street	artycrafts@btconnect.com	PL27 7DH	01208 812274	
Cumbria	Kendal	Williams Wools	3 Kirkland	adrienne@williamswools.co.uk	LA9 5AU	01539 724300	
Cumbria	Penrith	Indigo	Unit 15 Devonshire Arcade	carolyn@indigoknits.co.uk	CA11 7SX	01768 899917	www.indigoknits.co.uk
Cumbria	Whitehaven	The Knitting & Sewing Centre	28 Duke Street		CA28 7EU	01946 63091	
Derbyshire	Derby	Threads of Life	67 Borough St, Castle Donington	info@threadsoflife.co.uk	DE74 2LB	01332 811597	www.threadsoflife.co.uk
Derbyshire	Matlock	The Compleat Knit	22 Firs Parade	ann@patchworkdirect.com	DE4 3AS	01629 593700	www.patchworkdirect.com
Devon	**Bovey Tracy**	**Spin A Yarn (Rowan At)**	**26 Fore Street**	**info@spinayarndevon.co.uk**	**TQ13 9AD**	**01626 836203**	**www.spinayarndevon.co.uk**
Devon	**Exeter**	**Inspirations (Rowan At)**	**5 Central Station Buildings, Queen Street**			**EX4 3SB**	**01392 435115**
Devon	Modbury	Wild Goose Antiques	34 Church Street	wildgooseantiques@tiscali.co.uk	PL21 0QR	01548 830715	
Devon	Plymouth	The Pin Tin	17 Wilton Street	andie.thepintin@yahoo.co.uk	PL1 5LT	01752 313931	www.thepintin.co.uk
Devon	Shaldon	Lana Pura	49 Fore Street	enquiries@lanapura.com	TQ14 0EA	01626 873615	www.lanapura.com
Devon	Tavistock	Knitting Korner	9 Pepper Street		PH9 0BD	01822 617410	
Devon	Totnes	Creative Crafts & Needlework	18 High Street		TQ9 5RY	01803 866002	www.creative-crafts-needlework.co.uk
Dorset	Bournemouth	Carly's Crafts	Shop 1, 1a Cardigan Road, Winton	michelek1964@hotmail.com	BH9 1BJ	01202 512106	

Dorset	Christchurch	Honora	69 High Street, Christchurch	support@knittingyarns.co.uk	BH23 1AS	01202 486000	www.knittingyarns.co.uk
Dorset	**Sturminster Newton**	**Hansons Fabrics (Rowan At)**	**Station Road**		**DT10 1BD**	**01258 472698**	
Dorset	**Swanage**	**The Wool & Craft Shop (Rowan At)**	**17 Station Road**	**sales@craftywoolshop.co.uk**	**BH19 1AB**	**01929 422814**	**www.craftywoolshop.co.uk**
Dorset	Wimbourne	The Walnut Tree	1 West Borough		BH21 1NF	01202 840722	
Dumfries	Dumfries				DG8 6NH	01671 402627	
East Sussex	Brighton	Rowan At C & H Fabrics	179 Western Road,		BN1 2BA	01273 321959	www.candh.co.uk
East Sussex	Eastbourne	C & H Fabrics	82/86 Terminus Road		BN21 3LX	01323 410428	www.candh.co.uk
East Sussex	**Forest Row**	**Village Crafts (Rowan At)**	**The Square**	**shop@village-crafts.co.uk**	**RH18 5ES**	**01342 823238**	**www.village-crafts.co.uk**
East Yorkshire	**Pocklington**	**Poppy's (Rowan At)**	**20 Market Place**	**info@craftypoppycanknit.com**	**YO42 2AR**	**01759 303120**	**www.craftypoppycanknit.com**
Essex	Brentwood	We Three	16 Crown Street		CM14 4BA	01277 221709	
Essex	**Chelmsford**	**Franklins (Rowan At)**	**219 Moulsham St**		**CM2 0LR**	**01245 346300**	
Essex	**Colchester**	**Franklins (Rowan At)**	**13/15 St Botolphs St**		**CO2 7DU**	**01206 563955**	
Gloucestershire	Cricklade	Creative Crafts & Needlework	89a High Street	info@crickladecrafts.co.uk	SN6 6DF	01793 750604	www.crickladecrafts.co.uk
Greater London	Herne Hill	Sharp Designs	226 Croxted Road		SE24 9DJ	020 8674 4382	
Greater Manchester	**Didsbury**	**Sew In of Didsbury (Rowan At)**	**741 Wilmslow Road**	**enquiries@knitting-and-needlework.co.uk**	**M20 0RN**	**0161 445 5861**	**www.knitting-and-needlecraft.co.uk**
Greater Manchester	**Manchester**	**John Lewis (Rowan At)**	**Peel Avenue, The Trafford Centre**		**M17 8JL**	**0161 491 4040**	
Greater Manchester	**Marple**	**Sew In of Marple (Rowan At)**	**46 Market Street**	**enquiries@knitting-and-needlework.co.uk**	**M17 8JL**	**0161 427 2529**	**www.knitting-and-needlecraft.co.uk**
Hampshire	Basingstoke	Pack Lane Wool Shop	171 Pack Lane, Kempshott	enquires@packlanewool.co.uk	RG22 5HN	01256 462590	www.packlanewool.co.uk
Hampshire	Liss	Liss Wools	2 Station Road	hilary@lisswools.co.uk	GU33 7DT	01730 893941	www.lisswools.co.uk
Hampshire	**Southampton**	**John Lewis (Rowan At)**	**West Quay Shopping Centre**		**SO15 1GY**	**0238 021 6400**	
Hampshire	Winchester	C & H Fabrics	8 High St		SO23 9JX	01962 843355	www.candh.co.uk
Hants	Andover	Love Yarns Ltd	305 The Commercial Centre, Picket piece	fiona@loveyarn.com	SP11 6RY	01264 357333	www.loveyarn.com
Hemel hempstead	Needle Craft				HP1 1JQ	01442 245383	
Herefordshire	Hay-on-Wye	Bedecked.co.uk	5 Castle Street	thegirls@bedecked.co.uk,"	HR3 5DF	01497 822769	www.bedecked.co.uk
Herefordshire	Hereford	Doughty's	5 Capuchin Road, Church Street	sales@doughtysonline.co.uk	HR1 2LR	01432 267542	www.doughtysonline.co.uk
Hertfordshire	Boreham Wood	The Wool Shop	29 Shenley Road		WD6 1EB	0208 9052499	
Hertfordshire	Bushey	Mavis	44 High Street		WD23 3HL	0208 950 5445	www.mavis-crafts.com
Hertfordshire	St Albans	Alison's Wool Shop	63 Hatfield Road		AL1 4JE	01727 833738	
Hertfordshire	**Watford**	**John Lewis (Rowan At)**	**The Harlequin, High St**		**WD2 8HL**	**01923 244266**	
Hertfordshire	**Welwyn Garden City**	**John Lewis (Rowan At)**	**Bridge Road**		**AL8 6TP**	**01707 323456**	
Isle of Man	Onchan	Joan's Wools & Crafts	5B & 6B Village Walk	joans_wools_crafts@manx.net	IM3 4EA	01624 626009	
Kent	**Canterbury**	**C & H Fabrics (Rowan At)**	**2 St George's Street**		**CT1 2SR**	**01227 459760**	**www.candh.co.uk**
Kent	**Greenhithe**	**John Lewis (Rowan At)**	**Bluewater**		**DA9 9SA**	**01322 624123**	
Kent	Maidstone	C & H Fabrics	68 Week Street		ME14 1RJ	01622 762060	www.candh.co.uk
Kent	**Tunbridge Wells**	**C & H Fabrics (Rowan At)**	**113/115 Mount Pleasant**		**TN1 1QS**	**01892 522618**	**www.candh.co.uk**
Lancashire	Accrington	Sheila's Wool Shop	284 Union Road, Oswaldtwistle	sheila'swoolshop@aol.com	BB5 3JB	01254 875525	www.sheilaswoolshop.com
Lancashire	**Barnoldswick**	**Whichcrafts? (Rowan At)**	**29 Church St**	**crafts@whichcrafts.co.uk**	**BB18 5UR**	**01282 851003**	**www.whichcrafts.co.uk**
Lancashire	Chorley	& Sew What	247 Eaves Lane	info@sewwhat.gb.com	PR6 0AG	01257 267438	www.sewwhat.gb.com
Lancashire	Oldham	Yarn Barn	16 Milnrow Road, Shaw	info@yarnbarnshaw.co.uk	OL2 8EQ	01706 843538	www.yarnbarnshaw.co.uk
Lancashire	Preston	Bow Peep	136 Liverpool Road (next to the Red Lion), Longton		PR4 5AU	01772 614508	
Lancashire	Ramsbottom	Clark Craft Products	Empire Works, Railway Street, Bury		BL0 9AS	01706 826479	www.clarkcraft.co.uk
Lancashire	Thornton	Yarns of Lancashire Ltd	Unit 15, Marsh Mill Village, Fleetwood Road	yarns@tiscali.co.uk	FY5 4JZ	01253 822922	
Leicestershire	**Leicester**	**John Lewis (Rowan At)**	**2 Bath House Lane, Highcross**		**LE1 4SA**	**0116 242 5777**	
Leicestershire	Leicester	Mary Clare	4 Shaftesbury Road		LE3 0QN	0116 255 1866	
Leicestershire	Loughborough	Quorn Country Crafts	18 Churchgate	quorncountrycrafts@hotmail.com	LE11 1UD	01509 211604	www.quorncountrycrafts.com
London	Barnes	Creations	79 Church Road		SW13 9HH	020 8563 2970	
London	Central London	All the Fun of the Fair	Unit 2, 8 Kingly Court, Off Carnaby Street	buzzstokes@btinternet.com	W1B 5PW	0207 287 2303	www.allthefunofthefair.biz
London	**Central London**	**John Lewis (Rowan At)**	**Oxford Street**		**W1**	**020 7629 7711**	
London	**Central London**	**Liberty (Rowan At)**	**Regent St**		**W1**	**020 7734 1234**	
London	**Central London**	**Peter Jones (Rowan At)**	**Sloane Square**		**SW1**	**0207 881 6364**	
London	Chingford	JJ Wool & Crafts	89 Station Road	jjwoolandcrafts@yahoo.co.uk	E4 9RH	0208 523 7172	www.jjwoolandcrafts.co.uk
London	Chiswick	Creations	29 Turnham Green Terrace		W4 1RS	020 8747 9697	
London	Finsbury Park	Lenarow	169 Blackstock Road	michael@lenarow.co.uk	N4 2JS	020 7359 1274	www.lenarow.co.uk
London	Islington	Loop	41 Cross Street	info@loop.gb.com	N1 2BB	0207 288 1160	www.loop.gb.com
London	**North London**	**John Lewis (Rowan At)**	**Brent Cross Shopping Centre**		**NW4**	**020 8202 6535**	
Merseyside	**Liverpool**	**John Lewis (Rowan At)**	**70 South John Street**		**L1 8BJ**	**0151 709 7070**	
Merseyside	Liverpool	Purlesque	The Bluecoat, School Lane	purlesque@gmail.com	L1 3BX		
Merseyside	St Helens	The Knitting Centre	9 Westfield Street		WA10 1QA	01744 23993	
Middlesex	Twickenham	Mrs Moon	41 Crown Road, St Margarets	info@mrsmoon.co.uk	TW1 3EJ	020 8744 1190	www.mrsmoon.co.uk
Monmouthshire	Monmouth	Cotton Angel	2 Church Street	info@thecottonangel.com	NP25 3BU	01600 713548	www.thecottonangel.com
Norfolk	Dereham	Knitwits	1 Glencoe Court, Cherry Tree Car Park	knitwits.dereham@googlemail.com	NR19 2AX	01362 652961	www.knitwitsdereham.co.uk
Norfolk	Diss	Diss Wool & Craft Shop	2 Cobbs Yard, St Nicholas Street	sales@disswoolandcrafts.com	IP22 4LB	01379 650640	www.disswoolandcrafts.com
Norfolk	**Norwich**	**John Lewis (Rowan At)**	**All Saints Green**		**NR1 3LX**	**01603 660021**	
Norfolk	Sheringham	Creative Crafts	47 Station Road	info@creative-crafts.co.uk	NR26 8RG	01263 823153	www.creative-crafts.co.uk
North Yorkshire	Clapham	Beckside Yarn & Needlecraft	Church Avenue	info@becksideyarns.co.uk	LA2 8EA	01524 251122	www.beckside yarns.co.uk
North Yorkshire	**Embsay**	**Embsay Crafts (Rowan At)**	**Embsay Mills**	**enquiries@embsaycrafts.com**	**BD23 6QF**	**01756 700946**	**www.embsaycrafts.com**
North Yorkshire	Filey	Beachcomber	35 Belle Vue St		YO14 9HV	01723 514434	
North Yorkshire	Whitby	Bobbins	Wesley Hall, Church Street	bobbins@globalnet.co.uk	YO22 4DE	01947 600585	www.bobbins.co.uk
North Yorkshire	York	Craft Basics	9 Gillygate		YO31 7EA	01904 652840	
North Yorkshire	York	Poppy's	11 Colliergate	info@craftypoppycanknit.com	YO1 8BP	01904 270927	www.craftypoppycanknit.com
Northamptonshire	Northampton	House of Fraser	37 Newland Walk	Grosvenor Centre	NN1 2EP	0870 607 2835	
Northamptonshire	Rushden	Manfield Crafts	24 Griffiths Street	enquiries@manfieldcrafts.com	NN10 0RL	01933 314920	www.manfieldcrafts.com
Northamptonshire	Weedon	Crafts & Quilts	Unit 5 The Barn, Heart of the Shires Shop Village	tintindowton@aol.com	NN7 4LB	01327 349276	
Northern Ireland	Co Antrim	The Glen Gallery	48 Fenagh Road, Cullybackey		BT43 5PH	0282 588 0354	
Northumberland	Alnwick	Pavi Yarns	42 Royal Oak Gardens	info@paviyarns.com	NE66 2DA	01665 606062	www.paviyarns.com
Northumberland	Berwick upon Tweed	The Needleworks Ltd	54 Hide Hill	kp1612@btinternet.com	TD15 1AB	01289 330503	
Nottinghamshire	**Beeston**	**Yarns (Rowan At)**	**55 Chilwell Road**	**info@yarn-in-notts.co.uk**	**NG9 1EN**	**0115 925 3606**	**www.yarn-in-notts.co.uk**
Nottinghamshire	**Nottingham**	**John Lewis (Rowan At)**	**Victoria Centre**		**NG1 3QA**	**0115 941 8282**	
Nottinghamshire	Southwell	The Little Wool Shop	18 Queen Street	mac8142@aol.com	NG25 0AA	01636 814198	www.thelittlewoolshop.co.uk
Oxfordshire	Abingdon	Masons	39 Stert Street	sales@masonsneedlecraft.co.uk	OX14 3JF	01235 520107	www.masonsneedlecraft.co.uk
Oxfordshire	Burford	Burford Needlecraft	150 High Street	info@needlework.co.uk	OX18 4QU	01993 822136	www.needlework.co.uk
Oxfordshire	Oxford	Port Meadow Designs	104 Walton Street		OX2 6EB	01865 311008	
Scotand	Alloa	Wee County Yarns	Gartmonhill Farm	clare@wee-county-yarns.co.uk	FK10 3AU	01259 759000	www.wee-county-yarns.co.uk
Scotland	**Aberdeen**	**John Lewis (Rowan At)**	**George Street**		**AB9 1BT**	**01224 625000**	
Scotland	**Aberdeen**	**The Wool Shed (Rowan At)**	**Ryehill, Oyne**	**info@thewoolshed.co.uk**	**AB52 6QS**	**01464 851539**	**"www.thewoolshed.co.uk, "**
Scotland	Aberdeen	Wool for Ewe	83-85 Rosemount Place	info@woolforewe.co.uk	AB25 2YE	01224 643738	
Scotland	Berkwickshire	Woolfish	Northfield Farm, St Abbs	louise@woolfish.co.uk	TD14 5QF	01890 771133	www.woolfish.co.uk
Scotland	**Castle Douglas**	**Outback Yarns (Art 2 Go) (Rowan At)**	**130-132 King Street**	**sarahmckie@btinternet.com**	**DG7 1LU**	**01556 504900**	**www.outbackyarns.com**
Scotland	**Edinburgh**	**Jenners (Rowan At)**	**48 Princes Street**		**EH2 2YJ**	**0131 225 2442**	
Scotland	**Edinburgh**	**John Lewis (Rowan At)**	**St James Centre**		**EH1 3SP**	**0131 556 9121**	
Scotland	**Edinburgh**	**McAree Bros (Rowan At)**	**19 Howe Street**	**sales@mcadirect.com**	**EH3 6TE**	**0131 558 1747**	**www.mcadirect.com**
Scotland	Fife	Twist Fibre Craft Studio	88 High Street, Newburgh	enquiries@twistfibrecraft.co.uk	KY14 6AQ	01337 842843	www.twistfibrecraft.co.uk
Scotland	**Glasgow**	**John Lewis (Rowan At)**	**Buchanan Galleries**		**G4 0BZ**	**0141 353 6677**	
Scotland	Glasgow	Mandors	13 Renfrew Street	fabric@mandors.co.uk	G3 6ST	0141 332 7716	www.mandors.co.uk
Scotland	Gourock	Once A Sheep	60 Kempock Street	info@onceasheep.com	PA19 1ND	01475 648089	www.onceasheep.co.uk
Scotland	Hamilton	Stitching Time	14 Haddon Street	getit@stitchingtime.co.uk	ML3 7HX	01698 424025	
Scotland	St Andrews	Rowan At Di Gilpin @ The Wool Merchants	Burghers Close, 141 South St	shop@digilpin.com	KY16 9UN	01334 476193	www.digilpin.com
Scotland	**Stirling**	**McAree Bros (Rowan At)**	**55-59 King Street**	**sales@mcadirect.com**	**FK8 1DR**	**01786 465646**	**www.mcadirect.com**
Shropshire	**Ludlow**	**The Wool Shop (Rowan At)**	**13 Broad Street**		**SY8 1NG**	**01584 872988**	
Shropshire	Much Wenlock	Ippikin	59 The High Street	info@ippikin.com	TF13 6AE	01952 728371	www.ippikin.com
Shropshire	Telford	House of Fraser	244-250 New Row, Town Centre		TF3 4BS	0870 607 2838	
Somerset	Clevedon	The Spinning Weal	63 Hill Road	mail@spinningweal.com	BS21 7NZ	01275 876000	www.spinningweal.com
Somerset	Frome	Marmalade Yarns	11 Catherine Hill	CatrionaandMaxine@marmaladeyarns.co.uk	BA11 1BZ	01373 473557	www.marmaladeyarns.co.uk
Somerset	Minehead	Jana Henrie	High Street, Porlock	info@janahenrie.com	TA24 8SP	01643 862058	www.janahenrie.com
Somerset	Taunton	Hayes Wools Ltd	150 East Reach		TA1 3HT	01823 284768	
Somerset	Wool Limited				BA1 1JU	07788 6691800	www.woolbath.co.uk
South Yorkshire	**Sheffield**	**John Lewis (Rowan At)**	**Barkers Pool**		**S1 1EP**	**0114 2768511**	
Staffordshire	**Lichfield**	**The Knitting Corner (Rowan At)**	**Unit 3, Curborough Hall Farm, Watery Lane**	**theknittingcorner@btinternet.com**	**WS13 8ES**	**01543 415837**	
Staffordshire	**Newcastle under Lyme**	**K2Tog (Rowan At)**	**97 High Street, Wolstanton**	**sales@cucumberpatch.com**	**ST5 0EP**	**01782 862332**	**www.cucumberpatch.co.uk**
Suffolk	Bungay	Knit and Yarn	3 Upper Olland Street	gillybell@knitandyarn.co.uk	NR35 1BD	01986 895400	www.knitandyarn.co.uk
Suffolk	Bury St Edmunds	Wibbling Wools	24b Angel Hill	lynz@wibblingwools.co.uk	IP33 1UZ	01284 749555	www.wibblingwools.co.uk
Suffolk	Hadleigh	Threadneedle Fabrics	28 High Street		IP7 5AP	01473 824040	
Suffolk	Woodbridge	Anjays Fabrics	11 Gobbitts Yard		IP12 1DD	01394 387593	
Surrey	Camberley	House of Fraser	45-51 Park Street		GU15 3PG	08701 607230	
Surrey	Carshalton Beaches	Maxime Wools	68 Banstead Road		SM5 3NL	020 8661 5625	www.maximewools.co.uk
Surrey	Guildford	C & H Fabrics	6 Tunsgate Square		GU1 3QZ	01483 301380	www.candh.co.uk
Surrey	**Guildford**	**Pandora (Rowan At)**	**196 High Street**	**sales@craft-supplies-store.co.uk**	**GU1 3HZ**	**01483 572558**	**www.stitch1knit1.com**
Surrey	**Kingston**	**John Lewis (Rowan At)**	**Wood Street**		**KT1 1TE**	**020 8547 3000**	
Teeside	Guisborough	Leven Crafts	7-9 Chaloner Mews, Chaloner Street	info@levencrafts.co.uk	TS14 6SA	01287 610207	www.levencrafts.co.uk
The Wirrall	Brimstage	Voirrey Embroidery Centre	Brimstage Hall	mail@voirrey.com	CH63 6JA	"0151 342 3514, "	www.voirrey.com
Tyne & Wear	**Newcastle upon Tyne**	**John Lewis (Rowan At)**	**Eldon Square**		**NE99 1AB**	**0191 232 5000**	
Tyne & Wear	Newcastle upon Tyne	The Knit Studio	Blackfriars	annemakepeace@btopenworld.com	NE1 4XN	07540 277764	
Tyne & Wear	**Whitley Bay**	**Ring a Rosie (Rowan At)**	**272/274 Whitley Bay**	**loweringarosie@aol.com**	**NE26 2TG**	**0191 252 8874**	**www.ringarosie.co.uk**
Wales	Aberystwyth	Clare's Wools	13 Great Darkgate Street	webenquiries@clarewools.co.uk	SA23 1DE	01970 617786	www.clarewools.co.uk
Wales	Anglesey	"Copperfield, Four Mile "	Bridge Road Valley		LL65 4HB	01407 740982	
Wales	**Cardiff**	**John Lewis (Rowan At)**	**The Hayes**		**CF10 1EG**	**029 2053 6000**	
Wales	Conwy	Ar-y-Gweill	8 Heol Yr Orsaf, Llanrwst		LL26 0EP	01492 641149	
Wales	Fishguard	Jane's of Fishguard	14 High Street		SA65 9AR	01348 874443	www.janes-fishguard.co.uk
Wales	Monmouth	Cotton Angel	2 Church Street	info@thecottonangel.com	NP25 3BU	01600 713548	www.thecottonangel.com
Wales	Penarth	Yarn & Yarns	22 Cornerswell Road		CF64 2UZ	02920 712097	
Wales	Port Talbot	W T Hopkins (Port Talbot) Ltd.	110 Fairways, Sandfields	williamhopkins@btconnect.com	SA12 7HR	01639 889244	
Wales	**Whitland**	**Colourway (Rowan At)**	**Market Street**	**shop@colourway.co.uk**	**SA34 0AJ**	**01994 241333**	**www.colourway.co.uk**

ROWAN INTERNET STOCKISTS

All Rowan Internet stockists offer secure online shopping facilities of a wide selection of Rowan products. * denotes retail store and internet

ROWAN YARNS, GREEN LANE MILL, HOLMFIRTH, WEST YORKSHIRE, ENGLAND TEL: +44 (0)1484 681881

THE DESIGN GALLERY

WILDWOOD

HOLLY
Felted Tweed
Kaffe Fassett
Pattern page 159
Main image page 5, 6 & 7

ROBINIA
Felted Tweed
Marie Wallin
Pattern page 133
Main image page 8 & 9

HAWTHORNE CAPE
Felted Tweed Aran
Marie Wallin
Pattern page 126
Main image page 10 & 11

BEECH MITTENS
Felted Tweed Chunky
Erika Knight
Pattern page 126
Main image page 10

MAPLE
Felted Tweed
Marie Wallin
Pattern page 168
Main image page 12, 13, 14 & 15

HORNBEAM
Felted Tweed Aran
Martin Storey
Pattern page 178
Main image page 16 & 17

CHESTNUT
Kid Classic
Marie Wallin
Pattern page 131
Main image page 18 & 19

BIRCH
Felted Tweed Aran
Martin Storey
Pattern page 176
Main image page 20 & 21

FINESSE

MARTHA
Pure Wool DK
Sarah Dallas
Pattern page 162
Main image page 42, 44 & 45

LORETTA
Pure Wool DK
Marie Wallin
Pattern page 147
Main image page 46 & 47

BETTY
Pure Wool 4 ply
Marie Wallin
Pattern page 150
Main image page 48, 49, 50 & 51

CARRIE
Wool Cotton
Marie Wallin
Pattern page 151
Main image page 52 & 53

CINDY
Cashsoft 4ply
Lisa Richardson
Pattern page 154
Main image page 54, 55, 56 & 57

BONNIE
Cashsoft DK
Martin Storey
Pattern page 182
Main image page 58 & 59

GLENDA
Wool Cotton
Amanda Crawford
Pattern page 153
Main image page 60 & 61

JOYCE
Cashsoft DK
Lisa Richardson
Pattern page 166
Main image page 62 & 63

WINTER ESSENTIALS

COMPASSION
Cocoon
Martin Storey
Pattern page 128
Main image page 88, 90 & 91

SINCERE
Kid Classic
Marie Wallin
Pattern page 163
Main image page 92 & 93

LOVE
Kidsilk Haze & Baby Alpaca DK
Marie Wallin
Pattern page 175
Main image page 94 & 95

AFFECTION
Lima
Sarah Hatton
Pattern page 142
Main image page 96 & 97

CORDIAL
Big Wool
Sarah Hatton
Pattern page 156
Main image page 98 & 99

AMOUR
Silk Twist
Amanda Crawford
Pattern page 144
Main image page 100 & 101

GENEROUS
Silk Twist
Grace Melville
Pattern page 145
Main image page 102 & 103

KIND
Lima
Marie Wallin
Pattern page 170
Main image page 104 & 105